BEST DESERT HIKES

Washington

BEST DESERT HIKES
Washington

Alan Bauer
Dan A. Nelson

THE MOUNTAINEERS BOOKS

THE MOUNTAINEERS BOOKS
*is the nonprofit publishing arm of The Mountaineers Club, an organization
founded in 1906 and dedicated to the exploration, preservation, and
enjoyment of outdoor and wilderness areas.*

1001 SW Klickitat Way, Suite 201, Seattle, WA 98134

© 2004 by Dan A. Nelson and Alan L. Bauer

Distributed in the United Kingdom by Cordee, www.cordee.co.uk

Manufactured in the United States of America

Acquiring Editor: Christine U. Hosler, Project Editor: Kate Rogers, Copy Editor:
Heath Lynn Silberfeld, Cover and Book Design: The Mountaineers Books,
Layout Artist: Ani Rucki, Cartographer: Ben Pease

Maps shown in this book were produced using National Geographic's TOPO!
software. For more information, go to www.nationalgeographic.com/topo.

Unless otherwise noted, all photographs by Alan Bauer

Cover photograph: *Balsamroot and other flowers cover the rocky slopes of Selah Butte.*
Frontispiece: *Clump of blooming Bitterroot* (Lewisia rediviva) *on Manastash Ridge*
Page 254: *A huge inlet waterfall crashes down the basalt cliffs into one of the potholes at
Ancient Lake.*

Library of Congress Cataloging-in-Publication Data
Nelson, Dan.
  Best desert hikes : Washington / Dan Nelson and Alan Bauer.— 1st ed.
    p. cm.
  Includes index.
  ISBN 0-89886-537-9 (pbk.)
  1. Hiking—Washington (State)—Guidebooks. 2. Washington (State)—Guidebooks.
I. Bauer, Alan. II. Title.
  GV199.42.W2.N43 2004
  796.51'09797—dc22
                          2004012712

CONTENTS

Hikes at a Glance ▪ 9
Preface ▪ 15
Introduction ▪ 17

YAKIMA AND ELLENSBURG ▪ 33

1. Umtanum Creek Falls ▪ 34
2. Umtanum Creek Canyon ▪ 36
3. Durr Road and North Yakima Skyline ▪ 38
4. Yakima Skyline Ridge ▪ 41
5. Kelley Hollow ▪ 43
6. Robinson Canyon/Ainsley Canyon ▪ 46
7. Black Canyon ▪ 48
8. Shell Rock ▪ 50
9. Westberg Trail ▪ 52
10. Hardy Canyon ▪ 54
11. Big Burn Canyon ▪ 56
12. Cleman Mountain ▪ 57
13. Bear Canyon ▪ 59
14. Ginkgo Petrified Forest Interpretive Trails ▪ 61
15. Ginkgo Petrified Forest State Park Backcountry ▪ 63
16. Wild Horses Monument ▪ 64
17. Whiskey Dick Wildlife Area ▪ 66
18. John Wayne Trail, Army West ▪ 69
19. John Wayne Trail, Army East ▪ 72
20. Selah Butte ▪ 73
21. Cowiche Canyon ▪ 75

WENATCHEE ▪ 77

22. Ancient Lake ▪ 78
23. Dusty Lake ▪ 80
24. Frenchman Coulee ▪ 81
25. Steamboat Rock ▪ 83
26. Northrup Canyon ▪ 85
27. Old Wagon Road Trail ▪ 87
28. Umatilla Rock/Monument Coulee ▪ 89
29. Park Lake Side Canyon ▪ 91
30. Lenore Lake Caves ▪ 92
31. Trail Lake Coulee ▪ 94
32. Billy Clapp Lake ▪ 96
33. Douglas Creek Canyon–North ▪ 99

34. Douglas Creek Canyon–South ■ 101
35. Douglas Creek Canyon–Badger Mountain ■ 102
36. Duffy Creek ■ 103
37. Rock Island Creek ■ 105
38. Beezley Hills Preserve ■ 107
39. Moses Coulee Preserve ■ 109
40. Chester Butte Wildlife Area ■ 111
41. Swakane Canyon ■ 113

TRI-CITIES ■ 115
42. Saddle Mountain East ■ 117
43. Crab Creek Wildlife Area ■ 119
44. Milwaukee Railroad ■ 122
45. White Bluffs–North Slope ■ 123
46. Wahluke Lake ■ 126
47. White Bluffs–South Slope ■ 127
48. McGee Ranch ■ 130
49. Priest Rapids Wildlife Area ■ 132
50. Horsethief Butte ■ 135
51. The Dalles Mountain ■ 137
52. Columbia Hills Natural Area Preserve ■ 138
53. Catherine Creek ■ 140
54. Juniper Dunes Wilderness ■ 142
55. McNary National Wildlife Refuge ■ 145
56. Wallula Habitat Management Unit ■ 147
57. Twin Sisters Rock ■ 149
58. Chamna Natural Preserve ■ 151
59. Rattlesnake Slope Wildlife Area ■ 153
60. Horse Heaven Hills ■ 155
61. Chief Joseph Wildlife Area–Grande Ronde River ■ 156
62. Chief Joseph Wildlife Area–Green Gulch ■ 158
63. Marmes Pond/Lyons Ferry Park ■ 160
64. Palouse Falls ■ 163
65. Kamiak Butte ■ 166
66. Washtucna Coulee (Kahlotus Railroad Grade) ■ 168
67. Snake River/Columbia Plateau Trail ■ 170
68. Big Flat Habitat Management Unit ■ 172

SPOKANE ■ 175
69. Frog Lake/Crab Creek/Marsh Loop Trails ■ 177
70. Chukar Lake/Blythe Lake ■ 179
71. Goose Lake Plateau ■ 181
72. Desert Wildlife Area ■ 183
73. Potholes Wildlife Area–North ■ 185
74. Potholes Wildlife Area–Dunes Ramble ■ 186

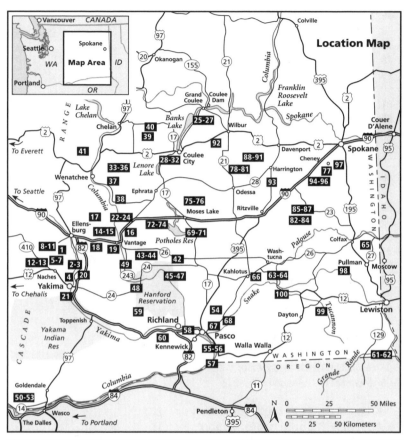

Location Map

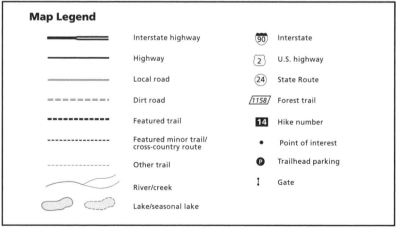

Map Legend

Interstate highway	90 Interstate		
Highway	2 U.S. highway		
Local road	24 State Route		
Dirt road	1158 Forest trail		
Featured trail	14 Hike number		
Featured minor trail/cross-country route	• Point of interest		
Other trail	P Trailhead parking		
River/creek	↕ Gate		
Lake/seasonal lake			

75. Gloyd Seeps–North ■ 188
76. Gloyd Seeps–South ■ 190
77. Columbia Plateau–Amber Lake ■ 192
78. Lakeview Ranch ■ 195
79. Bobs Lakes ■ 197
80. Odessa–Lake Creek Trail ■ 198
81. Odessa Craters ■ 201
82. Escure Ranch ■ 203
83. Breeden Road/Wall Lake ■ 205
84. Towell Falls ■ 207
85. Packer Creek ■ 209
86. Rock Creek Wildlife Area ■ 211
87. Rock Creek/Milwaukee Railroad Corridor ■ 212
88. Twin Lakes ■ 214
89. Florence Lake ■ 216
90. Reiber Road Loop ■ 218
91. Swanson Lakes ■ 220
92. Wilson Creek ■ 222
93. Rocky Ford–Crab Creek ■ 224
94. Hog Lake ■ 226
95. Fishtrap Lake–North ■ 228
96. Fishtrap Lake–Scroggie Loop ■ 230
97. Turnbull National Wildlife Refuge ■ 232
98. Boyer Park Bluffs ■ 234
99. Tucannon River Canyon (Camp Wooten) ■ 236
100. Mouth of the Tucannon ■ 238

Appendix A: Camping Information ■ 241
Appendix B: Contact Information ■ 243
Appendix C: Additional Resources ■ 246
Index ■ 247

HIKES AT A GLANCE

Hike	Hike Name	Distance	Hiking Time	Difficulty	Season
1	Umtanum Creek Falls	3–10 miles	3–6 hours	Moderate	Late winter–early spring
2	Umtanum Creek Canyon	6–10 miles	3–6 hours	Moderate	November–May
3	Durr Road and North Yakima Skyline	9–14 miles	4–7 hours	Difficult	May–June
4	Yakima Skyline Ridge	8+ miles	4–6 hours	Moderate	March–July
5	Kelley Hollow	12 miles	7 hours	Moderate	March–June
6	Robinson Canyon / Ainsley Canyon	10 miles	6 hours	Difficult	May–July
7	Black Canyon	7 miles	4 hours	Difficult	September–November
8	Shell Rock	6 miles	4 hours	Moderate	September–November
9	Westberg Trail	4 miles	3 hours	Moderate	April–July
10	Hardy Canyon	9 miles	6 hours	Moderate	May–June
11	Big Burn Canyon	16 miles	10 hours (or overnight)	Difficult	May–June
12	Cleman Mountain	6–8 miles	5 hours	Moderate	March–July
13	Bear Canyon	4 miles	3 hours	Moderate	April–July
14	Ginkgo Petrified Forest Interpretive Trails	3 miles	2 hours	Easy	Year-round
15	Ginkgo Petrified Forest State Park Backcountry	5 miles	3 hours	Easy	Year-round

Hike	Hike Name	Distance	Hiking Time	Difficulty	Season
16	Wild Horses Monument	1 mile	1 hour	Easy	Year-round
17	Whiskey Dick Wildlife Area	8+ miles	6 hours	Moderate	September–December
18	John Wayne Trail, Army West	8+ miles	5 hours	Easy	Year-round
19	John Wayne Trail, Army East	8+ miles	5 hours	Moderate	Year-round
20	Selah Butte	4 miles	3 hours	Moderate	June–October
21	Cowiche Canyon	6 miles	4 hours	Easy	Year-round
22	Ancient Lake	4–5 miles	3–4 hours	Easy	Year-round
23	Dusty Lake	6 miles	4 hours	Moderate	Year-round
24	Frenchman Coulee	4 miles	3 hours	Moderate	Year-round
25	Steamboat Rock	4 miles	3 hours	Difficult	March–November
26	Northrup Canyon	6 miles	4 hours	Difficult	January–May
27	Old Wagon Road Trail	3 miles	2 hours	Moderate	April–November
28	Umatilla Rock/Monument Coulee	5 miles	3 hours	Moderate	April–July
29	Park Lake Side Canyon	5 miles	3 hours	Moderate	April–July
30	Lenore Lake Caves	1.5–2 miles	1.5 hours	Easy	April–July
31	Trail Lake Coulee	5 miles	3 hours	Easy	March–July
32	Billy Clapp Lake	5 miles	4 hours	Easy	Year-round
33	Douglas Creek Canyon–North	3 miles	2.5 hours	Moderate	Year-round
34	Douglas Creek Canyon–South	5 miles	3 hours	Easy	Year-round
35	Douglas Creek Canyon–Badger Mountain	6 miles	4 hours	Moderate	September–November
36	Duffy Creek	8 miles	5 hours	Moderate	September–November

Hike	Hike Name	Distance	Hiking Time	Difficulty	Season
37	Rock Island Creek	2 miles	1.5 hours	Easy	May–November
38	Beezley Hills Preserve	3 miles	3 hours	Moderate	April–May
39	Moses Coulee Preserve	4 miles	3 hours	Easy	April–May
40	Chester Butte Wildlife Area	5 miles	3 hours	Moderate	May–November
41	Swakane Canyon	6 miles	4 hours	Difficult	October–December
42	Saddle Mountain East	4 miles	2 hours	Moderate	Year-round
43	Crab Creek Wildlife Area	4–6 miles	3–4 hours	Moderate	Year-round
44	Milwaukee Railroad	10+ miles	4 hours	Easy	Year-round
45	White Bluffs–North Slope	8 miles	4–5 hours	Easy	Year-round
46	Wahluke Lake	4 miles	2–3 hours	Easy	Year-round
47	White Bluffs–South Slope	10 miles	6 hours	Moderate	Year-round
48	McGee Ranch	5 miles	2–3 hours	Easy	Year-round
49	Priest Rapids Wildlife Area	5 miles	2–3 hours	Easy	Year-round
50	Horsethief Butte	1 mile	1 hour	Easy	Year-round
51	The Dalles Mountain	8 miles	5 hours	Difficult	March–November
52	Columbia Hills Natural Area Preserve	6 miles	3–4 hours	Difficult	March–November
53	Catherine Creek	1.5 miles	1 hour	Easy	March–November
54	Juniper Dunes Wilderness	Up to 15 miles	3–6 hours or overnight	Moderate	March–June or October–November
55	McNary National Wildlife Refuge	2 miles	1 hour	Easy	November–March
56	Wallula Habitat Management Unit	6 miles	3 hours	Easy	November–March
57	Twin Sisters Rock	1 mile	1 hour	Easy	Year-round

Hike	Hike Name	Distance	Hiking Time	Difficulty	Season
58	Channa Natural Preserve	3 miles	2 hours	Easy	Year-round
59	Rattlesnake Slope Wildlife Area	5 miles	2–3 hours	Moderate	Year-round
60	Horse Heaven Hills	5–6 miles	3 hours	Moderate	April–June and October–November
61	Chief Joseph Wildlife Area–Grand Ronde River	4–6 miles	3 hours	Moderate	April–June
62	Chief Joseph Wildlife Area–Green Gulch	4–6 miles	3–4 hours	Moderate	April–June
63	Marmes Pond/Lyons Ferry Park	4 miles	3 hours	Moderate	November–March
64	Palouse Falls	2–3 miles	Up to 3 hours	Moderate	March–June
65	Kamiak Butte	3.5 miles	2–3 hours	Moderate	March–November
66	Washtucna Coulee (Kaholotus Railroad Grade)	8 miles (13-mile option)	3–4 hours	Moderate	March–June
67	Snake River/Columbia Plateau Trail	6–8 miles	4 hours	Moderate	November–March
68	Big Flat Habitat Management Unit	6–7 miles	3–4 hours	Easy	Year-round
69	Frog Lake/Crab Creek/Marsh Loop Trails	3+ miles	2–3 hours	Easy	Year-round
70	Chukar Lake/Blythe Lake	4 miles	2–3 hours	Moderate	Year-round
71	Goose Lake Plateau	7–8 miles	4–5 hours	Moderate	Year-round
72	Desert Wildlife Area	6 miles	3–4 hours	Moderate	October–March
73	Potholes Wildlife Area–North	8 miles	3–4 hours	Easy	October–March
74	Potholes Wildlife Area–Dunes Ramble	4 miles	2–3 hours	Easy	Year-round
75	Gloyd Seeps–North	5+ miles	3 hours	Easy	Year-round

Hike	Hike Name	Distance	Hiking Time	Difficulty	Season
76	Gloyd Seeps–South	3.5 miles	2–3 hours	Easy	Year-round
77	Columbia Plateau–Amber Lake	Up to 23 miles	As long as you want	Moderate	Year-round
78	Lakeview Ranch	4 miles	3 hours	Moderate	Year-round
79	Bobs Lakes	3 miles	2 hours	Moderate	Year-round
80	Odessa–Lake Creek Trail	Up to 26 miles	6+ hours	Moderate	Year-round
81	Odessa Craters	2 miles	1–2 hours	Easy	Year-round
82	Escure Ranch	8+ miles	4–5 hours	Moderate	Year-round
83	Breeden Road/Wall Lake	8–10 miles	4–5 hours	Moderate	Year-round
84	Towell Falls	6+ miles	3 hours	Easy	Year-round
85	Packer Creek	4 miles	2–3 hours	Moderate	Year-round
86	Rock Creek Wildlife Area	6 miles	3 hours	Moderate	Year-round
87	Rock Creek/Milwaukee Railroad Corridor	12 miles	5–6 hours	Easy	Year-round
88	Twin Lakes	2–6 miles	1–4 hours	Moderate	Year-round
89	Florence Lake	4.5 miles	2 hours	Moderate	Year-round
90	Reiber Road Loop	9 miles	5 hours	Moderate	Year-round
91	Swanson Lakes	3–4 miles	2+ hours	Easy	Year-round
92	Wilson Creek	2–4 miles	2+ hours	Easy	Year-round
93	Rocky Ford–Crab Creek	6 miles	3 hours	Moderate	September–March
94	Hog Lake	5 miles	3 hours	Moderate	April–July
95	Fishtrap Lake–North	4–10 miles	3–5 hours	Moderate	April–July or September–December

Hike	Hike Name	Distance	Hiking Time	Difficulty	Season
96	Fishtrap Lake–Scroggie Loop	3+ miles	2–3 hours	Moderate	April–July or September–December
97	Turnbull National Wildlife Refuge	1–6 miles	1–3 hours	Moderate	March–October
98	Boyer Park Bluffs	4 miles	2 hours	Difficult	Year-round
99	Tucannon River Canyon (Camp Wooten)	4–6 miles	2–4 hours	Moderate	Year-round
100	Mouth of the Tucannon	4 miles	3 hours	Moderate	Year-round

PREFACE

I have a special affinity for the sagebrush and rimrock of the far southeast corner of Washington, having grown up hiking, hunting, and fishing in the open country there. That dry country is a far cry from the moisture-rich forests of the Olympics and western Cascades, but it is just as much a part of Washington as are the emerald forests of those mountains.

The popular image of stark, barren strands of blowing desert sand doesn't work as a definition for Washington's desert country. Nothing barren or lifeless characterizes this desert. Rather, the dry landscape is rich in both plant and animal life. Sun-loving desert plants add color to the already multihued earth. The black and russet rocks and soils are painted each spring and summer with the vibrant blues, purples, yellows, oranges, whites, and reds of wildflowers bursting into bloom. The deep gullies, high ridges, and long rolling plateaus echo with the calls of coyotes, the screams of raptors, and the "thump, thump, thump" of deer, elk, and bighorn sheep bounding across the landscape. Yes, this is desert, but it is vibrant and intensively beautiful.

The open country east of the Cascades and west of the Rockies sees rain only rarely, but life in great diversity has taken hold here. This land features upland plateaus, sagebrush steppes, dry coulees, and richly vegetated canyons. Running through the heart of this scenic and varied landscape is the mighty Columbia River. Indeed, most of central Washington comprises the Upper Columbia River Basin. From the Tri-Cities to Canada, the Columbia is the central artery through this arid country.

This oft-overlooked part of Washington contains much more than the river, though, and offers some of the most scenic, grandiose country in all of the majestic Pacific Northwest. The massive black basalt walls of Dry Falls—once (following the last great Ice Age) the largest waterfall on the planet and now just a series of dripping cliffs—drop away from the upland flats south of Banks Lake. The steep, rimrock-lined canyons of Swakane Canyon offer refuge to mule deer, bighorn sheep, coyotes, and cougars. Black bears occasionally roam the wild, remote canyons. The rolling hills of the Columbia National Wildlife Refuge flank the last untamed stretch of the wild Columbia along the Hanford Reach. The ravines and draws above Palouse Falls boast literal forests of sagebrush—bushes that tower 6, 10, even 15 feet over the sandy canyon floors. In spring, the entire desert country explodes in color as a plethora of wildflowers—from balsamroot to bitterroot—blossom in the sun.

The broad flatland between the Cascades and the Rockies of Idaho offers wonderful wintertime fun for snow-weary hikers. This part of eastern Washington seldom sees snow of any significance, and what light dustings it does receive merely serve to enhance the stark beauty of the landscape without hindering the hiking opportunities. Washington's desert country is prime winter hiking country.

This varied landscape, full of plants and animals, is a dynamic, exciting part of the state, ripe for recreational exploration. Deserts, yes—but not the Lawrence of Arabia sort. While eastern Washington's desert shares the sun and heat common to that sand-swept image, it is full of life.

In short, the area described in this book is one of the richest, most varied ecosystems in the state. Enjoy your explorations there.

Dan A. Nelson

Western bluebird pauses on a fencepost, Umtanum Ridge, L.T. Murray State Wildlife Recreation Area.

INTRODUCTION

THE JOYS OF DESERT HIKING

"Desert hiking" may seem an alien concept to western Washington hikers who spend all their trail time in the Cascade and Olympic Mountains. It may even seem alien, or at least unusual, to hikers from the metropolitan areas of eastern Washington. Most hikers gravitate toward mountains. In western Washington, hikers head for the Cascades and Olympics. Folks from Spokane may be more familiar with the Selkirk and Colville Ranges. Ellensburg and Yakima-based hikers hit the South Cascades. Hikers from Wenatchee head for the Central Cascades. Trail lovers from the Tri-Cities often explore the Blue Mountains of Washington and Oregon.

All too often, the dry sagebrush steppe country remains unnoticed and unvisited, but the desert country of eastern Washington represents some of the best hiking east of the Cascades. It also offers hikers a new experience in a world completely different from the more familiar mountain country they typically travel.

The desert country east of the Cascades offers wonderful hiking opportunities for nature lovers. The high deserts of eastern Washington are unique, with an amazing array of plant and animal species thriving in the dry climate of the upper Columbia Basin. The wildlife and wildflowers aren't the only sources of beauty and majesty in Washington's desert. This country constitutes some of the most rugged and remote in the state: Deep coulees—carved by Ice Age–era floods—cut across the desert country, and jagged rimrock bluffs line the river canyons.

The desert country east of the Cascades offers snow-weary hikers an escape during the long winter months. When snow clogs the trails and basins of the Cascades and Olympics, the desert routes remain open and largely snow-free. Some higher-elevation desert routes might receive a dusting of snow, but rather than hamper travel, that light snow cover enhances the beauty of this remarkable country. An inch or two of snow coating the sagebrush and black basalt rock of a deep coulee can create a glorious portrait in black and white through which hikers can make their way. Most routes, though, remain snow-free year-round. Hikers may not fully escape the cold bite of winter—indeed, the desert is often colder than the mountains—but the lack of precipitation that defines a desert means that snow is as scarce as rain. Dressed properly, hikers can trek through the desert country all winter without worrying about snow slowing their passage. Bear in mind, too, that most big animals like to avoid snow—snow buries the foliage on which browsers feed and saps the strength of animals that need every possible calorie to survive until spring. Thus, come winter, herds of deer and elk (and in some areas, bighorn sheep) drop out of the forested mountain slopes to browse the snow-free highland steppes of the high desert, providing terrific wildlife viewing for wintertime desert hikers.

What's more, hikers in the urban areas of eastern Washington can find phenomenal year-round hiking opportunities close at hand. Rather than drive hours from their homes to find mountain trails to explore, residents of the major eastern Washington cities and many surrounding communities can find remote wildlands in the open country close to home. The mountains of the Northwest are certainly deserving of visits, but all too often Eastern Washingtonians ignore the very heart of their home country. The desert steppes can be visited year-round, and often the desert routes are easier to access than the distant mountain trails usually traveled.

The desert routes, though, must be given proper consideration, and certain precautions must be observed. Hikers used to the tight tree-lined trails of the Cascades will experience a new sense of freedom when they first start exploring east of the mountains. In addition to a notable lack of trees, hikers will often find a lack of trails. Many of the best routes in the open sagebrush country follow contours of the land, rather than human-made trails.

This book, therefore, doesn't follow the exact model used by other guidebooks. Rather than describe the twists and turns of specific trails, our route descriptions—for the most part—are merely suggestions on how to explore some of these remote, wild, open spaces. Some areas contain well-defined trails, but you also can easily and freely move off trail in such places to explore any nearby ravines, ridges, and plateaus that interest you.

In researching this work, we found we could loosely group the best of the dry-side wild lands around the major urban centers of eastern Washington. With this organization, hikers can plan their adventures from home or from a "base camp" set up in one of these cities. The regions we include in this book are Spokane (northeast), Tri-Cities (southeast), Yakima/Ellensburg (southwest), and Wenatchee/Chelan (northwest).

At the start of each region, we provide a brief, general overview, followed by detailed route descriptions that can be modified with scenic rambles and side trips. To truly appreciate the splendor of the open desert country of eastern Washington, hikers must make each trip their own personal adventure— not just a carbon copy of our recommendations or someone else's trip.

PERMITS AND REGULATIONS

No matter how wild and remote public lands may seem, one generally can't visit them these days without some form of pass or permit. Regulations have pursued recreationists into the most primitive areas. That's not necessarily a bad thing. In an effort to keep our wild areas wild, local, state, and federal land managers have implemented a sometimes complex set of rules and regulations.

At the top of the permit and pass list are the federal lands programs. Virtually all trails in national forests in Washington (and Oregon) fall under the Region 6 Forest Pass Program. Simply stated, in order to park legally at any

U.S. Forest Service–maintained trailhead in USFS Region 6 (Washington and Oregon), you must display a Northwest Forest Pass decal on your windshield. The price as of this writing is $5 per day per vehicle or $30 for an annual pass good throughout Region 6. The Northwest Forest Pass is also required at most trailheads within North Cascades National Park.

The National Park Service has its own permit and fee programs, but those don't come into play in the areas covered by this book. The U.S. Fish and Wildlife Service works with the National Park Service (both agencies are part of the U.S. Department of the Interior), however, to manage national wildlife refuges. To visit these federal wildlife areas, you'll generally need to pay a day-use fee or have an annual Golden Eagle Pass, which covers admission fees for virtually all national park and national wildlife refuge lands.

At the time of this writing, the other big federal land agency—the Bureau of Land Management—doesn't require permits for personal recreational use of their lands.

State lands are a little more complex. The Washington Department of Natural Resources (DNR) asks that recreationists have a free DNR "recreational use permit" when venturing out on their lands. These can be acquired from any DNR field office or from the agency headquarters in Olympia.

The Washington Department of Fish and Wildlife (WDFW), which manages the state's wildlife refuges, requires all vehicles parked at its facilities to have a vehicle use permit displayed. These decals are included free with the purchase of fishing and hunting licenses. They can be bought separately for $10 from any WDFW office or from authorized sellers of Washington fishing and hunting licenses.

SAFETY ISSUES
Seasonal Considerations

Generally, most of the routes described in this book are hikeable year-round, though some will accumulate modest amounts of snow periodically in winter. Seldom will accumulated snow total more than 10 inches, but snow can fall in great depths anywhere in the state. The higher the elevation of the trail, and the farther north, the greater the likelihood of deeper snow.

Come summer, the risk is high temperatures. Parts of the central Columbia River Basin roast with daytime temperatures frequently topping 100 degrees F. for days at a time. Carrying plenty of water is essential when visiting any of these routes in the summer months.

Spring and autumn are the safest seasons to hike the desert, with milder conditions prevailing. Spring brings wildflowers to bloom throughout the region. However, winter often provides the most unique and memorable outings—nothing in the world compares to seeing the shimmering green-grey sage bushes dusted with a thin layer of snow, or the stark black basalt cliffs above the Snake River fringed in ice. Simply put, the desert can be enjoyed any time of the year, with seasonal allowances made for weather and conditions.

Weather

As the moist air comes rushing inland from the Pacific, it hits the western front of the Cascades. The air is pushed up the slopes of the mountains, often forming clouds and eventually rain, feeding the wet rain forests that dominate the western slopes. By the time the airstream crests the Cascades and starts down the east slopes, the clouds have lost their moisture loads, leaving the east side dry and forests filled with open stands of drought-resistant pine.

Where east meets west—roughly marked by the Cascade crest—the wet clouds hit the dry heat of the desert country, often creating thunderstorms. These storms frequently extend well out into the high deserts of eastern Washington, meaning hikers in the sagebrush flats can start a day hike under clear skies only to find their return muddied by heavy rains and dangerous bolts of lightning. The storms can blow up with little warning, and a hiker in the open country as a thunderstorm develops is a good target for a lightning bolt.

To reduce the dangers of lightning, if thunderstorms are forecast, or develop while you are hiking, do the following:

■ Use a National Oceanic and Atmospheric Administration (NOAA) weather radio (i.e., a radio set to tune in to one of the national weather forecast frequencies) to keep abreast of the latest weather information.

■ Avoid setting up camp in narrow valleys, gullies, or ridge tops. Instead, use campsites in broad, open valleys and meadows, away from large rock formations.

■ Stay well away from bodies of water.

■ If your hair stands on end, or you feel static shocks, move immediately— the static electricity you feel could very well be a precursor to a lightning strike.

■ If a shelter or building can be found nearby, get into it. Don't take shelter under trees, however, especially in open areas.

■ If no shelter is available, and lightning is flashing, remove your pack (the metal stays or frame are natural electrical conduits) and crouch down, balancing on the balls of your feet until the lighting clears the area.

Of course, thunderstorms aren't the only weather hazard desert hikers face. A sudden rain squall can push temperatures down 15 or 20 degrees in a matter of minutes. Folks dressed for hot summer hiking must be prepared for such temperature drops and the accompanying soaking rain if they want to avoid hypothermia.

The lack of trees in this country also makes flash floods a concern. With no forests to absorb and slow it, falling rainwater rushes downhill and fills ravines and gullies quickly, creating rushing torrents of water that can sweep hikers away with little warning. So when it starts raining in the high country, stay out of the low country.

Sun and Heat

Perhaps the greatest weather-related risk hikers face is the heat of summer. In July and August, hikers of many of the routes descibed in this book can experience daytime temperatures well in excess of 100 degrees F. Coupled with a general low humidity, that can lead to heat exhaustion or heat stroke in hikers who aren't properly prepared. The key to staying safe when the mercury rises is to stay hydrated. Plan to drink at least two or three quarts of water every day you are on the trail in warm weather—and plan to carry that much, plus an extra quart for emergency use. That means carrying upward of a gallon of water per day on the trail since you can't expect to find water sources on many of the routes. Even in the "shoulder" seasons—April through June and September through October—the sun can be scorching though the temperatures may be well below 80 degrees F. most days.

To counter the destructive nature of the sun, hikers should carry and use sunscreen that's rated at least 15 or 20 SPF, even on overcast days when ultraviolet (UV) light can be intense in these treeless areas. On bright days, it's also a good idea to wear long-sleeved shirts and pants made from fast-drying nylons and synthetics, which provide excellent UV protection and slow moisture loss in the dry climate without causing overheating. A wide-brimmed hat is also a great aid in blocking out the scorching sun.

Hydration and General Health

Even in winter, when the mercury rattles around at the bottom of the thermometer, the desert country of eastern Washington is dry. With an average rainfall of less than a foot per year in many parts of this region, spring, summer, winter, and fall are all dry. As a result, the humidity is low, and hikers are more prone than ever to dehydration.

Dehydration leads to an array of problems for hikers. It makes us tire and fatigue faster. It slows our reaction time and makes us more sluggish. It affects our thought processes and helps hasten other problems, such as heat exposure and heat exhaustion.

One way to easily test of our hydration level is to pay attention to our urination. First, if we aren't urinating regularly during the day, we aren't drinking enough. When we do urinate, if it is dark yellow in color, we need more water. Properly hydrated, we'll stop for a bathroom break every few hours, and our urine will be clear or pale yellow.

Staying hydrated in the dry desert country can be problematic, however, primarily because we have to carry all that water we are supposed to drink. The natural sources of water are few and far between in much of eastern Washington. We need to carry at least three liters of water per day and to drink a liter or two *before* starting a hike to make sure our cells are pumped full of H_2O (drink a bottle or two of water on the drive to the hiking area).

Rattlesnakes

We (the authors) love snakes, but we're in the minority. We actively look for rattlesnakes when we hike the desert country of Washington because we think they are some of the most beautiful—and misunderstood—critters on our wild lands. Most folks avoid the desert in summer for one reason only: snakes. That's unfortunate, because those hikers are more at danger from bees in the Cascades than they are from snakes in the desert.

Rattlesnakes act and react instinctually for the most part, and instinct tells them that it is better to run away or hide from big, lumbering beasts (humans) than it is to attack them. That being the case, if given even half a chance, rattlesnakes will avoid humans.

Personally, the only rattlesnake bites I know of have occurred when a foolish human decided to try to capture a snake. Grab for a rattlesnake, and it will strike. Walk up a trail and surprise a snake, and it will slither away as fast as possible.

That's not to say accidents don't happen. Rattlesnakes sometimes nap on the same sun-drenched rocks over which hikers like to scramble. When surprised or cornered, snakes will strike in self-defense.

Knowing this, hikers can minimize the chances of an accident by being aware of the dangers and working to minimize them. Hiking with a trekking pole or a walking stick helps immensely. Use your poles to push brush back when you're on the trail and to thump rocks and ledges before climbing onto them.

You'll never know how effective this action is because snakes seldom let you see them. In fact, the patterns on a rattlesnake provide camouflage from predators, which want to eat the snake, and from prey, which the snake wants to eat. If the snake senses a human, odds are good that it will simply lie motionless and hidden, even if it is mere feet from the trail. If a hiker gets too close and the snake has an open avenue of escape, it will disappear quickly and silently.

Only when surprised and cornered will a snake become defensive. It will coil up, raise its head into a strike posture, and shake its tail, producing that distinctive "buzz" that is impossible to mistake for something else. The rattle is the snake's last-ditch effort to avoid confrontation—it's basically a warning to anything threatening it to back off or there will be trouble.

If you hear that buzz, you should immediately freeze and locate the source of the sound—you don't want to start backpedaling only to realize you've already walked past the snake. Once you know more or less where the snake is, move away slowly and methodically in the most direct manner possible. Keep your hiking stick slightly off the ground between you and the snake as you move away: If the snake does strike, it may go for the stick rather than your leg.

Once you've moved 3 or 4 feet from the snake, you are pretty much in the clear: A snake can strike only a little more than half its body length, and seldom do Washington's rattlesnakes grow more than 3 or 4 feet in length.

All that said, snakebites do occur. The most recent data I've seen suggest 7,000 to 8,000 venomous snakebites occur each year in the United States, and 60 percent of those are from rattlesnakes. Still, fewer than ten deaths from snakebites occur every year, and most fatalities are from the more toxic species, such as cottonmouths and copperheads.

If you are one of the unfortunate few who receives a bite from a rattlesnake, don't panic. You'll immediately feel pain if the snake injects venom (frequently, a snake will initially pretend to strike, without biting, to intimidate and scare you away). Injected venom sets off a rapid response, producing pain, enormous swelling, and bruising.

Following are steps to take immediately following a snakebite:
1. Remain calm and inactive.
2. Rest.
3. Get medical aid as quickly as possible.

Some things should be avoided as well. Therefore:
1. *Do not panic.* (Panic increases heart rate, which circulates venom more quickly.)
2. *Do not elevate the bite site above the heart.*
3. *Do not suck the venom out by mouth.*
4. *Do not cut the bite wound to draw out the venom.*
5. *Do not apply a tourniquet or pressure dressing.*
6. *Do not apply ice to the bite.*

Getting to medical aid may be problematic when in a remote area, and especially if you are alone. Fortunately, the venom travels fairly slowly, and the most severe symptoms often do not occur for some time, so it is possible to calmly, slowly walk out to the trailhead to find aid.

In some instances, a snakebite kit can be of help, but only if it is the proper type of kit. According to new research from the Wilderness Medical Society—a group devoted to developing safe and effective medical treatments for wilderness travels—the only effective way to reduce venom in a bite wound is with an extractor-type device. These (mechanical) suction devices can remove up to 30 percent of the venom from a bite if used within 3 minutes of a strike.

Ticks

This is also tick country, so after each outing hikers should check themselves for the tiny bloodsuckers. Fortunately, ticks usually take 24 hours or more before attaching themselves, so ridding yourself of these pests is generally easy with a little care.

Other Wildlife

In the remote desert country, one is more likely to encounter wild mule deer, elk, and bighorn sheep—and to be at greater risk from any of them than from rattlesnakes. These big grass-eating beasts are vicious, and they are quick to defend themselves and their offspring if they feel threatened. Thus, please be careful around any wild animals. Observe them from a distance. Never try to move closer for a better view or camera angle because your approach could be taken as an act of aggression and the usually mild-mannered beasts could become frightened aggressors.

Hunting Seasons

The desert country of eastern Washington supports an incredible array of wildlife. That makes for great wildlife watching, but it also creates good hunting opportunities. Upland bird hunters prowl the sagebrush flats, desert canyons, and rimrock bluffs above river canyons in search of pheasant, quail, partridge, chukar, grouse, and dove. Deer and elk are also hunted throughout the region. In response to human suppression of natural predators, human hunters are needed to help maintain population balances. Deer especially can overpopulate an area quickly if they aren't hunted—and with no wolves available to do the job, humans must handle it. Whether or not you like the thought of hunting, it is a legitimate use of public lands, and it does occur. Understanding that and knowing the approximate dates of the hunting seasons will help you avoid any problems that might occur during a hunting season. Most hunters are extremely ethical, conscientious, and responsible outdoor enthusiasts and will welcome fair and responsible hikers into the field with them. If you want to hike during hunting season (typically, September though December for all the various seasons), you should—at the very least—wear a hunter's orange vest and hat. You should also pick up a copy of the "Washington Department of Fish and Wildlife's Hunting Regulations" (available anywhere hunting licenses are sold or online at *www.wa.gov/wdfw*).

GEAR AND EQUIPMENT
Navigation and Maps

Hikers everywhere should carry and understand how to use maps and compass. Unlike the Cascades and Olympics, however, no Green Trails maps are available for eastern Washington's open desert country, where established trails are few and far between, so basic navigation skills are absolutely essential there. Hikers should obtain the appropriate USGS 7.5-minute maps or one of the many topographic map sets available on CD-ROM. The Washington State Department of Natural Resources (DNR) also offers a series of 1:100,000-scale maps that delineate all public land boundaries and natural features, as well as most roads (including minor gravel and dirt roads). These maps can be found at all DNR regional offices or by contacting the DNR office in Olympia (details in Appendix B).

Before heading out on any hike in this—or any other—guidebook, hikers should obtain and—before leaving home—study the appropriate map for the area of travel. It is also important to practice navigation and route finding with a compass—including how to take bearings and transfer them to maps for accurate route finding. Because no trails will be available on many of these routes, map-and-compass navigation skills are essential. Fortunately, this open country provides wonderful places for practicing and perfecting route-finding skills. The landscape allows unobstructed views for many miles, and even when views are blocked, a scramble to a hilltop or ridgeline provides clear views to the distant horizon. The open space and unlimited viewing make taking a bearing and following a compass heading easy.

A map and compass are adequate for most travel, but a GPS receiver can make route finding easier. Many current models of GPS receivers allow users to transfer map and route information from a home computer to a handheld GPS unit. In the field, then, route information is easily accessible, and the satellite navigation system helps users stay on course. However, no one should rely solely on a GPS for navigation—batteries die, clouds and weather can obscure satellite signals, and disruptions in service (natural disruptions—such as solar flares—and technical disruptions—such as national defense emergencies) can render satellites unusable for varying periods of time. Thus, even when using a GPS receiver, hikers should have—and know how to use—a map and compass.

Gear

No hiker should venture far up a trail without being properly equipped. Starting with the feet, a good pair of *boots* can make the difference between a wonderful hike and a horrible death march. Keep your feet happy and you'll be happy.

Appropriate *socks* are also essential equipment. Only one rule applies here: *Wear whatever is most comfortable, unless it's cotton.*

Masses of arrowleafed balsamroot, Beezley Hills Nature Preserve

In fact, *never wear cotton.* Cotton is a wonderful fabric when your life isn't on the line: It is soft, light, and airy. But get it wet and it stays wet, which means blisters on your feet if you're wearing cotton socks. Wet cotton also lacks any insulation value. In fact, wet cotton sucks away body heat and increases susceptibility to hypothermia. Therefore, leave your cotton socks, cotton underwear, and cotton T-shirts at home. The only cotton we carry on the trail is a trusty bandanna.

A good, three-season *tent* for shelter and a fluffy, lightweight *sleeping bag*— with a *small pad* (used as much for insulation from the cold ground as for padding)—are the primary items to pack, along with a *pack stove* and *food.* In addition, a lot of little things should go into a pack, even on a day hike.

While the list of what to pack will vary from hiker to hiker on the same trail, each and every hiker should pack certain essentials. For instance, every hiker who ventures more than a few hundred yards from a road should be prepared to spend the night under the stars (or under the clouds, as may be more likely). Desert storms can whip up in a hurry, catching sunny-day hikers by surprise. What was an easy-to-follow trail during a calm, clear day can disappear into a confusing world of fog and rain—even snow—in a windy tempest. Therefore, every member of a party should carry a pack loaded with a few other items that can keep a group safe and comfortable in an emergency.

The Ten Essentials

The Mountaineers organization has long maintained a list of "Ten Essentials"—items that every wilderness traveler should carry to help them stay safe and healthy when delayed in the wilderness. Over the years, the list of essentials has changed a bit, but the bottom line has remained constant: Some basic essentials can help outdoor recreationists survive any emergency situation outdoors. The latest version of The Mountaineers' Ten Essentials (as published in the outdoor recreationists' bible, *Freedom of the Hills,* 7th edition) was devised to answer two basic questions: (1) Can you respond positively to an accident or emergency? (2) Can you safely spend one or more nights out in an emergency? Rather than list ten specific items, the new Ten Essentials list focuses on equipment systems. Here's the new list:

The Ten Essentials: A Systems Approach

1. **Navigation (map and compass).** This also includes knowledge of how to use a map and compass, as well as secondary aids such as GPS receivers and altimeters.
2. **Sun protection (sunglasses and sunscreen).**
3. **Insulation (extra clothing).** Hikers should carry extra clothing in their packs so that they always have another layer or two to add to what they are wearing if temperatures drop.
4. **Illumination (headlamp or flashlight).** New generations of LED lights mean it's easy to add effective light sources to a pack with only minimal additional weight.

5. **First-aid supplies.** Every hiker should carry a basic first aid kit and have the skills to handle any basic medical emergency, from burst blisters to lacerations and sprains.
6. **Fire (firestarter and matches/lighter).** Matches and/or lighters are useful, but it is also important to carry some basic tinder that will burn long enough to start a fire with damp wood. This can be as simple as a candle or some form of chemical tinder.
7. **Repair kit and tools (including knife).** Generally, a small roll of duct tape and some safety pins work well. You might also carry an extra quick-release buckle and webbing straps in case you break a buckle on your pack.
8. **Nutrition (extra food).** This can be as simple as adding an extra energy bar to your pack. Always carry a little more than you plan to eat over the regular course of your hike.
9. **Hydration (extra water).** Carry all you plan to drink during your hike, plus an extra quart.
10. **Emergency shelter.** At the minimum, carry a lightweight "space blanket" that you can wrap around yourself if you have to spend the night out.

LEAVE NO TRACE
Go Lightly on the Land

Despite the harsh, rugged nature of the landscape, desert ecosystems are often fragile and sensitive. Hikers should enjoy these resources, but wisely. That means traveling as lightly on the land as possible. When trails exist, hikers must use them—even if they are just game trails carved into the soil by years of use by passing deer and elk. When trails don't exist, hikers must choose paths wisely, sticking to the rocky, hard-packed earth as much as possible to avoid treading on the delicate wildflowers and plants that dot the desert floor. Backpackers should never make a campfire unless they find an established campsite with a concrete-lined fire ring.

When we provide driving directions to a hiking site, we frequently recommend stopping short of the road's end and walking the dirt tracks. This serves two purposes. First, it gets you out hiking that much faster. Second, it gets your vehicle off the desert floor that much sooner. Wheel tracks can make long-lasting impressions in the thin soils of the desert country. Indeed, in some areas, you'll find the deep wheel ruts of horse-drawn wagons from years gone by. By stopping your vehicle before the wheel tracks run out, you can help slow the erosion of some sensitive areas while enjoying more time walking.

General Trail Etiquette

Everyone who enjoys recreating in the backcountry should recognize their responsibility to the natural, wild lands and to other recreationists. We each must work to preserve the tranquility of wild lands by being sensitive to the environment as well as to other trail users.

Most of the lands described in this book are open to hikers, trail runners, horse riders, hunters, bird-watchers, dog owners, and sometimes bicyclists and motorcyclists. Upon encountering other trail users, the "Golden Rule of Trail Etiquette" is that common sense and simple courtesy must be observed. It's hard to overstate how vital common sense and courtesy are to maintaining an enjoyable, safe, and friendly situation on trails when different types of trail users meet.

With that rule firmly in mind, you can do some other things to make your trip, and that of others on the trail, most enjoyable:

■ When hikers meet other hikers, the group heading uphill has the right-of-way. There are two general reasons for this. First, on steep ascents, hikers may be watching the trail before them and not notice the approach of descending hikers until they are face-to-face. More importantly, it is easier for descending hikers to break their stride and step off the trail than it is for those who have fallen into a good, climbing plod. IF, however, the uphill hiker is in need of a rest, they may step-off the trail and yield the right-of-way to the downhill hikers, but this is the decision of the climbers alone.

■ When hikers meet other user groups, the hikers should move off the trail. This is because hikers are generally the most mobile and flexible users, so it is easier for hikers to step off the trail than for bicyclists to lift their bikes or for horse riders to get their animals off the trail.

■ When hikers meet horseback riders, the hikers should step off the downhill side of the trail unless the terrain makes this difficult or dangerous. In that case, move to the uphill side of the trail, but crouch down a bit so you do not tower over the horses' heads. Also, do not stand behind trees or brush if you can avoid it as this could make you invisible to the animals until they get close, and then your sudden appearance could startle them. Rather, stay in clear view and talk in a normal voice to the riders. This calms the horses.

■ Stay on trails and practice minimum impact. Don't cut switchbacks, take shortcuts, or make new trails. If your destination is off-trail, leave the trail in as direct a manner as possible—that is, move away from the trail in a line perpendicular to the trail. Once clear of the trail, adjust your route to your destination.

■ Obey the rules specific to the trail you are visiting. Many trails are closed to certain types of use, including hiking with dogs or riding horses.

■ Hikers who take their dogs on trails should have them on leashes—or immediately responsive to voice commands—at all times.

■ Avoid disturbing wildlife, especially in winter and in calving areas. Observe from a distance: If you cannot get the picture you want from a distance, resist the urge to move closer to wildlife. This not only keeps you safer but also prevents animals from having to exert themselves unnecessarily to flee from you.

■ Leave all natural objects and features as you found them so others can enjoy them.

■ Never roll rocks off trails or cliffs: You never know who or what is below.

These are just a few of the things hikers can do to maintain a safe and harmonious trail environment. While not every situation is addressed by these rules, hikers can avoid problems by always practicing the "Golden Rule of Trail Etiquette": Common sense and courtesy are the order of the day.

Low-Impact Camping

Everyone loves to sit around a campfire, letting the orange flames hypnotize them and stir up a wealth of thoughts and dreams. Unfortunately, if everyone who enters the wilderness were to build a fire, campsites would be filled with charcoal, and grasslands and forests would soon be picked clean of dead wood, leaving hordes of small critters with nowhere to scrounge for food (the insects that eat dead wood provide meals for an army of birds and other animals). Thus, fires should be restricted to campgrounds with structured fire pits and readily available supplies of firewood. Backcountry campers should stick to small pack stoves, even when regulations technically allow campfires.

Hikers must also remember that anything packed in must be packed out, even biodegradable items such as apple cores. The phrase "Leave only footprints, take only pictures" is a worthy slogan to live by when visiting the desert.

You must also give some thought to your campsites. When hardened sites are available, use them. Restricting campers to one or two sites around a lake prevents the entire shoreline from being trampled and stripped of its vegetation. If there is no established site, choose a rock surface or sandy area where you won't damage fragile vegetation.

If you must camp in a meadow, choose a location with good drainage and limit the amount of time your tent is set up. Rather than pitch the tent immediately upon reaching your camp, leave it in its stuff sack until you are done with dinner, and then set it up. First thing next morning, break it down before breakfast. This prevents the plants under a tent from being smothered. Most of the time, even though plants are a bit bent and crumpled, they'll spring back up again soon.

Also keep in mind that you aren't the only hikers enjoying the beauty of the desert. That rocky bench overlooking the mountains across the valley might seem the perfect place for a tent, but what if you set up there and someone comes along and wants to sit and enjoy the view for a few moments? With your camp established on the viewpoint, other hikers will feel uncomfortable stepping up for a look at the vista. It's a much better idea to set up away from the most scenic locations so that you can walk to them from camp and others sharing the trail with you can enjoy them also.

"Hey, you two! Get back here," seems to be the look on mom's face as her two young steers enjoy balsamroot on the other side of the fence at The Dalles Mountain. Most public lands border private ranch lands, and the boundaries need to be respected by us—not just the cattle.

The same goes for water. Keep your camps at least 100 feet away from lakeshores and stream banks. This not only lets other hikers—and animals—get to the water without having to bypass you, but it helps keep the water clean.

Another important leave no trace principle focuses on bathroom etiquette. The first backcountry rule is that if an outhouse exists, it should be used. This may seem obvious, but all too often folks find backcountry toilets to be dark, dank affairs and they choose to use the woods rather than the rickety wooden structure provided by the land manager. It may be easier on your nose to head off into the woods, but this disperses human waste around popular camping areas. Privies, on the other hand, keep the waste concentrated in a single site, minimizing contamination of area waters. The outhouses get even higher environmental marks if they feature removal holding tanks that can be airlifted out. These johns and their accompanying tanks aren't exactly aesthetically pleasing, but having an ugly outhouse tucked into a corner of the woods is better than finding toilet paper strewn throughout.

When privies aren't provided, the key factor to consider is location. You'll want to choose a site at least 200 to 300 feet from water, campsites, and trails. A location well out of sight of trails and viewpoints will give you privacy and will reduce the odds of other hikers stumbling into the site after you leave. Other factors to consider are ecological: A good surrounding of vegetation, with some direct sunlight, will aid decomposition.

Once you pick your place, start digging. The idea is to make like a cat and bury your waste. You need to dig down through the organic duff into the mineral soil below—a hole six to eight inches deep is usually adequate. When you've taken care of business, refill the hole and camouflage it with rocks and sticks—this helps prevent other humans, or animals, from digging in the same location before decomposition has done its job.

Water

Always treat your drinking water. Wherever humans have gone—and humans have gone just about everywhere—germs have gone with them. What's more, domestic livestock and wild ruminants (deer and elk), have no compunction against relieving themselves in waterways, and use much of the open grassland of eastern Washington. That means that even the most pristine desert and mountain streams may harbor microscopic nasties such as giardia cysts, cryptosporidium, and *E. coli.*

Treating water can be as simple as boiling it, chemically purifying it (adding tiny iodine tablets), or pumping it through one of the new generation of water filters or purifiers (*Note:* Pump units labeled as filters generally remove everything but viruses, which are too small to be filtered out. Pumps labeled as purifiers must have a chemical element—usually iodine—that kills viruses after filtering out all the other microorganisms). Never drink untreated water, or your intestines will never forgive you.

Cleanup

When it comes time to wash yourself or your utensils, give a thought to what you want in the water you drink. You get your drinking water from the nearby lake or stream, right? Would you want to find someone's leftover macaroni and cheese in it? Or their soap scum? Of course not, and neither would other folks, so be careful with your cleanups.

When washing your hands, first rinse off as much dust and dirt as you can in plain water. If you still feel the need for a soapy wash, collect a pot of water from the lake or stream and move away at least 100 feet. Apply a tiny bit of biodegradable soap to your hands, dribble on a little water, and lather up. Use a bandanna or towel to wipe away most of the soap, and then rinse with the water in the pot. Follow the same procedure with your pots and pans, making sure you eat all the food first (never dump leftover food in water or on the ground. If you can't eat it, pack it into a plastic bag and store it with your other food: In other words, carry it out!

Private and Public Property

Throughout this book, we've made every effort to point you toward public lands and away from private property. However, land ownership changes, sometimes quickly. Also, some landowners who are adjacent to public lands try to quietly limit the use of those public lands by placing "No Trespassing" signs on property boundaries in a way that suggests the public lands and/ or public roads are closed to use.

The best way to deal with this is to always have current maps in hand, call the land management agency before you head out for a hike, and be willing to turn around and go somewhere else if a landowner challenges you. It is far better to walk away and come back another day than it is to raise a ruckus over an issue that is at best unclear. For the most part, though, the ranchers, farmers, and other landowners of eastern Washington are warm, caring, and gracious folks who don't mind hikers skirting their property, as long as they are respectful and courteous.

That said, you should always do the following:

- Leave gates as you find them (close them if they were closed, leave them open if they were open).
- Don't drive (or walk unless absolutely necessary) on planted crops or tilled fields.
- Leave livestock alone.
- Say hello to any ranchers, farmers, hunters, and hikers you encounter.

A Note on Driving Routes and National Security

The concrete dams along the Columbia and Snake Rivers have long been used as part of the road system in eastern Washington. With bridges sometimes few and far between, locals appreciate the availability of the dams as secondary routes across the great rivers of the desert country. Following the horrific events of September 11, 2001, however, public access to the dams has been restricted, and the Department of Homeland Security and Army Corps of Engineers have prohibited public vehicle use over the dams.

While the driving directions within this book avoid requiring the crossing of hydroelectric dams, many maps and atlases still list the dams as viable driving routes. Please make note of the changes in dam regulations to avoid getting caught on the wrong side of the river far from the nearest bridge.

A Note About Safety

Safety is an important concern in all outdoor activities. No guidebook can alert you to every hazard or anticipate the limitations of every reader. Therefore, the descriptions of roads, trails, routes, and natural features in this book are not representations that a particular place or excursion will be safe for your party. When you follow any of the routes described in this book, you assume responsibility for your own safety. Under normal conditions, such excursions require the usual attention to traffic, road and trail conditions, weather, terrain, the capabilities of your party, and other factors. Keeping informed on current conditions and exercising common sense are the keys to a safe, enjoyable outing.

The Mountaineers Books

Facing page: Grasswidow (Olsynium inflatum)

YAKIMA AND ELLENSBURG

he areas surrounding the urban centers of Yakima and Ellensburg represent some of the richest ecosystems in all of Washington. Vast state-managed wildlife refuges sprawl over remote hills, valleys, and coulees from the foothills of the Cascades to the lower Yakima River basin. Herds of the great beasts known to native tribes as wapiti (Rocky Mountain elk) roam the pine-studded hills of the L. T. Murray State Wildlife Recreation Area. Bighorn sheep prowl the high, craggy bluffs above the Yakima River Canyon. Mule deer browse the sagebrush slopes of the Oak Creek State Wildlife Area, and birds of all sizes and colors soar through the desert air above the entire region.

The rugged desert country between Ellensburg and Yakima is also some of the easiest to reach, with good access from Interstate 90 and Interstate 82. Rain-weary west-side hikers can find themselves deep in the dry desert country in just a few hours.

1 UMTANUM CREEK FALLS

Round trip ■	3 to 10 miles
Hiking time ■	3 to 6 hours
Difficulty ■	Moderate
Starting elevation ■	2000 feet
Low point ■	1300 feet
Best season ■	Late winter, early spring
Maps ■	Washington State Department of Natural Resources (DNR) Yakima
Contact ■	Washington Department of Fish and Wildlife
Permits/passes ■	Washington Department of Fish and Wildlife Vehicle Permit required

From Seattle, drive east on Interstate 90 to exit 109 in Ellensburg. At the end of the exit ramp, turn right to drive under the freeway and at 0.7 mile turn left at Umtanum Road at the traffic light. Stay on this road, which turns to gravel at 5.2 miles, for a total of 10 miles from the freeway exit. At 10 miles, find a small signed parking area at a sharp turn in the road.

A diversity of landscape and ecosystems are found along this canyon trek. Starting high and hiking downhill, the route begins in open, Douglas fir forest and ends in sagebrush and scrub grass desert canyons. Elk roam the upper woods, and bighorn sheep prowl the steep canyon walls around the pounding waterfall. Visit in early spring to enjoy the best wildlife viewing (beasts of all sizes stick to this canyon while the snows still fill the high country). Spring also means the waterfall is running full with snowmelt water. The area in and around the falls is very icy in winter.

From the parking area, start down the Umtanum Falls Trail, noting that the first 0.5 mile no longer rolls between sections of private property. The Washington Department of Fish and Wildlife purchased this land in 2006, and it is now part of the state-owned L. T. Murray State Wildlife Recreation Area lands. For the next 0.5 mile, you'll pass through the transition zone between the lowland forest and the high desert. At times the canyon narrows and the north wall looms higher. With more shade and less scorching sun in the summer, trees thrive. Douglas firs tower high on the shaded slopes, while the canyon floor sports a dense forest of pine and fir. As you near the 1-mile mark, the canyon walls mellow, opening the entire chasm to the full glare of sun day in and day out. The result is dramatic: Gone are the towering firs and pines, and instead the canyon is filled with fragrant sagebrush groves.

At just over 1 mile, the stunning punchbowl surrounding Umtanum Falls opens before you. The creek falls about 40 feet into an oval-shaped basalt bowl. Throughout winter and spring, ice plasters the black rock alongside the falls as the water cascades into the bowl and then out a narrow canyon. In this water-rich basin, ponderosa pines thrive.

Hikers may continue down the creek valley for several miles along the

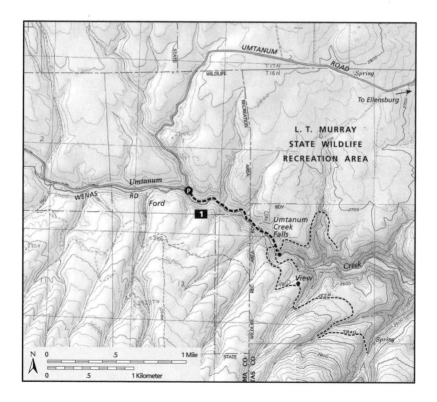

Umtanum Creek Falls in winter

"official" trail (brushy scramble in places), though we recommend exploring. Rock-hop across the creek well above the falls, where you'll find an easily scrambled slope to the top of the south wall of the canyon. Follow the canyon rim to view amazing rock formations: myriad volcanic basalt forms that boggle the mind. Later in spring, the ridge top also sports the first color of the local wildflower show. Buckwheat and balsamroot are especially abundant.

For a good daylong outing, follow the south canyon rim about 3 miles until it is broken by a broad side canyon, then turn back and head home.

2 UMTANUM CREEK CANYON

Round trip ■	6 to 10 miles
Hiking time ■	3 to 6 hours
Difficulty ■	Moderate
Starting elevation ■	1300 feet
High point ■	2000 feet
Best season ■	November through May
Maps ■	Washington State Department of Natural Resources (DNR) Yakima
Contact ■	Washington Department of Fish and Wildlife
Permits/passes ■	In 2008, the Bureau of Land Management (BLM) implemented its own parking pass program. BLM Day Use pass now required (available at trailhead, $5 per day); federal "America the Beautiful Pass" also accepted ($80 per year, accepted at all BLM, National Park, and Forest Service locations).

From Seattle, drive east on Interstate 90 to exit 110. After exiting, continue east on Interstate 82 about 3.5 miles to exit 3 (Thrall Road). At the stop sign, turn

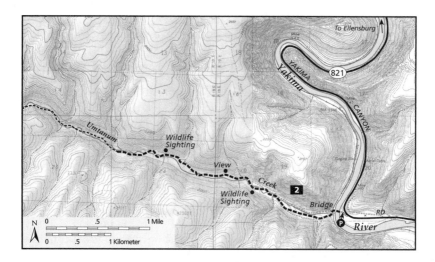

right on State Route 821. Turn left at the next stop sign to continue southeast along State Route 821 into Yakima Canyon (signed "Yakima Canyon") and continue about 8 miles to the Umtanum Recreation Area (between mileposts 16 and 17). A large gravel parking lot is on the right (west) side of the road.

Begin with a walk over a bouncy suspension bridge above the trout-rich waters of the Yakima River. This trail meanders up an ever-narrowing canyon, but it also seems to be a path to the past. The trail leaves behind the highway and clusters of anglers and rolls up past an old homestead (complete with an overgrown, brambly apple orchard) and leads into pristine desert wildlife habitat. The year-round waters of Umtanum Creek draw a vast collection of critters to this canyon. Bighorn sheep roam the canyon walls and browse the grass-rich bottoms. Deer abound throughout the area. Coyotes hunt the heavy populations of rabbits, rock chucks (marmots), and upland birds (quail, pheasant, chukar, grouse, Hungarian partridge, and others). Rattle-snakes are frequently seen in the summer (another reason to visit in winter months) when they congregate to take advantage of the mice, voles, and ground squirrels that thrive in the creek-fed grasses and tree stands. Beavers and muskrats build homes in the creek, creating an endless series of pools and ponds throughout the length of the valley. All around, underfoot and on the canyon walls, desert wildflowers color the canyon.

From the trailhead parking area, cross the Yakima River via the broad foot-traffic-only suspension bridge, then cross the high berm of the railroad tracks. Once over the railroad route, enter the L. T. Murray State Wildlife Rec-reation Area. The trail meanders through a broad sagebrush flat for 0.5 mile or so before crossing an old fence line (a few rotten posts and a low mound of dirt are about all that remains of the fence). Around this old homestead site you'll see the remnants of an old cabin—mostly just its rock foundation and a scraggly grove of apple trees.

That's the last real imprint of humans in this wild canyon. Various species of sage provide texture and fragrance to the canyon floor, while the canyon walls tower overhead.

Visit in winter and you might find a dusting of snow (possibly a few inches). A thin blanket of snow is actually a benefit to hikers as it serves as a tapestry on which the comings and goings of the local population are recorded. If you find snow, you'll also find tracks left by deer, bighorns, coyotes, small mammals, and game birds. The creek is the only water source for miles around, and it's easy to see the pathways of animals that come down from the canyon rim to get water.

The trail crosses the creek at about 1 mile. The crossing is typically an easy rock-hop, though at times you'll be forced to find a shallow spot between beaver ponds—or to carefully cross on a beaver dam. Extensive beaver activity is visible on this small desert creek. Some dams (made primarily from the local aspen, cottonwood, and alder) stand 6 to 8 feet tall, creating ponds that stretch several dozen yards upstream. Frequently the dams are built back to back with a new one standing at the upper edge of the lower dam's pond.

About 2 miles up the trail, the trail skirts around a stand of low alder. On several visits to the area, we've encountered a portion of the resident herd of bighorn sheep (usually numbering 50 or 60 animals) either bedded down in this area or vacating their beds. The alder grove apparently provides good shelter for them on cold winter nights.

The trail continues up the canyon, but past the 3-mile mark it becomes narrow and largely overgrown and many creek crossings are needed. Rather than push on through the brush, turn around here and return through the rich canyon, remembering that you will find plenty to see on your way back.

3 DURR ROAD AND NORTH YAKIMA SKYLINE

Round trip ■	9 to 14 miles
Hiking time ■	4 to 7 hours
Difficulty ■	Difficult
Starting elevation ■	3450 feet
Low point ■	2000 feet
Best season ■	May through June
Maps ■	Washington State Department of Natural Resources (DNR) Yakima
Contact ■	Washington Department of Fish and Wildlife
Permits/passes ■	Washington Department of Fish and Wildlife Vehicle Permit required

Old corner fence posts atop Umtanum Ridge near Durr Road trailhead

From Seattle, drive east on Interstate 90 to exit 109 in Ellensburg. After exiting the freeway, turn right to drive under the freeway. At 0.7 mile from the freeway, turn left at Umtanum Road (at second traffic light). Continue on this road as it leaves town. At 5.1 miles from the traffic light, turn left onto Durr Road. Drive on Durr Road (rough in places and occasionally steep) for 4 miles as it winds down to a crossing of Umtanum Creek (the ford is generally shallow and well cobbled for safe use by most vehicles in fall and winter, but spring runoff can cause problems). After crossing the creek, continue another 3.2 miles on Durr Road as it climbs to the trailhead. Park at a broad pullout on the left by an old wooden sign-hanger, a total of 7.2 miles along Durr Road.

Just the drive to this glorious area can be an adventure! The road is steep at times, rough in places, and sometimes totally blocked by high waters at the creek ford. However, patience and perseverance on the drive yield high payoffs on the hike. Wildlife abounds here, from flocks of mountain bluebirds to herds of elk. The lovely desert landscape is backed up by the craggy summits of the Cascades to the west and the deep, rocky cut of Yakima Canyon to the east. Additionally, the area is rich in human history as the Durr Road route in use today is the same route used by settlers traveling through the area in the 1880s. At times, the deep ruts carved by the steel-rimmed wheels on horse-drawn wagons are still visible parallel to the road.

From the trailhead, hike east along the dirt road that cuts away in that direction. After about 0.25 mile, you have a choice to make. The first option continues along the old wagon road as it rolls for 5 miles along the

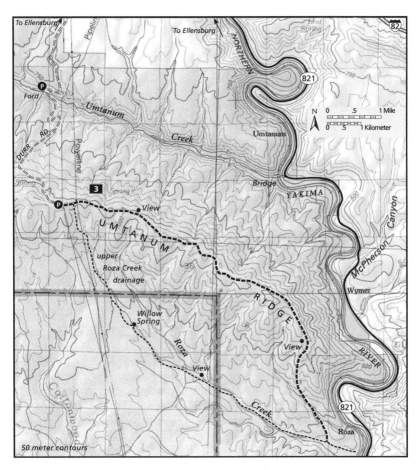

crest of Umtanum Ridge. This easy ridge-top walk leads through a garden of wildflowers in the late spring and early summer. Look for the bright bitterroot, spreading phlox, three species of balsamroot, shooting stars, yellow bells, desert bluebells, sage, death camas, and (with a reminder to look but not touch) prickly pear cactus. Folks who want to backpack in the desert country will find this route an excellent overnight choice. Make a dry camp on the ridge top or, by dropping an additional 2 miles from the end of the ridge route, you'll find camping opportunities near the Yakima River (dropping to the river stretches the trek to 14 miles round trip).

The other option leaves the ridge-top road after that first 0.25 mile and descends to the right (south) along an even more primitive road track. This jeep path winds down bird-rich draws and gullies. Seasonal creeks dribble out of these gullies, sporting narrow bands of lush, green vegetation, which are home to birds and animals.

About 1 mile down the road, the route angles back to join Durr Road. From this point, pick a path—continue down the slope by following the game trails down the Roza Creek valley as far as you'd like. At about 3 miles (2300 feet elevation), you'll find Willow Spring merging with Roza Creek. At about 4.5 miles, you'll reach the place where Roza Creek Road runs alongside the creek (2000 feet elevation). Turn around here for the long slog back up to the trailhead.

4 YAKIMA SKYLINE RIDGE

Round trip ■	**8+ miles**
Hiking time ■	4 to 6 hours
Difficulty ■	Moderate
Starting elevation ■	2000 feet
High point ■	3000 feet
Best season ■	March through July
Maps ■	Washington State Department of Natural Resources (DNR) Yakima
Contact ■	Washington Department of Fish and Wildlife
Permits/passes ■	Washington Department of Fish and Wildlife Vehicle Permit required

From Seattle, drive east on Interstate 90 to exit 110 and Interstate 82. Drive I-82 to the Selah/Canyon Road exit 26. Turn right off the exit and immediately turn left onto Harrison Road and drive 1.9 miles southwest before turning right onto Wenas Road. Continue 2.8 miles to a Y junction (near a rural fire station). Stay right (straight ahead on Gibson Road). In 0.3 mile after turning onto Gibson Road, turn right on Buffalo Road, where the pavement ends and the L. T. Murray State Wildlife Recreation Area begins. Turn left into a large parking area surrounded by an elk drift fence. Park here or drive through the gate (close it behind you) and proceed up a dirt track another 1.5 miles to the official trailhead. Start walking toward the rim from anywhere between the two parking areas.

The L. T. Murray State Wildlife Recreation Area offers some of the best desert hiking in the state, and this far-eastern edge of the preserve boasts the best of the best. Unmatched desert wildflowers bless the dry brown hills with vibrant colors. You'll also find an array of birds and animals— swallows, swifts, bluebirds, chukars, quails, magpies, partridges, hawks, and eagles grace the sky while deer, elk, bighorn sheep, coyotes, rock chucks (marmots), badgers, hares, and an army of other small mammals roam the desert floor.

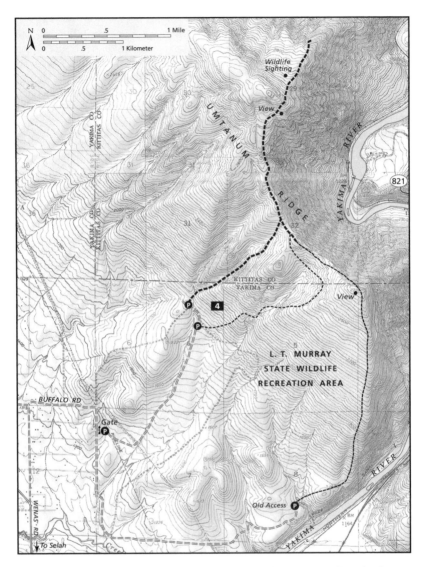

While an official trail leads up a broad ravine from the trailhead, a better hiking option is to park 0.5 mile short of the trailhead area and climb the open grass slopes toward the ridge top to experience the desert environment more directly. This route puts you among the plants and animals—it's literally a stroll in a wild garden. What's more, you'll find it impossible to get lost doing this. The open terrain and gentle slope ensure that the road and your vehicle are in sight for the entire first mile of your trek to the ridge

A hiker on the Yakima Skyline Trail passes through masses of blooming spring wildflowers.

top. Once at the top of the slope, you'll notice the far side of the ridge drops off in a steep cliff down to the Yakima River. By turning left and following this rim, you'll soon intercept the official trail, which hugs the rim, keeping the river far below always in sight. Journey out as far as you like before returning. (You can also head south on the trail along the rim.)

As the flowers color the landscape, they also perfume the air. Sage provides a constant, steady background on the wind, but as the warm sun heats the new plant growth, an intoxicating blend of scents awaits you. The air itself becomes a veritable stew of aromas as the ever-present sage is joined by the pungent odors wafting from the leaves of wild parsleys and onions. Through it all swirls the sweet aroma of new grasses and blooming flowers.

5 KELLEY HOLLOW

Round trip	12 miles
Hiking time	7 hours
Difficulty	Moderate
Starting elevation	1800 feet
High point	3800 feet
Best season	March through June
Maps	Washington State Department of Natural Resources (DNR) Yakima
Contact	Washington Department of Fish and Wildlife
Permits/passes	Washington Department of Fish and Wildlife Vehicle Permit required

From Seattle, drive east on Interstate 90 to exit 109 in Ellensburg. After exiting the freeway, turn right to drive under the freeway. At 0.7 mile, turn left

A coyote den dug into a sandy outcropping in Kelley Hollow

at Umtanum Road (at second traffic light). Continue on this road for 18.4 miles (turns to gravel at 5.2 miles) until it turns to pavement again upon entering the upper Wenas Valley. Stay on the pavement (Wenas Road). In 8 miles (26.4 miles total from the traffic light in Ellensburg), turn left onto a very rough dirt road. Park in the wide spot at the start of the road (room only for a couple of vehicles). To get to the trailhead, walk 0.2 mile up the rough road to the trailhead.

As is often the case when hiking in the desert, the best walking route is actually an old road. These rough, four-wheel-drive dirt roads are legally open for driving, but only occasionally do folks drive them—mostly a stray hunter or two late in the fall. The two-track trails are too rough for most motorists, but they are perfect for hikers. This one leads into a glorious desert wildlife haven.

You'll find the official trailhead at the elk drift fence along the boundary of the L. T. Murray State Wildlife Recreation Area. Pass through the gate (closing it securely behind you) and continue to trek along the increasingly rough road. The track climbs 1 mile past stunning little draws and gullies. At 1.2 miles from your vehicle, you'll reach a junction. Heading left leads you up a long, straight road along the flank of Umtanum Ridge, which climbs above you on the right the entire way. In 2 miles, the road turns left to angle back toward Wenas Lake. At this turn, enjoy the view down to the lake, then turn back and return the way you came.

A better option at the road junction is to go right. This track climbs steeply through a series of tight turns to top out on Umtanum Ridge. Keep

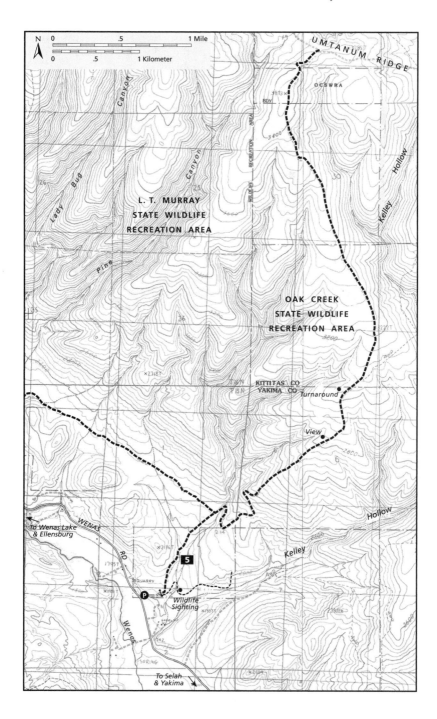

an eye out for deer and elk as you pass the assortment of side canyons and gullies. This road leads to the far end of the ridge at 4.8 miles from the junction, for a total of 6 miles from your vehicle.

6 ROBINSON CANYON/AINSLEY CANYON

Round trip ■	**10 miles**
Hiking time ■	6 hours
Difficulty ■	Difficult
Starting elevation ■	2200 feet
High point ■	3200 feet
Best season ■	May through July
Maps ■	Washington State Department of Natural Resources (DNR) Wenatchee
Contact ■	Washington Department of Fish and Wildlife
Permits/passes ■	Washington Department of Fish and Wildlife Vehicle Permit required

Note: This area and the access road for hiking into it are typically closed November 1 through May 1 each year to protect wintering elk herds.

From Seattle, drive east on Interstate 90 to exit 101 for Thorp. At the end of the exit ramp, turn right. Drive about 0.75 mile before turning right on Killmoor Road (where main road veers to the left). Drive Killmoor Road 2.5 miles, then turn right on Robinson Canyon Road (pavement gives way to gravel in 0.5 mile) and drive 1.5 miles to reach the trailhead parking area at the elk fence gate. Park outside the gate and hike in (closing the gate behind you).

This is a gem of a hike, providing you easy access to the best of the best of the rich L. T. Murray State Wildlife Recreation Area. This is prime elk country and a major wintering and calving ground for the great wapiti (as elk are

Remarkable desert survival: a ponderosa pine seedling grows out of a rocky hillside crevice.

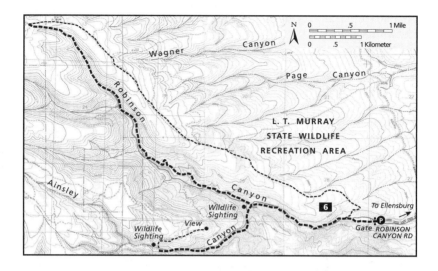

known to Native Americans in the region), which has led to the seasonal closure that keeps vehicles well away from the area during calving season. After mid-April, when the closure order is lifted, you can find herds of the big beasts—especially groupings of elk cows with young calves.

More than elk can be found here. Mule deer (some nearly as big as elk) also take advantage of the rich browse to get through the long winter months. The entire area is a diverse conglomeration of ecosystems: Thick forest characterizes the north slopes, while south-facing slopes are barren basalt cliffs and sage. Aspen trees and cottonwoods grace the creek basins and, in season, wildflowers fill all the lands between. It is also an area where rattlenakes are known to be present in large numbers in May when coming out of their dens.

After going through the gate, follow the dirt two-track through the broad meadows. In about 0.3 mile, you'll find Robinson Creek as it bisects the meadows. All vehicle use of the primitive road ends at the creek crossing: Beyond this point, vehicles are prohibited.

Just past Robinson Creek, a side track climbs out of the canyon to the right (Page Pasture Road). Stay on the main road and, about 1 mile from your vehicle, recross Robinson Creek in a nicely wooded area. In another 0.5 mile, reach a second road junction where Ainsley Canyon angles down from the south. Beaver dams can be found all along Robinson Creek, with new ones going up in new locations each year as old ones are washed out or damaged.

Hiking up the road into Ainsley Canyon leads to stunning views in just 0.5 mile (2 miles from your vehicle) of steep basalt cliffs paralleling the creek far below. The thin forests of this area provides comforting shelter for deer and elk, so keep a close eye on the trees. Continue on another 0.5 mile or so in this open flat area, then head north off the road, cross Ainsley Creek, and scramble up to an incredible viewpoint looking across the canyon and over the Kittitas Valley.

To extend your hike, return to the main road trail and continue left up the Robinson Canyon valley. At mile 4 (from your vehicle), the road leaves the bank of Robinson Creek and the best scenery is now behind you. A loop is possible here, but it is a long hike and not recommended. Instead, turn around for a leg-stretching outing of 10 miles with the 1-mile side trip up Ainsley Canyon.

7 BLACK CANYON

Round trip ■	**7 miles**
Hiking time ■	4 hours
Difficulty ■	Difficult
Starting elevation ■	2600 feet
High point ■	3850 feet
Best season ■	September through November
Maps ■	Washington State Department of Natural Resources (DNR) Yakima
Contact ■	Washington Department of Fish and Wildlife
Permits/passes ■	Washington Department of Fish and Wildlife Vehicle Permit required

From Seattle, drive east on Interstate 90 to exit 109 in Ellensburg. After exiting the freeway, turn right to drive under the freeway. At 0.7 mile, turn left at Umtanum Road (at second traffic light). Continue on this road for 18.4 miles (turns to gravel at 5.2 miles) until it turns to pavement again upon entering the upper Wenas Valley. Stay on the pavement (Wenas Road), and in 3.9 miles (22.3 miles total from the traffic light in Ellensburg), turn left onto a very rough dirt road. Drive along this rough road 0.5 mile to a gate at the boundary of the L. T. Murray State Wildlife Recreation Area. Pass through the gate (close it behind you) and continue another 0.8 mile to the parking area at the end of the (drivable) road.

This canyon is stunning! It offers black basalt talus slopes below steep cliffs, hillsides of brilliant wildflowers, and an array of birds. That's right: Bird lovers, take note. This is an avian paradise. In addition to the ever-present raptors that soar above virtually all desert country, Black Canyon boasts stunning populations of mourning doves and western kingbirds. You'll also find grouse, Hungarian partridge, and chukar.

The road continues from the parking area, though the huge berm of dirt prevents further vehicle access. Follow the road as it climbs the canyon. In a

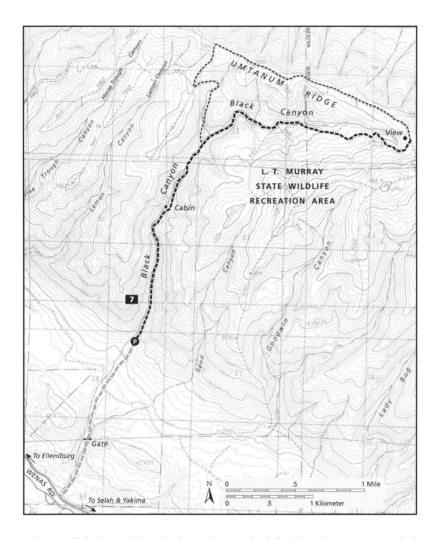

mile you'll find an old settler log cabin on the left. The cabin is surrounded by a lovely stand of cottonwoods and aspens—glorious golden during the peak of fall color season (usually early October).

At 1.5 miles, the road splits. The best bet here is to bear right and stroll up another 2 miles through increasingly thick stands of ponderosa pine and white pine. Between the forest stands are lush high desert ecosystems, with an array of seasonal wildflowers filling the meadows. Elk abound here as they use the forests for cover and the meadows for feeding. Birds also appreciate the merging environments, with bluebirds nesting throughout the area in spring.

A hiker wanders around old cabin remains found in Black Canyon.

At about 3.5 miles total from the trailhead, the road crests out on Umtanum Ridge, providing outstanding views: Look northeast to the Kittitas Valley near Ellensburg and west to the jagged summits of the snowcapped Cascades.

8 SHELL ROCK

Round trip ■	**6 miles**
Hiking time ■	4 hours
Difficulty ■	Moderate
Starting elevation ■	2700 feet
High point ■	3800 feet
Best season ■	September through November
Maps ■	Washington State Department of Natural Resources (DNR) Yakima
Contact ■	Washington Department of Fish and Wildlife
Permits/passes ■	Washington Department of Fish and Wildlife Vehicle Permit required

From Seattle, drive east on Interstate 90 to exit 101 for Thorp. Turn right onto South Thorp Highway and continue 2 miles. Turn right (south) onto

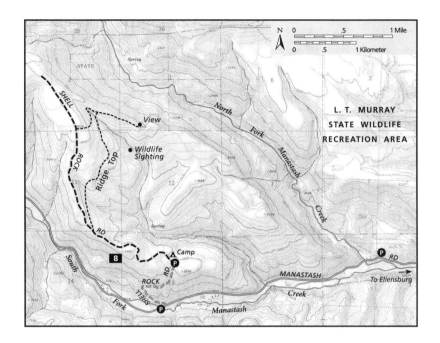

Cove Road, then drive 4.2 miles before turning right (west) onto Manastash Road. Continue 7.1 miles along Manastash Road to the junction with Shell Rock Road on the right. Park here, or if you have a high-clearance vehicle, you can drive 0.75 mile up Shell Rock Road to park at a flat clearing at an elevation of 3200 feet.

All you'll find here are rolling meadows, broad stands of fragrant ponderosa pine, wonderful views, and wildlife ranging from badgers to black bears. All that, and a modest elevation gain to boot. What more could you want from a desert escape?

If you park at the start of Shell Rock Road (and for the sake of your vehicle's oil pan, you should), walk up the road for about 1.2 miles as it climbs through the trees to the ridge top. Continue another 0.5 mile through a series of small clearings in the thinning ponderosa forest before breaking out in broad, open wildflower fields atop the ridge. You may continue along the road as it angles back along the ridge, but the better choice is to angle off the track heading to the right to explore the ridge top at your fancy. Loop back down to the road to hike back to your car.

The western edge of the ridge sports a good forest of pine and fir, while the east flank opens onto views of the Manastash drainage. Hike as far as you like, though after about 3 miles, the route enters the trees for good, which makes a great place for turning around.

9 WESTBERG TRAIL

Round trip	■	**4 miles**
Hiking time	■	3 hours
Difficulty	■	Moderate
Starting elevation	■	1850 feet
High point	■	3560 feet
Best season	■	April through July
Maps	■	Washington State Department of Natural Resources (DNR) Yakima
Contact	■	Washington Department of Fish and Wildlife
Permits/passes	■	None

From Seattle, drive east on Interstate 90 to exit 101 for Thorp. Turn right onto South Thorp Highway and continue 2 miles. Then turn right (south) onto Cove Road and drive 6 miles. At the second stop sign, continue straight, crossing Manastash Road. In 0.2 mile, find the large parking area on the right side of the soon-to-dead-end road.

Ray Westberg was the popular wrestling coach in Ellensburg who died in 1997 at the young age of 47. This trail was built and dedicated to him, with a memorial placed at the high point on the ridge. The route isn't heavily

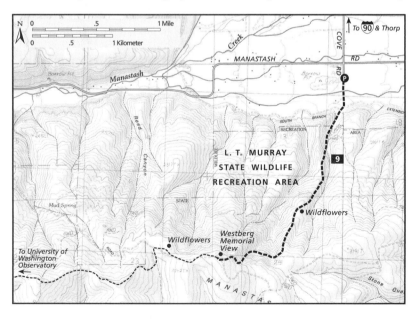

The Ray Westberg Memorial site on Manastash Ridge

used by hikers, but it is popular with birds—birds on the ground and in the air. You can expect to find grouse scurrying through the brush and Lewis's woodpecker pounding on the trees. In the air, look for a mix of northern flickers, bluebirds, meadowlarks, and the ever-present red-tailed hawks. If birds aren't enough of an aerial display, this is also butterfly heaven in late spring. Birds don't do it for you? Well, deer and elk also roam the region, and no one can find fault with the spectacular views—especially from the site of the Westberg Memorial at the top of the ridge.

The trail starts on an old jeep track that first crosses an irrigation canal on a set of railroad timbers, and then heads up a steep gully. Be cautious because this stretch of trail is prime snake terrain. At about 0.3 mile, the trail splits, with both paths leading to the same junction about a mile farther up the route, so you can actually turn this into a short loop. We went left. From the split, the trail (both of them) climbs steeply. Indeed, in the 1.5 miles from the split to the memorial site, the trail gains almost 1800 feet in elevation, all without benefit of switchbacks.

As the trail climbs, the scenery gets even better. Birds are likely to keep you company along the entire trek, and amazing flower displays are possible all around: brodiaea, lupine, balsamroot, phlox, paintbrush, yellow asterlike beauties, microsensis, and others. When the bitterroot is in bloom, any exposed rocky soil area flushes pink with its blooms.

The memorial site, which can be seen from all along the trail, offers stunning views of the Kittitas Valley and the sweep of the Cascade Range, with Mount Stuart capping the mountain scene. Continue another 3.0 miles if you want to get to the University of Washington's Manastash Ridge Observatory.

10 HARDY CANYON

Round trip ■	**9 miles**
Hiking time ■	6 hours
Difficulty ■	Moderate
Starting elevation ■	2000 feet
High point ■	4500 feet
Best season ■	May through June
Maps ■	Washington State Department of Natural Resources (DNR) Yakima
Contact ■	Washington Department of Fish and Wildlife
Permits/passes ■	Washington Department of Fish and Wildlife Vehicle Permit required

From Seattle, drive east on Interstate 90 to exit 109 in Ellensburg. After exiting the freeway, turn right to drive under the freeway. At 0.7 mile, turn left at Umtanum Road (at second traffic light). Continue on this road for 18.4 miles (turns to gravel at 5.2 miles) until it turns to pavement again upon entering the upper Wenas Valley. Stay on the pavement (Wenas Road). In 4 miles (22.4 miles total from the traffic light in Ellensburg), find the gated road signed "Hardy Canyon" on your right. Park in the pullout area and start hiking. **Note:** This area and the access road for hiking into it are typically closed November 1 through May 1 each year to protect wintering elk herds.

This unique desert canyon is part of the Oak Creek State Wildlife Area. Nestled between the sprawling expanse of the L. T. Murray State Wildlife Recreation Area and the Wenatchee National Forest, the Oak Creek State Wildlife Area holds some of the richest wildlife habitat in the state. The dry desert country is popular wintering country for deer and elk and home to countless birds. The Hardy Canyon Trail leads you through a dense thicket

An eight-spotted skimmer (Libellula forensis) *species of dragonfly along the way up Hardy Canyon*

of wild rose that, when in bloom, provides one of the most wonderfully fragrant wilderness treks we've encountered. The canyon is also home to an assortment of birds, including barred owls, and seems to be an early-summer gathering place for a host of butterflies. It's definitely not desolate here.

From the parking area, begin your trek along an old dirt jeep track by winding through thick aspen, birch, and cottonwood stands on the valley floor. The collection of deciduous trees here makes this a colorful autumn outing. In just 0.2 mile, the trail climbs into Hardy Canyon proper. The lower section of the canyon boasts a collection of bluebird houses—built and placed to help protect and enhance these colorful western songbirds. After 0.5 mile or so, the canyon narrows and forest stands give way to brushy sections filled with chokecherry, serviceberry, and other lush plant life.

The thick foliage provides well-appreciated cover for birds of all sizes and colors, including ground-hugging grouse, trilling meadowlarks, and beautiful western kingbirds. The brush also shelters rattlesnakes, so be careful as you walk this canyon during snake season, typically the warmer months of May through September.

Aside from the protective cover, the brush provides food for critters. Mule deer flock to the area, and even coyotes browse on the berries. Continue up the valley as far as you want to go, reaching the summit ridge of Cleman Mountain at 4.5 miles. Turn around and return the way you came.

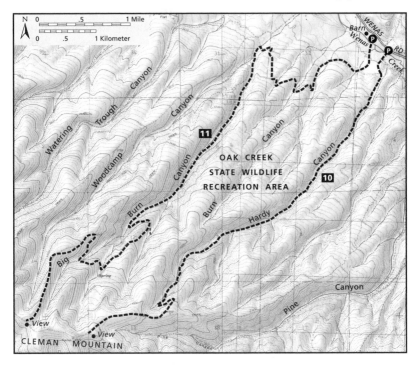

11 BIG BURN CANYON

Round trip ■ **16 miles**
Hiking time ■ 10 hours (or overnight)
Difficulty ■ Difficult
Starting elevation ■ 2000 feet
High point ■ 4850 feet
Best season ■ May through June
Maps ■ Washington State Department of
Natural Resources (DNR) Yakima
Contact ■ Washington Department of
Fish and Wildlife
Permits/passes ■ Washington Department of Fish and
Wildlife Vehicle Permit required

From Seattle, drive east on Interstate 90 to exit 109 in Ellensburg. After exiting the freeway, turn right to drive under freeway. At 0.7 mile turn left at Umtanum Road (at second traffic light). Continue on this road for 18.4 miles (turns to gravel at 5.2 miles) until it turns to pavement again upon entering the upper Wenas Valley. Stay on the pavement (Wenas Road). In another 3.6 miles (22 miles total from the traffic light in Ellensburg), find the gated road and "Wenas Wildlife Area" on the right near a large barn and silo. Park in the pullout area and start hiking. (See page 55 for trail map.) **Note:** This area and the access road for hiking into it are typically closed November 1 through

Views across the valley to Umtanum Ridge from lower Big Burn Canyon

May 1 each year to protect wintering elk herds.

The sprawling public land preserve of the Oak Creek State Wildlife Area offers some of Washington's best extended desert hiking. This route allows you to enjoy a mild day hike or a gentle backpacking trip. You'll find an array of wildlife, and bighorn sheep prowl the upper slopes of Cleman Mountain. Since being reintroduced in 1967, the large curly-horned beasts have thrived on the rich desert mountain.

From the parking area, hike south almost 0.5 mile; near the mountain's base, reach a junction with a road and go right (the left route links with the Hardy Canyon trail), then veer northward for 1.5 miles, winding around the base of the mountain. When you reach a junction with what appears to be a main road, turn left to head up the main Big Burn Canyon. As the trail climbs higher in the long, narrow canyon, you'll find more conifers at the higher elevation. Lots of pines and even a few firs grow in this isolated region as it receives a bit more moisture than even the similar canyons just 8 miles southeast in the L. T. Murray State Wildlife Recreation Area. Snow lingers long here, too—well into late March on the upper slopes of Cleman Mountain.

When you reach the first Y in the road near the 5-mile mark, go right. The left fork drops 0.25 mile to cross the creek (pick up water here if you are planning to camp farther up) and then disappears under thick brush. The right fork climbs steeply to the summit of Cleman Mountain.

12 | CLEMAN MOUNTAIN

Round trip ■	6 to 8 miles
Hiking time ■	5 hours
Difficulty ■	Moderate
Starting elevation ■	2600 feet
High point ■	3400 feet
Best season ■	March through July
Maps ■	Washington State Department of Natural Resources (DNR) Yakima
Contact ■	Washington Department of Fish and Wildlife
Permits/passes ■	Washington Department of Fish and Wildlife Vehicle Permit required

From Ellensburg, drive southeast on Interstate 82 to exit 31 near Yakima. Take the exit signed "Hwy 12–West/Naches" and drive west on US 12 for 16 miles, passing through the town of Naches, to a Y junction. Stay right to merge onto westbound State Route 410. In 2 miles, turn right onto a gravel road signed "Public Access." This steep, rough road (four-wheel-drive recommended) leads past Mud Lake in 1.5 miles. Continue another mile past the lake and park in a small pullout alongside the road just after the road levels off. **Note:** The access road is gated just off State Route 410 from December 15 through May 1 every year to protect wintering elk. This closure may be extended in the future. Call the managing agency prior to venturing out or be prepared to hike the gated road.

Cleman Mountain stretches west to east above the Naches River Valley to the south and the Wenas Valley to the north. The mountain offers an endless array of hiking opportunities, and hikers can create their own adventures by heading off on the network of game trails that weave around the upper slopes of the mountain. These trails are carved into the desert soils by browsing herds of bighorn sheep, mule deer, and elk. Keep your eyes open and active: You might see some of the big beasts during your wandering.

From the parking area, hike up the road for about 0.1 mile. At the first sharp left turn in the road, head off to the right (north) on one of the many game trails

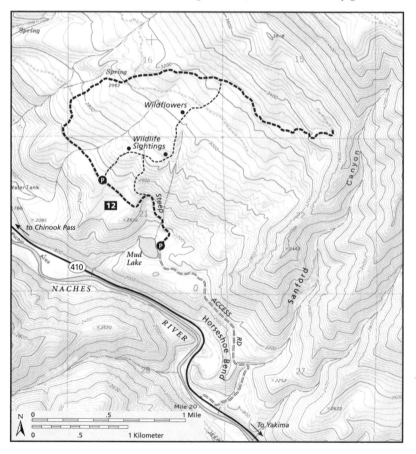

that come down to cross the road. The slope is steep, but after gaining 400 feet or so, the climb moderates and you can head out across the vast expanse of a relatively flat plateau on this western slope of Cleman Mountain.

The flowers here are intensely beautiful. Look for yellow bells, desert bluebells, buckwheat, sagebrush, butter-cups, lupines, grass widows, and carpets of prairie star flowers. Deer and elk love the sweet treats of these meadows—and they appreciate the stands of forest that line the side canyons and gullies as they provide secure places to rest and relax (hikers would do well to keep that in mind when trekking here during the heat of the day). You can hike to your heart's content along these open slopes and on up to the ridge crest.

One of many mule deer typically seen along the slopes of Cleman Mountain

If you prefer a more structured outing, from the parking area, hike up the main road a mile or so to reach a side road on the right that leads toward the crest of Cleman Mountain. You can then head southeast along the spine of the ridge (never really all the way on the top ridge of Cleman here, but you can hike back down on a lower spine) for at least 2 miles, enjoying the incredible views west along the Naches River Valley.

13 BEAR CANYON

Round trip ■	**4 miles**
Hiking time ■	3 hours
Difficulty ■	Moderate
Starting elevation ■	2000 feet
High point ■	2900 feet
Best season ■	April through July
Maps ■	Washington State Department of Natural Resources (DNR) Yakima
Contact ■	Wenatchee National Forest, Naches Ranger District
Permits/passes ■	USFS Region 6 Trail Park Pass required

From Ellensburg, drive southeast on Interstate 82 to exit 31 near Yakima. Take the exit, signed "Hwy 12–West/Naches" and drive west on US 12 for

Ponderosa pine and cliff walls of Bear Canyon

16 miles, passing through the town of Naches to a Y junction. Stay left to continue on US 12. At 6.6 miles from the Y, turn right into a gravel parking area at the head of the gated road for Bear Canyon Trail 1158.

Desert? Well, this really is a transition zone where pines and even some fir trees cover the more protected north slopes. South slopes are a different story, however, and here you will find bare rocky talus slopes of basalt beneath towering basalt cliffs. Only a few aspens and cottonwoods grow near wet areas. This mix makes the area prime wildlife habitat. Cover and water are abundant, and so are the birds. Many avid bird watchers know about this place, but few other special-interest users do. White-headed, hairy, downy, and acorn woodpeckers call this area home. Nesting cavities are seen all along the way, and flicker boxes are located along Bear Creek every ⅛ mile or so. Elk can be expected along with the mule deer. All in all, this is a wildlife haven.

That trail crosses Bear Creek numerous times in the first miles, making this a hike to avoid until at least late April so you don't have trouble with a creek swollen by snowmelt.

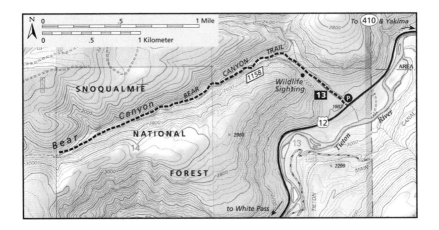

About 0.5 mile in from the trailhead, the path tapers down from an old, abandoned roadbed and turns into a soft single-track trail. It then crosses the creek once more before veering westward to lead up a very narrow canyon. Cliff swallows zoom around the bluffs here—mostly violet green swallows feeding on bugs. If birds aren't your pleasure, enjoy the blooming bushes along the trail. Look for serviceberry, mock orange, and wild rose along the entire route. Turn around after 2 miles of walking to return to your car.

14 GINKGO PETRIFIED FOREST INTERPRETIVE TRAILS

Round trip ■	**3 miles**
Hiking time ■	2 hours
Difficulty ■	Easy
Starting elevation ■	2400 feet
High point ■	2600 feet
Best season ■	Year-round
Maps ■	Washington State Department of Natural Resources (DNR) Yakima
Contact ■	Washington State Parks and Recreation
Permits/passes ■	Washington State Parks and Recreation Parking Pass required

From Ellensburg, drive east on Interstate 90 to exit 136 for Huntzinger Road. At the end of the exit ramp, turn left and drive 2.3 miles past Vantage on the

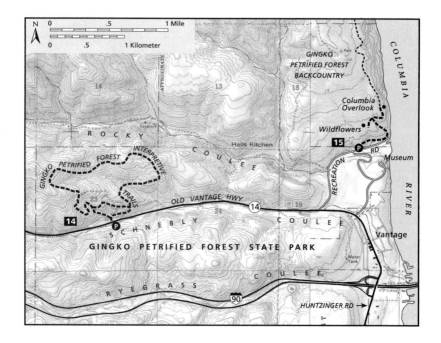

Old Vantage highway to the Ginkgo Petrified Forest Interpretive Trails parking lot at the park ranger building.

One of the largest petrified forests on the planet sits in the center of Washington State. The ancient trees were mineralized into rock during the great lava flows that swept the inland Northwest. In addition to petrified ginkgos (one of the oldest tree species in the world), the "rock forest" includes mineralized Douglas fir, spruce, walnut, and elm.

The trails here offer the perfect introduction to the desert landscape of the basin for newbie desert rats. The first 0.25-mile loop is paved for access to one and all, while the longer loops lead up to 3 miles back through the desert. You'll find stunning examples of the incredible diversity of trees that lived and died here millions of years ago. The petrified remains of these long-gone trees dot the landscape bisected by the interpretive trails. Little bits of petrified wood dot the landscape as well, and you'll find shards on other trails in the broad area surrounding this valley.

This trail provides easy access as well to great examples of the springtime flora and fauna known to the region: yellow bells, mariposa lily, grass widow, prairie star flower, salt and pepper desert parsley and other desert parsleys, buckwheats, and buttercups. Meadowlarks sing for you as you walk, and bluebirds keep a wary eye on all passersby. Interpretive signing is provided along the trail.

15 | GINKGO PETRIFIED FOREST STATE PARK BACKCOUNTRY

Round trip ■ **5 miles**
Hiking time ■ 3 hours
Difficulty ■ Easy
Starting elevation ■ 650 feet
High point ■ 1200 feet
Best season ■ Year-round
Maps ■ Washington State Department of Natural Resources (DNR) Yakima
Contact ■ Washington State Parks and Recreation
Permits/passes ■ Washington State Parks and Recreation Parking Pass required

From Ellensburg, drive east on Interstate 90 to exit 136 for Huntzinger Road. At the end of the exit, turn left and drive 1 mile before turning turn right on Recreation Road. Continue 0.8 mile on Recreation Road (also known as Old

View toward the Vantage Bridge from the backcountry highlands above the Columbia River in Ginkgo Petrified Forest State Park

Highway 10), which used to be the crossing of the Columbia River, nearly to the road end. Park on the left where you see the trail/old jeep track heading up the slope. If you reach the barrier signs in the roadway, you have driven 100 yards too far.

The old highway from Vantage, an old settlers' road, drops down a steep canyon to a crossing of the Columbia River—before the Wanapum Dam went in, the road crossed the river here. Now the roadway simply disappears into the river. Still, from this route, you can enjoy outstanding views of the Columbia River as it rolls through the basalt canyon.

From the parking area, hike up the old roadway as it climbs from the road/river. The road quickly narrows into a trail as it leads up to a high bluff overlooking the Columbia River. From here, follow a well-trod footpath/game trail leading onward and upward through a stunning side canyon. About 0.75 mile from the trailhead, you'll top out on the highlands above the Columbia River. Peer down onto the Ginkgo Petrified Forest region from here. The views are outstanding!

For additional exercise, hike north, staying to the edge of this highland area overlooking the Columbia River. The views east across the Columbia River toward the Babcock Bench are impressive, while to the south the views encompass Wanapum Break, Vantage Bridge, and Wanapum. The entire area is awash in flowers during spring and early summer, with a mixed bag of bitterroot, larkspur, sage violets, and Hooker's balsamroot.

16 ┇ WILD HORSES MONUMENT

Round trip ■	1 mile
Hiking time ■	1 hour
Difficulty ■	Easy
Starting elevation ■	1150 feet
High point ■	1300 feet
Best season ■	Year-round
Maps ■	Washington State Department of Natural Resources (DNR) Priest Rapids
Contact ■	Washington State Department of Transportation
Permits/passes ■	None

From Ellensburg drive east on Interstate 90 to exit 139 (just after crossing the Columbia River). The exit, signed "Scenic Viewpoint," leads to a large parking area. In winter, park at the closed gate and walk in. In any season, though, stop here for a quiet, relaxing, hour-long break when traveling across the state on I-90.

This simple little trek offers visitors some of the most impressive geologic and historic views of the Columbia River area. The uniquely beautiful sculptures at the top of the ridge offer great exposure to one of the most impressive outdoor art pieces in the Northwest.

The trail leads out of the parking area and climbs steeply to the fifteen surprisingly lifelike horse sculptures. These beauties stand on a bluff overlooking the Columbia River. Constructed out of welded steel plates, they are the work of Spokane artist David Govedare. The tempered steel ponies were put on the bluff in 1989 for Washington State's Centennial Celebration.

A short hike up the path leads to the base of the hill, from where you can peer up to admire the monument. To really experience the horses, though, and to connect with the desert landscape, follow the scramble trail from the viewpoint up to the horses. This steep, rocky path is only a few hundred yards long, but it's enough to lead you to some beautiful wildflowers and increasingly open views down to the river.

Once at the side of the horses, enjoy them up close, then continue to hike along the slope behind them until you can frame the horses against the blue

Who let loose the horses? Groups of horse statues make up the Wild Horses Monument.

ribbon of the Columbia down in the canyon to the southwest. You'll feel like you are watching a real herd of wild mustangs running over the hills when you look back on them! You'll also feel transported back hundreds of years to a time when horses first migrated into the area and ran wild through these hills.

Amble around the sagebrush flats above the monument at your leisure, enjoying the views before heading back down. To the west, look out over the rugged landscape of the Ginkgo Petrified Forest State Park highlands; north of that you'll see the Colockum Wildlife Area wildlands climbing more than 5000 feet above the river.

17 WHISKEY DICK WILDLIFE AREA

Round trip ■	**8+ miles**
Hiking time ■	6 hours
Difficulty ■	Moderate
Starting elevation ■	2000 feet
High point ■	3750 feet
Best season ■	September through December
Maps ■	Washington State Department of Natural Resources (DNR) Yakima
Contact ■	Washington Department of Fish and Wildlife
Permits/passes ■	Washington Department of Fish and Wildlife Vehicle Permit required

From Seattle, drive east on Interstate 90 to exit 115 for Kittitas. Go north over the freeway. At 1.2 miles, turn right at the stop sign. Veer to the left onto County Road 81 and continue 1.2 miles from the stop sign (2.4 miles

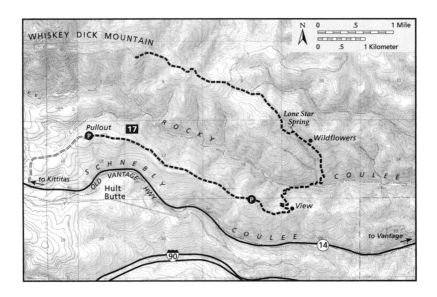

from I-90), then turn right onto the Vantage Highway. Drive past the first access to the Quilomene Wildlife Area at 12 miles, and at 13.7 miles turn left onto the rough dirt road accessing the Quilomene Wildlife Area. At 0.4 mile on this rough road, veer right at the Y, and at 0.6 mile veer right at the second Y. A good place to park is at the pullout 1.2 miles from the Old Vantage Highway.

Though this land is called a "wildlife area," it could as easily be named a state *wildflower* area. On any given spring day, hikers can expect to see an array of wildflowers that puts the pretty alpine meadows to shame. Among the plethora of blooms spotted during visits here are thyme-leaf desert parsley, Douglas buckwheat (huge masses of it), thyme-leaved buckwheat, shaggy daisy/shaggy fleabane, linear-leaf daisy (also called line-leaved fleabane), Cusick's sunflower, Hooker's onion, woolly-pod milk vetch, brodiaea, silky lupines, rock penstemon, Thompson's paintbrush, thread-leaved phacelia, Hooker's balsamroot, white phlox, Scouler's penstemon, small-flowered penstemon, cushion fleabane, large-flowered collomia, narrow-leaf collomia, bitterroot, and bitterbrush. Bring your wildflower guide to keep track of the plants, but keeping in mind that this is a wildlife area, expect to see some critters, too.

Our recommended route has you bypassing the first access road into the Quilomene Wildlife Area (that first access is just past highway milepost 18). Our route takes you along the long ridge across from Whiskey Dick Mountain before plunging down into Rocky Coulee and then hiking up the easternmost end of Whiskey Dick Mountain to roam the ridgeline along that peak.

The hike along the old road goes fast since the path is wide, smooth, and relatively level as it contours along the ridge. After a quick couple of miles, the road drops 800 feet in elevation to the bottom of Rocky Coulee. (With high-clearance vehicles, it might be possible to drive this far, but doing so has you driving over some of the most beautiful wildflower fields). The wildflowers carpet the entire desert floor, from the ridge top to the coulee bottom. This section of the route is rich in bitterroots, hedgehog cactus, and balsamroot, as well as various species of buckwheat, lupine, and daisies.

Coyotes hunt throughout this coulee country, and they can often be heard, if not actually seen, in the morning and evening—their yips and howls echoing off the coulee walls. After following the coulee basin for a mile or so (remaining alert for poison ivy), the route turns up the side of Whiskey Dick Mountain. More stunning wildflowers abound, with increasingly clear

Sunburst through wildflowers on Whiskey Dick Mountain

and stunning views over the rest of the wildlife area. Keep an eye on the sky to watch the raptors soaring, and another eye on the brush to look for mule and white-tailed deer.

You'll top out on the low summit of Whiskey Dick, a bit more than 4 miles from your starting point. This is the place to turn around and enjoy the long, scenic desert stroll back to your vehicle.

18 ┇ JOHN WAYNE TRAIL, ARMY WEST

Round trip ■	8+ miles
Hiking time ■	5 hours
Difficulty ■	Easy
Starting elevation ■	2000 feet
High point ■	2500 feet
Best season ■	Year-round
Maps ■	Washington State Department of Natural Resources (DNR) Yakima
Contact ■	Washington State Parks and Recreation
Permits/passes ■	Sign-in permit system (also requires return of permit stub before leaving)

From Seattle, drive east on Interstate 90 to exit 115 for Kittitas. After exiting, turn left over the freeway and reach the heart of Kittitas in 1 mile. Turn right onto First Avenue and continue east out of town on this road for 2.6 miles before turning right onto Prater Road. Drive 0.3 mile, passing over the freeway overpass, before turning left onto Boylston Road. Continue out Boylston Road for 3.3 miles. Just after you've passed under a large railroad trestle spanning I-90, turn right. In 100 yards, turn left into the large trailhead parking area for the John Wayne Trailhead.

A sign-in permit is required due to the fact that the trail passes through the highly active U.S. Army's Yakima Training Center. *You must not leave the trail.* The John Wayne Trail (which rolls through the heart of the linear Iron Horse Trail State Park) follows the historic route of the Milwaukee Railroad from North Bend to the Columbia River (the trail will eventually be a true cross-state trail, but the stretch from the Columbia River to Idaho is still to be developed). This far eastern section of the completed trail explores some incredibly wild, pristine land—the designation of the surrounding lands as an Army training base actually helped preserve the area's wild beauty.

From the trailhead, a short path leads up to the ridge to the actual rail-trail. The permit sign-in box is located at the end of this path. Carry

A hiker admires the rock formation at the west entrance to the Boylston Tunnel.

the permit with you, then put it in a drop box upon exit. The process is simple, free, and allows the Army to track usage by those wishing to hike this easement through their Yakima Training Center lands.

Once on the trail, you have a relatively flat, well-graded trail leading 4.5 miles to the old railway stop site of Boylston. The actual goal, though, is at the pass just east of that old rail stop: the Boylston Tunnel. The trail grade angles away from the freeway, taking you into the desert quiet. Within the first mile of trail, signs of local wildlife can be found. Badgers thrive here, as evidenced by a large system of burrows dug into the hills just off the trail. The burrows are easy to spot—just look for disturbed earth around dark holes. You can step off the trail and examine these since they are well within the 200-foot easement (staying off the restricted lands is easy since fences parallel both sides of the trail at a distance of 100 feet from the center line of the path).

Keep an eye on the sky as you walk: You'll likely see soaring red-tailed hawks, turkey vultures, and other raptors. Watch the ground around the trail, and you might see hares, rabbits, and other forms of dinner for the big birds. If the critters aren't showing themselves, simply enjoy the beautiful flora: Sage violets, yellow bells, cinquefoils, and phlox seem to be blooming for several months each spring and summer.

Near the end of the 4.5 miles, you'll see a large black void ahead. This is the tunnel door. As you draw nearer, feel the cold air rushing out—even in the heat of summer, the tunnel temperature stays down in the 50s.

The tunnel isn't a straight-through cut. A slight curve in the 1973-foot tunnel prevents those entering one end from seeing the other end. As a result, as you near the middle of the tunnel, the light at the entrance twinkles out, while the light from the exit slowly comes into view.

Caution: Do not enter the tunnel unless each person going in has a steady, dependable light source.

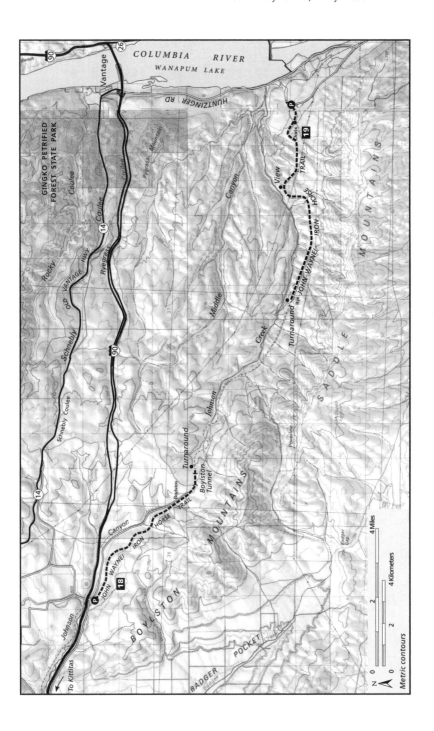

19 JOHN WAYNE TRAIL, ARMY EAST

Round trip ■	8+ miles (with a great 34-mile option for mountain bike riders)
Hiking time ■	5 hours
Difficulty ■	Moderate
Starting elevation ■	1000 feet
High point ■	1500 feet (2500 feet at the end of the longest route)
Best season ■	Year-round
Maps ■	Washington State Department of Natural Resources (DNR) Yakima
Contact ■	Washington State Parks and Recreation
Permits/passes ■	Sign-in permit system (also requires return of permit stub before leaving)

From Seattle, drive east on Interstate 90 to exit 136 for Huntzinger Road. After exiting, turn right onto Huntzinger Road, and at 7.1 miles (2 miles past the Wanapum Dam) turn right just after crossing the railroad-grade trail. The turn is signed "John Wayne Trail 2.5 miles." In 2.5 miles, park in the trailhead area. The sign-in requirement is due to the fact that the trail passes through the highly active Yakima Training Center of the U.S. Army. *You must not leave the trail.* (See page 71 for trail map.)

The desert here appears to be carpeted with flowers come spring! The most common colorful ground cover includes numerous species of phlox, adding the colors of white, pink, and creamy yellow to the hills. Both Hooker's and Carey's balsamroot add brilliant golds and greens, and microsensis adds a shiny yellow to the tapestry.

In the first 2 miles out from the trailhead, the railroad-turned-trail slices through an endless garden of wildflowers.

Balsamroot grows along the John Wayne Trail near the old town site of Doris.

In addition to those named above, look for locoweed as well buckwheat, which puts on a gorgeous yellow-to-red flower show.

At about 0.75 mile, the trail passes the remnants of the old townsite of Doris, Washington—one of numerous long-gone railroad stops along this stretch of the old Milwaukee–Chicago–St. Paul Railroad. All that remains now is a fallen roof of an ancient building (it now rests on the ground) and another collapsed shack. A few old cottonwood trees dot the edge of the railroad grade, and a number of old relics litter the ground: railroad spikes and broken power insulators being the most numerous.

At 4 miles, at the old whistlestop of Rye, the trail slices into the scenic Boylston Mountains. This makes a good turnaround point for those who don't have time (or leg strength) to make the 17 miles (one way) to the Boylston Tunnel. The trail pushes through deep cuts in the hills, some of which are occupied by swallows, and even raptors.

20 SELAH BUTTE

Round trip ■	**4 miles**
Hiking time ■	3 hours
Difficulty ■	Moderate
Starting elevation ■	3050 feet
High point ■	3024 feet
Low point ■	2700 feet or lower
Best season ■	June through October
Maps ■	Washington State Department of Natural Resources (DNR) Yakima
Contact ■	Bureau of Land Management, Spokane
Permits/passes ■	None

From Ellensburg, drive east on Interstate 82 to exit 26 for Canyon Road/Selah. After exiting, turn and drive 2.5 miles on Canyon Road (State Route 821). At 2.5 miles, turn right onto a gravel road and drive the steep washboarded road up the steep slope. At 1.6 miles, you'll pass through a gate (leave it as you found it: open or closed). This is the start of the BLM lands. Continue another 1.6 miles (a total of 3.2 miles from State Route 821). At a sharp right bend in the road, find a cleared parking area (may be partially grass covered) just off the left side of the road.

With its crown of radio towers, Selah Butte doesn't seem, at first glance, like a desert wilderness. But the expanse of open public lands that surround this massive butte harbors some of the best desert ecosystems in the area. Selah stands on the eastern edge of the Yakima River Canyon, offering

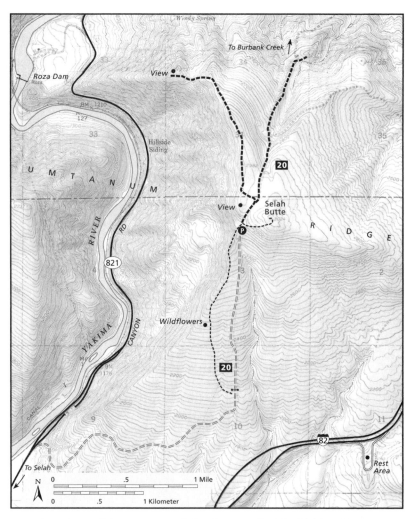

amazing views of the canyon and the sheer wall of the Yakima Rim.

The parking area puts you in the middle of a vast 10-acre carpet of Hooker's balsamroot. The golden glowers stretch out over the edge of the butte, creating a wonderful foreground for the stellar scenic backdrop of Yakima Canyon.

There are no trails here, so simply wander north along the ridge, stepping carefully to avoid the prickly hedgehog cactus that's common here.

After more than a mile of walking, the views get better and better. A long spinelike ridge juts out into Yakima Canyon and provides awesome views back along the ridge you've been following and the canyon to the next big

View down into the Yakima Canyon of the Roza Dam from a ridge on Selah Butte

hill: Baldy Butte. On clear days, look for paragliders soaring above that knob (they sometimes fly from Selah, too).

Roam north and west at your leisure, going as far and as fast as you like. The hike is the goal here, with no real destination.

21 | COWICHE CANYON

Round trip ■	**6 miles**
Hiking time ■	4 hours
Difficulty ■	Easy
Starting elevation ■	1400 feet
High point ■	1500 feet
Best season ■	Year-round
Maps ■	Washington State Department of Natural Resources (DNR) Yakima
Contact ■	Bureau of Land Management, Spokane
Permits/passes ■	None

From Ellensburg, drive east on Interstate 82 to exit 31A to get on westbound US 12. Take the second exit off US 12 —the exit is signed "N. 40th Ave. and Fruitvale Blvd." Drive under the freeway, across Fruitvale, and in 1.5 miles

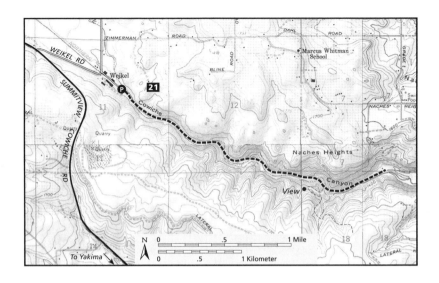

from US 12 turn right onto Summitview. Continue for 7.1 miles and turn right on Weikel Road (signs on Summitview indicate Cowiche Canyon turn-off). Drive 0.4 mile on Weikel Road, and turn right at the sign for Cowiche Canyon.

A group of dedicated volunteers with the Cowiche Canyon Conservancy worked for years to develop this trail—or, rather, to un-develop this trail—because this old railroad right-of-way is now a path through a wild wonderland. In short, this trail could be the crown jewel in Washington's collection of rails-to-trails. The old train line path weaves through an astounding set of deep road cuts and over a double handful of trestle bridges spanning Cowiche Creek as it climbs through this stunning canyon.

The path in the canyon bottom follows a portion of the old 1880s railroad route that stretched from Yakima to the Tieton area in the Cascade foothills. Today the gentle grade makes a terrific 3-mile one-way trek end to end.

Just the rock formations found throughout the canyon make this a worthwhile trail to explore. However, those towering rock sculptures are highlighted by the brilliance of the local wildflower show, which kicks off in mid-April each year. In the canyon lowlands, the first arrowleaf balsamroot are just starting to bloom. Not enough for you? As you stroll the gentle trail through the natural splendor of the canyon, keep one eye on the sky to watch for kestrels, hawks, eagles, and ravens. You might also see swallows, swifts, bluebirds, and flycatchers. You should also keep an eye on the ground, looking for marmots, badgers, rabbits, and rattlesnakes. Simply put, this old railroad grade is now a pristine wildlands trail.

Facing page: Trail Lake Coulee

WENATCHEE

The area surrounding the Wenatchee basin offers some of the most classically desertlike landscape in the state. From the blowing sand dunes of the Potholes region near Moses Lake to the broad flatlands and sagebrush prairies of the Waterville Plateau, this section of the state harbors some of the harshest ecosystems in Washington. Less than 10 inches of rain falls on many parts of this area each year, and the blazing sun often pushes summertime temperatures well above 100 degrees F. for weeks at a time.

Yet even with all that, the area offers wonderful wild country adventures. Desert plants provide plenty of color and fragrance, and a veritable host of wild critters call this brutal landscape home. If you hate the heat, visit in winter—unless you hate the cold, too (winter temperatures frequently drop well below freezing for weeks at a time). Spring and fall are wonderfully balmy most years.

22 ANCIENT LAKE

Round trip ■	4 to 5 miles
Hiking time ■	3 to 4 hours
Difficulty ■	Easy
Starting elevation ■	850 feet
High point ■	860 feet
Best season ■	Year-round
Maps ■	Washington State Department of Natural Resources (DNR) Moses Lake
Contact ■	Washington Department of Fish and Wildlife
Permits/passes ■	Washington Department of Fish and Wildlife Vehicle Permit required

From Ellensburg, drive east on Interstate 90 to exit 149 for George. After exiting, turn left and drive north on State Route 281 toward Quincy. After 5.6 miles turn left onto White Trail Road. Continue 7.8 miles on White Trail Road, then turn left onto Road 9-NW. Continue 5.9 miles on this road (pavement ends at 2.0 miles) as it winds steeply down onto Babcock Bench to the road's end. Seven to eight vehicles can park here. Do not block the gate or the road on the right (marked with a "Snake X-ing" sign): This is a private driveway and not open to the public.

This route through part of the Quincy Wildlife Recreation Area offers something you seldom find in the desert: a waterfall. But not just any waterfall; here you'll find a waterfall plunging into a lake. Did I mention this watery world is in the desert? Well it is—a quick glance at the areas around the lake reveals that. Prickly hedgehog cactus dot the slopes around the trail as does an array of desert wildflowers. In the heart of this 15,266-acre wildlife area, you'll find sparkling potholes surrounded by massive basalt cliffs. The geological wonders are a product of the erosion of lava flows by ancient glacial floodwaters. The many layers of basalt are exposed, and several of the potholes are filled with water that has seeped from the irrigation systems that feed the Quincy basin farmlands upslope. These wetlands, ponds, and lakes have added important habitat diversity to this area. Ancient Lake is one such set of numerous "filled potholes" that dot this coulee.

Start hiking down the old jeep road that rolls on past the gates at the road's end. Through the first mile or so of the track, keep an eye on the brush—upland game birds abound here, with quail, Hungarian partridge, and even a few chukar living among the rocks and sage.

This is a rich historical area, as evidenced by the archeological dig occurring just 0.25 mile from the trailhead (the bone hunters were excavating a giant ground sloth). At 0.7 mile, leave the jeep track and head east (left) on a single-track trail as it angles up into the heart of a vast coulee that contains

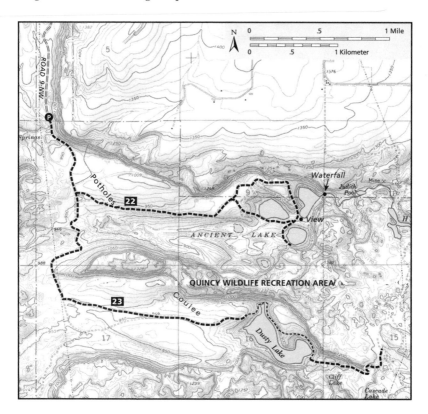

the Ancient Lake potholes. Come spring, wildflowers begin to wake up. By late May, the floor of the coulee is covered with flowering plants. Above the trail, the coulee's vertical basalt walls are startlingly colorful (russet reds mixed with the blues and blacks common to all basalt). At about 2 miles in, you'll reach the lake basin. Silvery gray cottonwood snags line portions of the lakeshore, and waterfowl frequently feed in the lake. Explore the lake basin—a deep bowl ringed with black basalt cliffs—before heading back down the coulee.

23 ┆ DUSTY LAKE

Round trip ■	**6 miles**
Hiking time ■	4 hours
Difficulty ■	Moderate
Starting elevation ■	800 feet
High point ■	1000 feet
Best season ■	Year-round
Maps ■	Washington State Department of Natural Resources (DNR) Moses Lake
Contact ■	Washington Department of Fish and Wildlife
Permits/passes ■	Washington Department of Fish and Wildlife Vehicle Permit required

From Ellensburg, drive east on Interstate 90 to exit 149 for George. After exiting, turn left and drive north on State Route 281 toward Quincy. After 5.6 miles turn left onto White Trail Road. Continue 7.8 miles on White Trail Road, then turn left onto Road 9-NW. Continue 5.9 miles on this road (pavement ends at 2.0 miles) as it winds steeply down onto Babcock Bench to the road's end. Seven or eight vehicles can park here. Do not block the gate or the road on the right (marked with a "Snake X-ing" sign): This is a private driveway and not open to the public. (See page 79 for trail map.)

Whispering stands of cottonwoods shine against the brilliantly polarized eastern Washington blue sky, while cool blue pools reflect their graceful beauty. The Quincy Wildlife Recreation Area boasts several sparkling lakes nestled in the long, deep coulees of the area. Hiking around these remarkable desert gems provides an immersion not only in desert ecology but also in the more uncommon desert riparian ecology. The common desert community of quails and chukars is joined by the less common desert population of waterfowl—including mallards, mergansers, and teals.

Start hiking along the old jeep road as if heading to the Ancient Lakes.

Instead of turning off the jeep track to climb into the coulee holding those lakes, continue on the dirt two-track as it angles southeast toward Dusty Lake. After hiking a total of about 1.6 miles, all the while enjoying amazing views of the towering cliffs that are the coulee walls, look for a road leading to the left. Climb up this track a bit more than a mile as it ascends into the Dusty Lake basin. As you near the basin, you'll slowly come in sight of the sheer beauty of the tall headwall of the coulee towering over the blue-green gem of Dusty Lake.

A huge inlet waterfall crashes down the basalt cliffs into one of the potholes at Ancient Lake.

24 FRENCHMAN COULEE

Round trip ■	**4 miles**
Hiking time ■	3 hours
Difficulty ■	Moderate
Starting elevation ■	1000 feet
Low point ■	800 feet
Best season ■	Year-round
Maps ■	Washington State Department of Natural Resources (DNR) Moses Lake
Contact ■	Washington Department of Fish and Wildlife
Permits/passes ■	Washington Department of Fish and Wildlife Vehicle Permit required

From Ellensburg, drive east on Interstate 90 to exit 143. After exiting, turn left under the freeway. At 0.8 mile, turn left onto Vantage Road. Drive 2.7 miles to the parking area on the right (north) side of the road.

An "aerial" view down into Frenchman Coulee

On summer weekends, rock climbers flock to the nearby Frenchman Coulee climbing area, drawn to the tall vertical columns of basalt that line the coulee walls. Hikers, who prefer their lands more horizontal than vertical, will also find great enjoyment here.

From the trailhead, the path leads straight up the bottom of the coulee. As you hike, watch the coulee walls for agile rock climbers doing their Spiderman impersonations on the black rock. If no climbers are in evidence, just

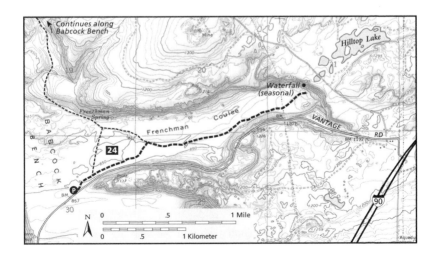

enjoy the natural spectacle of the coulee. The towering columnar walls frame a valley filled with sage and wildflowers.

At about 2 miles from the trailhead, you'll find yourself near the base of a seasonal waterfall that tumbles into the coulee—during the spring, this is truly a beautiful sight to behold. Flowers dot the entire coulee floor but are more numerous in this well-watered far end of the coulee. Turn around here.

25 STEAMBOAT ROCK

Round trip ■	**4 miles**
Hiking time ■	3 hours
Difficulty ■	Difficult
Starting elevation ■	1600 feet
High point ■	2250 feet
Best season ■	March through November
Maps ■	Washington State Department of Natural Resources (DNR) Banks Lake
Contact ■	Washington State Parks and Recreation
Permits/passes ■	Washington State Parks and Recreation Parking Pass required

From Ellensburg, drive east on Interstate 90 to exit 151 (State Route 283), signed "Ephrata/Soap Lake." Drive through Ephrata. At Soap Lake, turn north on State Route 17. Drive through Soap Lake and keep going about 20 miles to SR 2. Turn right onto SR 2. In 4.2 miles, you'll come to a Y junction. Stay straight to merge onto SR 155. At 15.5 miles from the Y junction, turn left into Steamboat Rock State Park. In 2 miles, pass through the entrance station, to arrive in another 0.5 mile at the trailhead area.

Steamboat Rock is a massive "island" of a rock mountain floating on the shore of Banks Lake. The durable rock was left behind through all of the Great Missoula Floods and was later nearly surrounded by the waters diverted by the Grand Coulee Dam. The top of the rock is a broad, flat plateau offering stunning views across the scablands of coulee country.

From the parking area, the trail tracks across the lower slope of the rocky butte. Wildflowers abound along the lower foot of the butte: arrowleaf balsamroot and prairie star flowers are particularly prominent. Within the first few hundred yards, the trail becomes very rough and steep for about 0.15 mile as it runs up through a slot in the cliffs.

Halfway up the butte, the trail slides across a broad ledge, which is carpeted with sagebrush buttercups. The trail splits here (both forks lead to the top). Go left to climb another couple hundred vertical feet to the western end

Balsamroot covers the landscape at the base of Steamboat Rock.

of Steamboat Rock's top. Stroll over to the sharp edge of the butte to peer down to the lake far below. The top of the rock here is blanketed in foliage, with a large garden of prairie lupines.

Drop back down the trail and head up the eastern spur trail to reach the eastern flank of the butte's top. Keep an eye out for deer here as a small herd lives on the rock, and they generally browse up high during the day but come down for water in the morning. Scramble around the butte as much as you desire before heading back down.

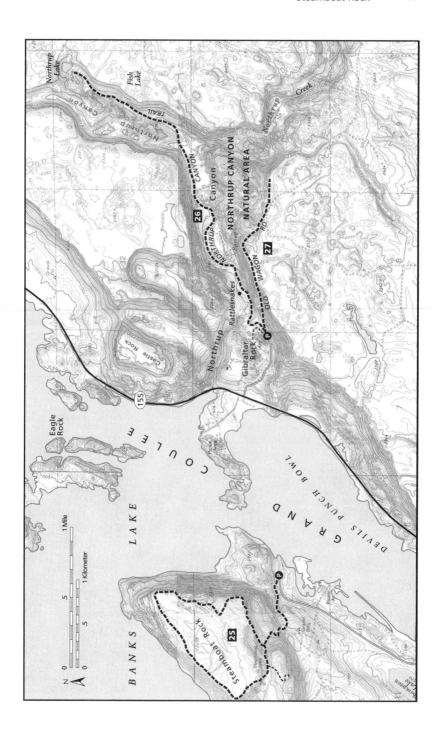

26 NORTHRUP CANYON

Round trip ■	**3 miles**
Hiking time ■	2 hours
Difficulty ■	Difficult
Starting elevation ■	1750 feet
High point ■	2134 feet
Best season ■	January through May
Maps ■	Washington State Department of Natural Resources (DNR) Banks Lake
Contact ■	Washington State Parks and Recreation
Permits/passes ■	Washington State Parks and Recreation Parking Pass required

From Ellensburg, drive east on Interstate 90 to exit 151 (State Route 283) signed "Ephrata/Soap Lake." Drive through Ephrata. At Soap Lake turn north on State Route 17. Drive through Soap Lake and keep going about 20 miles to State Route 2. Turn right onto SR 2. In 4.2 miles, you'll come to a Y junction. Stay straight to merge onto SR 155. At 18.8 miles from the Y junction, turn right onto a gravel road marked Northrup Canyon Natural

Spring views up Northrup Canyon

Area. Continue 0.7 mile to the new trailhead. (See page 85 for trail map.)

Bald eagles, icons of the mossy forests and deep rivers of the Pacific Coast, flock to this desert canyon each winter, and their presence is reason to visit in winter. Up to 200 of the big birds roost in the trees along the south side of the canyon each night—get to the trailhead early to see the squadrons of eagles flying out of the canyon as they head to the fishing areas of Banks Lake. Even without the baldies, the area offers a great experience with nature. While the eagles focus on fish, the local populations of red-tailed and Cooper's hawks hunt inland for upland birds, rodents, and small mammals. The prey animals find shelter in the rich ground cover of the canyon. Ever-present sagebrush provides the best cover, but the little beasts also scurry under the clumps of balsamroot and other desert wildflowers.

The trail climbs into the canyon, which holds the only native forest in Grant County. The forest is mostly pine (ponderosa and lodgepole pine), but some Douglas fir also is in the mix. Those trees make this canyon a logical home to birds of all kinds, and the result is a bird lover's paradise. Following the track as it meanders through the heart of the canyon, look and listen for avians such as great horned owls and barred owls, woodpeckers and flickers, grouse and quail, swallows and sparrows, hawks and eagles.

Hike up the canyon for a good 1.5 miles, and you'll find the forest diversifying with the inclusion of willow and aspen trees. Continue up the canyon to find an abandoned farmhouse, and scramble around the forest at your leisure before heading back the way you came.

27 ┆ OLD WAGON ROAD TRAIL

Round trip ■	3 miles
Hiking time ■	2 hours
Difficulty ■	Moderate
Starting elevation ■	1750 feet
High point ■	2300 feet
Best season ■	April through November
Maps ■	Washington State Department of Natural Resources (DNR) Banks Lake
Contact ■	Washington State Parks and Recreation
Permits/passes ■	Washington State Parks and Recreation Parking Pass required

From Ellensburg, drive east on Interstate 90 to exit 151 (State Route 283, signed "Ephrata/Soap Lake"). Drive through Ephrata. At Soap Lake, turn

Morning moisture drops on tiny desert bluebells that dot the landscape.

north on SR 17. Drive through Soap Lake and keep going about 20 miles to State Route 2. Turn right onto SR 2. In another 4.2 miles, you'll come to a Y junction. Stay straight to merge onto SR 155. At 18.8 miles from the Y junction, turn right onto a gravel road marked Northrup Canyon Natural Area. Continue 0.7 mile to the new trailhead. (See page 85 for trail map.)

Like the adjacent Northrup Canyon trek, this trail leads through a portion of the old wild forest in Grant County, a mixed forest of pine and fir that provides shelter each winter to a large population of bald eagles. Because the big, majestic eagles roost here throughout the winter, the trail—which climbs to the canyon rim, putting you at eye level with some of the prime roosting trees—is closed from November to March each year to ensure the eagles aren't disturbed during the hard winter months.

Come spring, though, the trail opens up and plenty of birds are still around for you to see (and hear). The old settlers' road leads to the canyon rim with views down onto scenic Northrup Canyon and out over the Banks Lake basin.

As the name suggests, from the trailhead the hiking route follows an old wagon road. This old road was an important link in the regional road system a century ago. Now the rutted track offers a nice hike as it climbs up the south side of Northrup Canyon before leveling out above. This path offers amazing views up and down the canyon. At 0.6 mile, you reach a viewpoint from which you can look back toward Banks Lake and see Steamboat Rock poking out of the dark waters. Continue up to the top of the canyon wall and stride along the canyon rim, enjoying the open views out over Banks Lake and down into Northrup Canyon.

At 1.5 miles, the road is crossed by a fence. Though the track continues on the far side of the fence, this is the turnaround point for hikers.

28 | UMATILLA ROCK/MONUMENT COULEE

Round trip ■	5 miles
Hiking time ■	3 hours
Difficulty ■	Moderate
Starting elevation ■	1200 feet
High point ■	1300 feet
Best season ■	April through July
Maps ■	Washington State Department of Natural Resources (DNR) Banks Lake
Contact ■	Washington State Parks and Recreation
Permits/passes ■	Washington State Parks and Recreation Parking Pass required

From Ellensburg, drive east on Interstate 90 to exit 151 (State Route 283, signed "Soap/Soap Lake"). Drive through Ephrata. At Soap Lake, turn north on State Route 17. Drive through Soap Lake, and 17 miles north of Soap Lake turn right into the Sun Lakes State Park. Continue along the park road. At 1.3 miles, turn left at the road (signed "Dry Falls Lake 3.0/ Camp Delany 1.3/Deep Lake 3.0") that heads up into the coulee (gated in winter). Park off the road near the gate if it is locked (November through March) or continue up the paved road another mile and park at any available pullout.

Dry Falls was once the world's largest (in water volume) waterfall in the world, but that was during the Great Missoula Floods at the end of the last Ice Age. Today the falls is a massive cirque of basalt: Dry Falls Lake. Dry water channels from the Banks Lake area slide south to the lip of the falls, and then the land falls away in great basaltic cliffs. What was once an ancient splash pool at the base of the falls is now a broad desert meadow dotted with lakes and ponds, swarming with birds and animals of all kinds, shapes, and sizes. This is a uniquely beautiful area to explore, both to delve into the geologic history of the area and to reach out and touch the native flora and fauna of the Washington desert.

Umatilla Rock towers like a giant fin in the middle of Grand Coulee in the basin below Dry Falls. This rock would have been an island in the midst of swirling waters during the great floods. Today it offers a clear look at the

Umatilla Rock during a winter visit

multiple layers of geologic soils and rock that make up these lands. At the junction where the road splits (left to Dry Falls Lake, right to Camp Delany), head left along the gravel road at the southwestern base of Umatilla Rock. Stray off the road and hike cross-country through the open sage prairie and you might kick up a few squawking birds—pheasant and quail are very common here. In the first mile or so, you'll pass Perch Lake (good fishing for panfish—perch, sunfish, and crappie) and climb a small rise for views of the lake basin.

The lake draws people though, so stick close to the hulky rock on your right to maintain your solitude and stay closer to the wildlife. Coyotes often establish dens near voids between fallen hunks of basalt at the base of the rock, and several species of birds nest in the area. Between the open cliff faces and the broad expanses of reeds along the lakeshores are ample nesting opportunities for swallows and flycatchers.

After a couple miles, you'll pass the eastern edge of Dry Falls Lake. Turn east and cross through a gap in the coulee on the north side of Umatilla Rock. Here a trail heads up and through the gap/pass to drop you into Monument Coulee on the east side of Umatilla Rock. Turn south and follow the game trails south to Camp Delany. Then stick to the road to get back to your vehicle.

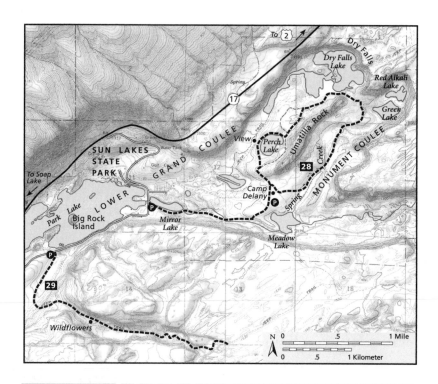

29 ┆ PARK LAKE SIDE CANYON

Round trip ■ 5 miles
Hiking time ■ 3 hours
Difficulty ■ Moderate
Starting elevation ■ 1150 feet
High point ■ 1500 feet
Best season ■ April through July
Maps ■ Washington State Department of Natural Resources (DNR) Banks Lake
Contact ■ Washington State Parks and Recreation
Permits/passes ■ Washington State Parks and Recreation Parking Pass required

From Ellensburg, drive east on Interstate 90 to exit 151 (State Route 283, signed "Soap/Soap Lake). Drive through Ephrata. At Soap Lake, turn north on SR 17. Drive through Soap Lake, and 17 miles north of Soap Lake turn right into the Sun Lakes State Park. Continue along the park road. At 2.4 miles, turn left into a broad parking area at the base of the jeep track heading east. Park here. At times, especially during winter months, the road is gated just inside the park. If that is the case, park near the gate (do not block it) and hike the road to the start of the route.

The land that comprises Sun Lakes State Park was purchased over the years in fifteen pieces. The last big chunk was obtained by the state in 1972, when it was bought from the Bureau of Land Management. The desert- and lake-filled park now encompasses more than 4000 acres in and around Grand Coulee. Park Lake is the largest of the lakes in the park, and this trail climbs a picturesque canyon along the lake's eastern flank, providing stunning views of the park.

The trail/jeep track climbs an unnamed canyon angling east away from Grand Coulee and Park Lake. The route is steep at times, and in a mile or so it reaches the top of the bluff above the lake. Follow the track as it rolls across the flat lands above the coulees, stopping periodically to look back down to Park Lake.

From the top of the hill, you'll enjoy tremendous views across Grand Coulee. You can continue along the track as it angles north. At 2.5 miles, you can look north to Deep Lake. Multitudes of flowers grow all along the canyon. Birds in the area include a population of huge, raucous ravens and swarms of black-billed magpies.

30 LENORE LAKE CAVES

Round trip ■	1.5 to 2 miles
Hiking time ■	1.5 hours
Difficulty ■	Easy
Starting elevation ■	1100 feet
High point ■	1300 feet
Best season ■	April through July
Maps ■	Washington State Department of Natural Resources (DNR) Banks Lake
Contact ■	Washington State Parks and Recreation
Permits/passes ■	Washington State Parks and Recreation Parking Pass required

From Ellensburg drive east on Interstate 90 to exit 151 (State Route 283) signed "Soap/Soap Lake). Drive through Ephrata. At Soap Lake, turn north on SR 17. At 8.5 miles north of the Soap Lake campground area, turn right onto a well-signed road leading to the Lenore Lake Caves. Drive 0.5 mile up

View looking out from one of the Lenore Lake Caves

the gravel road to the large turnaround parking area.

Lenore Lake Caves were formed 12,000 years ago when the area was flooded by melting ice. The "Shelter" part of the name comes from the fact that the caves were used by native tribes thousands of years ago. Today, visitors may view petroglyphs inside the caves. Seven caves are accessible by the maintained trail.

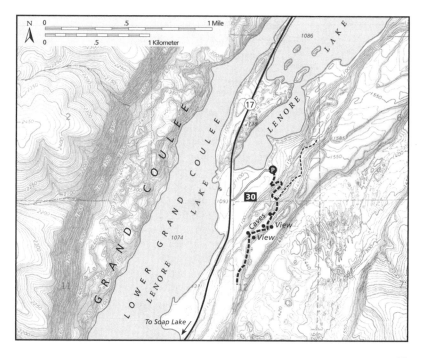

Prairie falcons nest in the sheer cliffs of the Grand Coulee, and this route brings you close to them. Watch the majestic raptors soar over the coulees as they hunt for birds, small mammals, and reptiles—yes, there are reptiles aplenty here. Rattlesnakes, rubber boas, and bull snakes can all be found in the vicinity. Be especially alert as you near the cave entrances as the snakes frequently use the cool cave environments to help regulate their body temperatures in the heat of summer.

The well-marked trail from the parking area leads to the series of caves, but while the caves are the primary draw to the area, don't forget to pay attention to what's outside them. In addition to the birds and other animals, enjoy the flora of the area. Look for desert shooting stars, which are thick along the trail. Also in evidence are nine-leaf desert parsley and fern-leaf desert parsley.

31 TRAIL LAKE COULEE

Round trip ■	5 miles (with longer option)
Hiking time ■	3 hours
Difficulty ■	Easy
Starting elevation ■	1500 feet
High point ■	1600 feet
Best season ■	March through July
Maps ■	Washington State Department of Natural Resources (DNR) Banks Lake
Contact ■	Washington Department of Fish and Wildlife
Permits/passes ■	Washington Department of Fish and Wildlife Vehicle Permit required

From Ellensburg, drive east on Interstate 90 to exit 151 (State Route 283, signed "Soap/Soap Lake). Drive through Ephrata. At Soap Lake, turn north on SR 17. Continue to the junction with SR 2 near the Dry Falls Dam. Turn right (east) onto SR 2 and continue 2 miles to Coulee City. Veer onto Fourth Street, and in 0.3 mile turn left onto Main Street. In 0.2 mile turn right onto Pinto Ridge Road. Drive 6.1 miles and, just before crossing the bridge over the main canal, turn right onto a dirt jeep track. Park by the gate, making certain you don't block the roadway or the gate.

Waterfowl flocking to the desert? You bet—when the desert is the coulee country of eastern Washington, with its plethora of lakes nestled in the rocky basins at the bottoms of the coulees. Trail Lake, a tiny gem of a lake just south of the massive impoundment of Banks Lake, draws more than its fair share of waterfowl, and not just during the winter migration. Year-

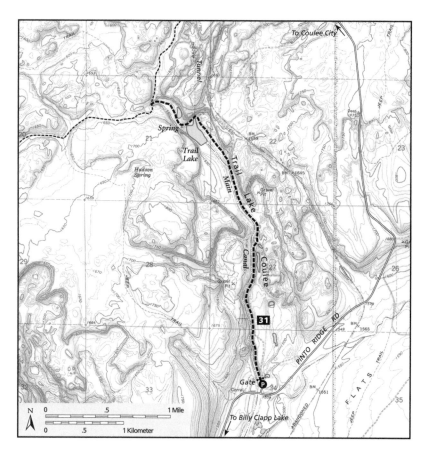

round populations of mallards, mergansers, herons, and scaups call this lake basin home.

Hike through the gate and begin your journey. For more than 2 miles, you'll follow a narrow dirt road atop the dike that forms one of the walls of an irrigation canal bringing water down from Banks Lake, over Summer Falls, and into Billy Clapp Lake. Grand views across the coulee are to be had all along the dike. At nearly 2.5 miles, you'll reach the edge of Trail Lake, which is a popular destination for hunters in duck hunting season (a good reason to visit in spring).

Reaching Trail Lake's north end at 2.5 miles you have many options. You could stop and enjoy the views of the lake and its resident waterfowl before heading home for a 5-mile round trip, or you could head up the jeep track that leads west from the end of the lake and climbs into a small unnamed coulee, where you can explore the local desert flora. This latter option could add between 1 and 5 miles, depending on how far you want to ramble.

Sage and gray rabbitbrush along the lakeshore in Trail Lake Coulee

32 | BILLY CLAPP LAKE

Round trip ■	5 miles
Hiking time ■	4 hours
Difficulty ■	Easy
Starting elevation ■	1200 feet
High point ■	1500 feet
Best season ■	Year-round
Maps ■	Washington State Department of Natural Resources (DNR) Moses Lake
Contact ■	Washington Department of Fish and Wildlife
Permits/passes ■	Washington Department of Fish and Wildlife Vehicle Permit required

From Ellensburg, drive east on Interstate 90 to exit 151 (State Route 283, signed "Soap/Soap Lake). Drive through Ephrata. At Soap Lake, veer right to continue east on SR 28. Drive east another 10.3 miles. Turn left (north) onto a road signed "Pinto Dam/Billy Clapp Lake." Continue 2.5 miles to the end of the road and large parking area by the boat launch and community beach. Hike up the path behind the outhouse to begin the trek.

Trail leading up through basalt columns along Billy Clapp Lake

Billy Clapp Lake, more than 3 miles long, is a stunning body of water behind a shallow earthen dam. The lake is fed by waters coming down the main canal from Banks Lake, which gets its water from the Columbia River backed up by the Grand Coulee Dam. The main canal from Banks dumps its water into Billy Clapp Lake in a thundering waterfall known as Summer Falls (water is released to the falls only in spring and summer to serve irrigation needs throughout the Columbia Basin). Though the lake is man-made, its beauty is entirely natural. A host of animals makes use of the wealth of water here, and native plants thrive in the irrigated basin.

Begin climbing the trail and almost immediately enjoy stunning views across the basalt cliff-lined lake. The trail climbs to a low viewpoint, then drops down through a beautiful canyon lined with incredibly colorful lichen-covered basalt rocks and cliffs. After this short (0.2 mile or so) section of rolling terrain, the trail flattens out for the next mile until you reach a bay on the lakeshore. All along this stretch are numerous side paths leading down to wonderful overlooks of the lake—and some of the sidetracks drop down secretive inlet bays with (wintertime) sandy beaches.

From the bay, the trail leads upward into the open sage plain along the lakeshore. This prairie is covered with springtime flowers: penstemon, balsamroot, buckwheat, and more. Obvious den sites on the cliffs above make it easy to see why the coyote population is so strong here, and the paths you follow are constantly dotted with coyote scat.

As you climb above the lakeshore, you'll gain about 400 feet of elevation above lake level. This height is sufficient to provide views that seem to stretch all the way up the Grand Coulee. Hiking another 1.5 to 2 miles brings you to the high bench areas near Summer Falls.

33 | Douglas Creek Canyon–North

Round trip ■	3 miles
Hiking time ■	2.5 hours
Difficulty ■	Moderate
Starting elevation ■	1600 feet
High point ■	1700 feet
Best season ■	Year-round
Maps ■	Washington State Department of Natural Resources (DNR) Moses Lake
Contact ■	Bureau of Land Management, Spokane
Permits/passes ■	None

From Wenatchee, drive east on State Route 2 through Waterville and into the small town of Douglas. Make note of the mileage by the fire station in Douglas. Continue east on SR 2 for 4.4 miles and pass the fire station in Douglas, then turn right (south) on Road H-SW (just after milepost 158). Drive this gravel road 6.7 miles to a "Road Closed Ahead" sign. Here the road roughens and begins a steep decent into Douglas Creek Canyon. At 8.1 miles from SR 2, you reach the bottom of the canyon as you pass a wooden signboard for the BLM land. Immediately to your right is the first spur road. Park near here. The side road is gated just 0.1 mile ahead.

Douglas Creek carves through the bottom of a deep, foliage-rich canyon in the heart of Washington's central plains. The views of the deep canyon are spectacular, and the stark rock walls and structures provide fascinating lessons in geology. The floor of the canyon is a veritable natural garden, blanketed as it is with wild rose, serviceberry, desert parsley, desert lupine, arrowleaf balsamroot, and—towering overhead—ancient hawthorn trees. Within this garden roams and flies an array of wildlife. Mule deer, coyotes, and rattlesnakes seem to be the most common

A hiker roams the trail up the north portion of Douglas Creek Canyon.

creatures in the valley, except for the birds—birds galore. Canyon wrens fill the canyon with song, and raptors dance aloft on the thermals.

Head up the rough dirt road, crossing through the gate to head into the northern reach of Douglas Creek Canyon. As you stroll along the brushy road, admire the towering basalt cliffs on both sides. Walk quietly and you'll likely hear the canyon wrens calling. Others will add to the song—listen for the trilling of meadowlarks, the screams of raptors, and a chorus of crickets.

Douglas Creek is a year-round stream of good flow, and that abundance of water fuels the rich ecosystems here. The creek hosts an array of insects, which feed the birds that fill the air with their songs and graceful flight.

The trail continues for more than 2 miles, but past about the 1.5-mile point it becomes overgrown and brushy. The path crosses Douglas Creek a few times, but you can avoid fording the creek by moving cross-country— just stick to the creek shore and you'll soon pick up the trail again when it re-crosses the creek.

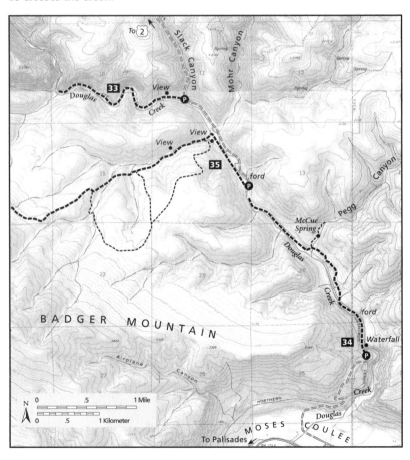

34 DOUGLAS CREEK CANYON–SOUTH

Round trip ■	**5 miles**
Hiking time ■	3 hours
Difficulty ■	Easy
Starting elevation ■	1400 feet
High point ■	1500 feet
Best season ■	Year-round
Maps ■	Washington State Department of Natural Resources (DNR) Moses Lake
Contact ■	Bureau of Land Management, Spokane
Permits/passes ■	None

From Ellensburg, drive east on Interstate 90 to exit 149 for George. After exiting, turn left and drive north on State Route 281 to Quincy. In town, turn left onto SR 28 and drive 15.3 miles to turn right onto Palisades Road. Continue 14.3 miles up Moses Coulee before turning left onto Wagon Road. Veer to the left at the Y that you encounter 100 yards up the road. In another 1.1 miles (at a sharp turn) you are at the crossing of the railroad grade. Park here or continue another 0.7 mile of rough steep driving (1.8 total from the turn onto Wagon Road) to the road end.

The drive up glorious Moses Coulee alone is worth the trip to this area, even if you never leave your vehicle. If you do decide to stretch your legs, the payoff is all the more fantastic: desert prairies, steep canyons, crashing waterfalls, fields of flowers, aerial antics of birds large and small, and more pure natural splendor than you'd expect from a desert canyon.

The trail follows the creek upstream from the trailhead. Though this is desert country, the rich riparian habitat around the creek supports some decidedly nondesert species. Most notably, a thriving population of belted kingfishers is found here. Indeed, the creek provides a long oasis through the heart of the canyon.

The trail crosses the creek at 0.5 mile. There is no bridge at the crossing, but large rocks and boulders are well spaced to allow for a dry-footed crossing.

About 1.5 miles up the canyon, look for a track leading into Pegg Canyon—a side canyon to the east of Douglas Creek. You can only go about 0.5 mile up Pegg Canyon before encountering the end of public land, but the views up and down it into Douglas Creek provide a splendid perspective on the area.

Back on the Douglas Creek trail, continue another mile up the canyon. At 2.5 miles from the trailhead, you'll reach the area near the junction with the Douglas Creek Canyon–Badger Mountain route (Hike 35). Turning back here creates a 5-mile hike and eliminates the need to ford Douglas Creek again.

With the ready availability of water, this canyon offers a fine destination for anyone interested in camping in the desert country.

35 DOUGLAS CREEK CANYON– BADGER MOUNTAIN

Round trip ■	**6 miles**
Hiking time ■	4 hours
Difficulty ■	Moderate
Starting elevation ■	1500 feet
High point ■	2400 feet
Best season ■	September through November
Maps ■	Washington State Department of Natural Resources (DNR) Moses Lake
Contact ■	Bureau of Land Management, Spokane
Permits/passes ■	None

From Wenatchee, drive east on State Route 2 through Waterville and into the small town of Douglas. Make note of the mileage by the fire station in Douglas. Continuing east on SR 2 for 4.4 miles, past the fire station in Douglas, turn right (south) on Road H-SW (just after milepost 158). Drive this gravel road 6.7 miles to a "Road Closed Ahead" sign. Here the road roughens and begins a steep descent into Douglas Creek Canyon. At 8.1 miles from SR 2, you reach the bottom of the canyon as you pass a wooden signboard for the BLM land. Continue another 1.1 miles from the BLM sign (9.2 miles from SR 2) to reach Douglas Creek. Here, you face a choice: Find parking near here off the road and ford Douglas Creek, or drive through Douglas Creek and park in the wide area on the far side. Warning: No attempt of this crossing should be made in a passenger car as the water is fast-moving and frequently more than 14 to 16 inches deep. Only high-clearance four-wheel-drive vehicles should attempt to drive through the ford. Most people should get wet feet instead. Once across the creek, you'll find a pullout area signed "Four Corners Sopher Flat." Park here and hike around the bend to access the railroad grade. (See page 100 for trail map.)

Great views await you here, as well as a total desert experience—complete with rattlesnakes. This area seems to be a haven for the serpents, so be careful while trekking through the brushy canyons. The snakes hole up when the temperature drops, so restrict your visits to autumn through spring and you'll have no worries about vipers. While the snakes dig in, the other animals come out in the cooler temperatures. Coyotes and jackrabbits play out their life-and-death dance here. Mule deer browse on the rich foliage. Badgers burrow in the sandy banks along the canyon walls.

A huge Northern Pacific rattlesnake crosses the jeep track in the Badger Mountain side canyon off of Douglas Creek Canyon.

From the creek crossing, hike north on the railroad grade. In just 0.7 mile, you'll encounter an old fence line and decrepit watering troughs. These relics create a very rustic Old West feel. Here you'll turn west and climb along a dirt road angling up a side canyon on the eastern flank of Badger Mountain. After another mile or so of steep climbing, the road veers left (south) and tops out on the highlands above Douglas Canyon. Use the various jeep tracks that cross the terrain to explore a mile or more along the highlands with their stunning views before returning the way you came.

36 DUFFY CREEK

Round trip ■	8 miles
Hiking time ■	5 hours
Difficulty ■	Moderate
Starting elevation ■	2900 feet
High point ■	2900 feet
Best season ■	September through November
Maps ■	Washington State Department of Natural Resources (DNR) Moses Lake Wenatchee, Chelan, and Banks Lake
Contact ■	Bureau of Land Management, Spokane
Permits/passes ■	None

From Ellensburg, drive east on Interstate 90 to exit 149 for George. After exiting, turn left and drive north on State Route 281 to Quincy. Once in

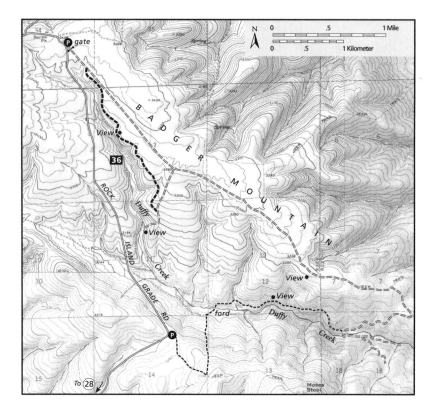

town, turn left onto SR 28. Drive 19.2 miles from Quincy and turn right onto Rock Island Grade Road. Continue up the very steep grade for 12.2 miles to a wide pullout near a small dirt road leading away to the southeast. Park here.

In 1995, the Richard King Mellon Foundation donated approximately 5661 acres to the Bureau of Land Management's (BLM) Spokane District, and that formed the core of the Duffy Creek Allotment, which totals 6580 acres of public land. The area is maintained by the BLM as a wildlife refuge and recreational area. Some of the critters that call the wild area home are mule deer, coyote, porcupine, house finch, black-billed magpie, black-capped chickadee, northern flicker, red-tailed hawk, gopher snake, and western rattlesnake.

Hike southeast along the jeep track that leaves the main road and enjoy the increasingly expansive views from Badger Mountain as you near the rim of Duffy Creek Canyon. Several dirt roads mix and merge throughout the area, so you have plenty of opportunity to explore—and the area is well worth exploring. You'll find outstanding wildflowers throughout the Badger Mountain area. In late spring, the flowers carpet the prairie with varied colors

A lone coyote trots over a ridge in the Duffy Creek area, with mountains near Wenatchee in the distance.

and textures. The nature of the flowers changes with the topography: On the rocky barren slopes buckwheat is dominant. In the lush open sagelands, you'll find desert lupine, balsamroot, white lupine, and brodiaea.

Along the first 2 miles of the jeep track, you'll find a series of bluebird houses posted along the fence line. Wander at will before heading back to your vehicle.

37 ROCK ISLAND CREEK

Round trip ■	**2 miles**
Hiking time ■	1.5 hours
Difficulty ■	Easy
Starting elevation ■	1700 feet
High point ■	1700 feet
Best season ■	May through November
Maps ■	Washington State Department of Natural Resources (DNR) Wenatchee
Contact ■	Bureau of Land Management, Spokane
Permits/passes ■	None

From Ellensburg, drive east on Interstate 90 to exit 149 for George. After exiting, turn left and drive north on State Route 281 to Quincy. In town,

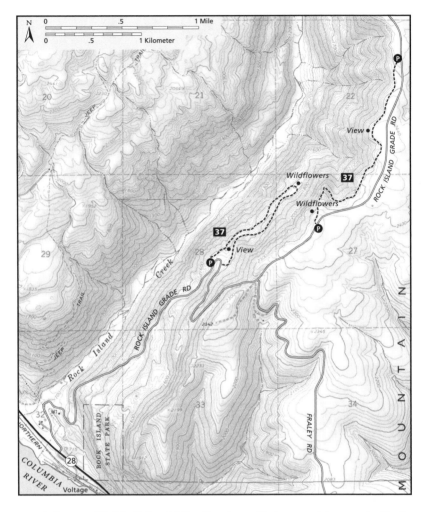

turn left onto SR 28. Drive 19.2 miles from Quincy and turn onto Rock Island Grade Road. Continue up the very steep grade for 2.2 miles to the first pullout on the curve. You can also hike from other pullouts further along the road (one is just past the radio towers; another is about 2 miles beyond).

Few areas can match the panoramic splendor of the view that sweeps over the pretty desert canyon of Rock Island Creek with a broad field of wildflowers filling the foreground. This BLM land is one of the areas described within that agency's "Watchable Wildflower" booklet.

By hiking just below the bluff cliffs, hikers can explore for some time. There are no definitive trails to follow, but the open slope offers unobstructed routes of exploration. Work your way northeast from the parking area and hug the slope. Watch for mule deer under the bluff as they frequently browse among the buckwheat that thrives here.

This is also prime habitat of chukar—a beautiful upland game bird that prefers steep slopes and arid landscapes. However, chukar is just one of the upland bird species that call this rich, sloped prairie home. Look for quail, Hungarian partridge (aka Huns), and pheasant.

As you trek along the bluffs, peer into the canyon below and up at the stark bluffs towering overhead.

38 BEEZLEY HILLS PRESERVE

Round trip ■	**3 miles**
Hiking time ■	3 hours
Difficulty ■	Moderate
Starting elevation ■	2800 feet
Low point ■	2400 feet
Best season ■	April through May
Maps ■	Washington State Department of Natural Resources (DNR) Moses Lake
Contact ■	The Nature Conservancy
Permits/passes ■	None

From Ellensburg, drive east on Interstate 90 to exit 149 for George. After exiting, turn left and drive north on State Route 281 to Quincy. In town, turn right onto SR 28 toward Ephrata. Drive 0.8 mile and turn left onto P-NW Road (also known as Monument Road on some maps). Drive up P-NW Road for 3.1 miles, to where it turns to gravel. At 7.1 miles from SR 28, look for the entry through the fence at a gate marked "Nature Preserve—Foot Travel Only" immediately across from a side road that leads off to the radio towers 200 feet away.

The Beezley Hills Preserve is an area of 4788 acres north of Quincy that is protected by The Nature Conservancy, which started buying up the land in 1998. From this high vantage point, hikers can peer out at the expanse of eastern Washington. The views to the south sweep in the broad lands of the middle Columbia Basin and the greater Quincy area, while to the east you can see all the way to Moses Lake on clear days. The preserve protects a diversity of wildlife and a huge array of wild plants. Indeed, this area is home to one of the largest populations of hedgehog cactus we've ever seen— thousands of the squat little spiny plants are tucked into the sandy loam of the preserve. Watch your step, and keep the kids close at hand if you don't want to be picking spines out of ankles.

Beezley Hills hosts an amazing flower display each spring, and the plethora of hedgehog cactus all seem to come in bloom at the same time—usually late April or early May. The spiny ground-hugging cactus sport bright, fluorescent-pink flowers that add a tropical feel to the desert.

The star of the Beezley Hills Preserve: blooming hedgehog cactus in late April!

Passing through the gate near the road at the top of the ridge leads you down an old jeep track. You can follow this two-track trail or head east to create a loop hike. Walk east along the first ridge spine you encounter to enter a wild garden filled with phlox, Hooker's balsamroot, daggerpod, and several examples of the very uncommon sulphur lupine—one of the only white lupine species in Washington State.

Once you leave the ridge-top area, the soils become more fertile and full, and as a result the flora changes. Look for arrowleaf balsamroot, death

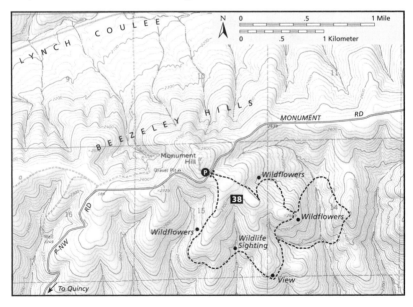

camas, lupine, fern-leaf desert parsley, squaw current, bearded owl-clover, larkspur, prairie star flower, long-flowered bluebells, thyme desert buckwheat, and more.

Continue east down one long deep draw and up to another highpoint ridge. Turning southward, drop into a deep draw filled with towering sage "trees"—this sagebrush is at times 8 feet tall! As you climb out of this draw, turn to the west and hike up to the original ridge to catch the jeep track.

The route provides a nice 3-mile loop, and the abundance of flowers and views means you can enjoy 3 or more hours of walking, moving slowly over that distance to savor the natural richness of the area. Hikers can roam at will within the fenced property, but no one should cross the fences—the adjacent landowners value their private property rights and visitors aren't welcome there.

39 | MOSES COULEE PRESERVE

Round trip ■	**4 miles**
Hiking time ■	3 hours
Difficulty ■	Easy
Starting elevation ■	1750 feet
High point ■	1750 feet
Best season ■	April through May
Maps ■	Washington State Department of Natural Resources (DNR) Banks Lake
Contact ■	The Nature Conservancy
Permits/passes ■	None

From Wenatchee, drive east on State Route 2 past Waterville and Douglas. About 17 miles east of Douglas, turn left onto Jameson Lake Road and continue 4 miles to the trail, found on the left side of the road. Park well off the road.

By our estimation, and from a mature geologist's point of view, this area is equally as grand as the aptly named Grand Coulee. Geology on a mind-blowing scale can be seen here. Moses Coulee boasts towering, sheer basalt walls, intricately sculpted rock forms, and an astounding array of flora and fauna. The desert scenery is just as great as what you'll find at the Grand Coulee.

The trail begins as a short trail to Dusty Hill Falls, but the route provides access to trails going both directions from there as well. The trail leads away from the road for more than 0.5 mile to the falls through a maze of sagebrush and wildflowers. The falls have their source in the drainage of Dutch Henry

The stunning basalt cliffs of the Moses Coulee Preserve region make it second only to Grand Coulee for inspiring geologic awe.

Draw to the northwest, and beyond that, far up at McCarteney Creek. Dusty Hill Falls thunders down the coulee walls briefly during spring runoff, but by early summer the falls is as dry as the great Dry Falls to the northeast.

As noted, the trail splits away from the falls in both directions, providing full access to the pristine basin of Moses Coulee. To make the most of the

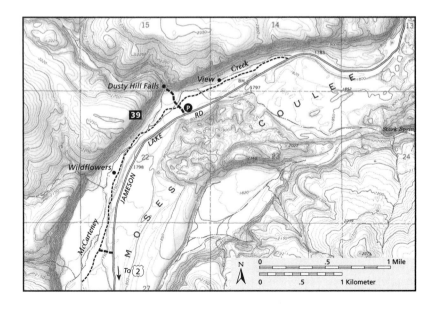

picturesque canyon, hike nearly a mile in each direction as each path offers novel experiences. Turning north from the falls leads you under the bluffs where we saw a falcon nest site as well as plenty of aerial activity of merlins and kestrels. Hawks of many species soar over this area as well.

Heading out along the southern trail, you'll find yourself entering a forest of towering sagebrush about a mile from the falls. These 8-foot tall sage bushes are the desert version of old growth forest. The massive sage plants are several centuries old.

40 CHESTER BUTTE WILDLIFE AREA

Round trip ■	**5 miles**
Hiking time ■	3 hours
Difficulty ■	Moderate
Starting elevation ■	2185 feet
High point ■	2394 feet
Best season ■	May through November
Maps ■	Washington State Department of Natural Resources (DNR) Banks Lake
Contact ■	Washington Department of Fish and Wildlife
Permits/passes ■	Washington Department of Fish and Wildlife Vehicle Permit required

From Wenatchee, drive east on State Route 2 to Waterville. There, turn north on SR 172 and continue to Mansfield. Continue 6.5 miles east of Mansfield and turn right onto a gravel road signed "Heritage Road." Drive 5 miles on Heritage Road to 9-NE Road. Chester Butte is visible 2 miles to the west. Park off the shoulder here.

This area was one of the most recent additions to the Washington Department of Fish and Wildlife's inventory of protected wildlife habitat lands. It is also one of the most important pieces of protected wildlife habitat in the state. Chester Butte Wildlife Area contains some of the last habitat in Washington for the desert sage grouse. This bird, a native of the area, is now rare in the Northwest, and the smallish population in the Chester Butte area might be the largest, most vital population in the entire state. What's more, the Chester Butte addition to the state wildlife area inventory helps protect the last wild population of northern pygmy rabbits in the state (perhaps as few as ten to fourteen individuals). This minuscule population is so small that the regional species is destined to become extinct. The land protection came too late to save this species, but it may have been perfectly timed to save the sage grouse. Visiting this area will help you understand why these species are

Winter hike toward Chester Butte in the distance

so sensitive—the harsh desert environment in which they live allows little room for error in their lives, and when humans interfere, that margin of error shrinks to nothing.

Start hiking on the old dirt jeep track that wanders 2 miles back to Chester Butte (legally, the road can be driven, but it's not advisable to do so). The dirt track is flat and it rolls through a pretty, if rugged, prairie of sage. As you stroll through the sagelands, you'll see wildflowers of many species and possibly some of the multitude of upland birds that live here. Hungarian partridges are the most common species, but sage grouse are the most impressive.

After covering the 2 miles to the butte, hike another 0.25 mile around the butte's north side to find a short trail that climbs the western side to the top of the butte. Here you'll find great views across the surrounding lands: massive areas of protected sagelands stretching to the south and east overlooking the Sagebrush Flats area. To the north, huge swatches of farmlands stretch out as far as you can see. Across it all you can see large blobs of rock that seem totally out of place. These are erratics—large rocks that were carried long distances by migrating glaciers before being dropped as the ice rivers receded. The rocks can be found throughout the coulee country, and some of the erratics are the size of small houses.

After enjoying the views from the top of the butte, head back the way you came.

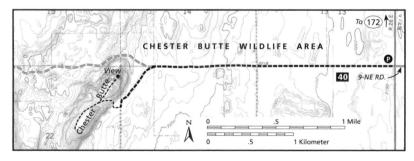

41 Swakane Canyon

Round trip ■	**6 miles**
Hiking time ■	4 hours
Difficulty ■	Difficult
Starting elevation ■	1550 feet
High point ■	3000 feet
Best season ■	October through December
Maps ■	Washington State Department of Natural Resources (DNR) Chelan
Contact ■	Washington Department of Fish and Wildlife
Permits/passes ■	Washington Department of Fish and Wildlife Vehicle Permit required

From Wenatchee, drive north on US 97-A (west side of Columbia River). Drive 5.4 miles before turning left onto a dirt road signed "Swakane Canyon." Continue up this very rough dirt road 2.9 miles to reach a Y. Turn onto the right fork and park at the trailhead area just yards beyond the junction. Start hiking up the road signed "5215." The road is gated closed just around the first bend.

Wow! That was our first reaction when we saw this desolate desert canyon. Though you'll be following an old road, this canyon seems to have been carved just for hikers. Enjoy views up and down the foliage-rich canyon, watch the antics of countless animals (aloft and on the ground), and scramble periodically to a viewpoint on the canyon wall to peer east to the broad basalt-line of the Columbia River Canyon. Golden eagles have been seen nesting on the high cliffs near the base of the canyon, and rugged bighorn sheep—some with massive full curls on their horns, showing their advanced age—prowl the steep canyon and its side gullies.

From the trailhead hike up the road, passing the gate that keeps out vehicles and makes the dusty road a fine wide trail. The road climbs somewhat steeply, but the rewards start coming immediately. At about 0.75 mile up the road, stop and enjoy a long look up Swakane Canyon as

A hiker walks up the road that leads up out of Swakane Canyon.

it stretches westward. This could be one of the most stunning views in the state. Pine trees dot the canyon hills on the south side of the canyon, creating a lovely pattern of shadows in the early morning light. In autumn, the brush along the canyon floor glows with bright reds, oranges, and yellows. The sheep can frequently be seen up among the pines, and mule deer wander throughout the entire canyon. The road continues to climb for 3 miles, leading to a flat area at the head of the canyon.

From here, enjoy a short walk along a faint side path out to the viewpoint overlooking the Columbia River. A spring-fed livestock-watering tank sits out along this ridge and is frequently visited by birds. Quail flock around the ridge as well as down in the canyon, and red-tailed hawks soar endlessly overhead.

The road continues across the rolling highlands for several more miles, allowing you to stretch your journey out, but the best of the area is found in the first 3 miles, giving you a nice 6-mile leg stretcher.

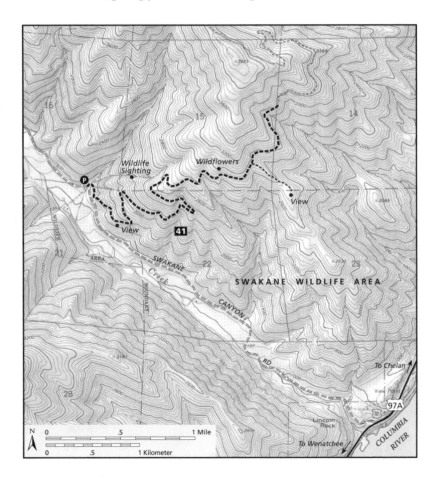

TRI-CITIES

ome 10 million years ago, great cracks in the earth ripped open and oceans of molten rock poured out. These massive flows of basalt lava formed a deep layer of basalt over much of eastern Washington.

In the intervening eons, weather and climate changes have carved and sculpted the rocky landscape. The Columbia and Snake Rivers cut deep chasms through the basalt, the great floods following the last Ice Age sluiced out endless coulees and canyons. Winds have nibbled away at the rock in some places while piling sand and dirt in others.

Much of the sand and dirt that came from the erosion processes ended in the area surrounding the mouth of the Snake River where it empties into the Columbia—in present-day Tri-Cities. The broad, flat basin accumulated shifting sands year after year until much of the basalt was buried under deep layers of sandy loam. The parched, dry weather of this region kept vegetation to a minimum, except around the rivers that lace the desert. Few humans delved into this desolate country, with the exception of a handful of hardy ranchers who recognized the richness of the soil.

In the mid-twentieth century, though, the Tri-Cities came to life. The United States was building a new weapon to help win World War II, and the secluded desert near the tiny ranch community of Pasco proved the perfect place to work on the weapon. The area was secluded, and therefore out of sight from the eyes of spies. There was plenty of power, thanks to the nearness of several hydropower plants (dams) on the Snake and Columbia Rivers. Thousands of acres were open, unsettled public lands. The Hanford Nuclear Reservation was born.

That reservation proved to be one of the greatest environmental aids in the history of the state of Washington. That is, putting aside the whole nuclear power issue, the government's drive for secrecy and seclusion of this installation helped set aside a vast area of natural landscape, protecting it from irrigation and other forms of development. Indeed, the last untouched free-flowing section of the Columbia River (the Hanford Reach) owes its existence to the Hanford Nuclear Reservation. If not for the protections afforded this government installation, the Reach would have been dammed and the adjacent lands plowed, tilled, and irrigated. Instead, we have the Reach as well as the Saddle Mountain Wildlife Refuge and Wahluke Slope Wildlife Area—an incredibly rich, vibrant desert area. We have, in short, an incredible natural landscape, complete with all the native wildlife that existed here hundreds of years ago.

Preceding page: Gazing up at the beautiful clouds, Wahluke Slope Wildlife Area–White Bluffs North

42 : SADDLE MOUNTAIN EAST

Round trip ■	**4 miles**
Hiking time ■	2 hours
Difficulty ■	Moderate
Starting elevation ■	1974 feet
High point ■	2050 feet
Best season ■	Year-round
Maps ■	Washington State Department of Natural Resources (DNR) Priest Rapids
Contact ■	Washington Department of Fish and Wildlife
Permits/passes ■	Washington Department of Fish and Wildlife Vehicle Permit required

From Ellensburg, drive east on Interstate 90 to Vantage and across the Columbia River. Immediately after crossing the river, turn right (south) at exit 137 onto State Route 26 and continue 0.9 mile to a junction with SR 243. Turn right onto SR 243 and drive 14.3 miles, then turn left (east) onto Mattawa Highway / SR 24 Cutoff Road (signed as "24SW"). Drive 13.8 miles along this straight road to its junction with SR 24. Turn left onto SR 24. Just past milepost 60, turn left onto a single-lane road signed "Wahluke National Wildlife Refuge." Drive north on this road for 4.2 miles to a Y junction. Turn right and continue 1.2 miles to a turnaround at the road's end.

Views from the entire top of Saddle Mountain are expansive. The urban sprawl of the Tri-Cities can be seen to the south, while the long, pristine stretch of the Hanford Reach portion of the Columbia Basin lies before you.

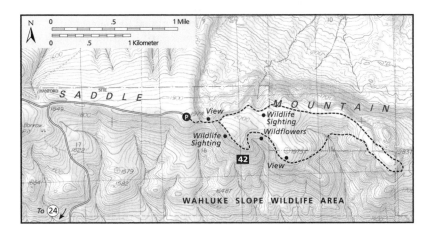

To the north and directly below you, you'll see the dramatic coulee of Lower Crab Creek, and beyond that the flat farmlands of the Columbia Basin that extend to Othello and Moses Lake.

Saddle Mountain stands tall between the deep and broad canyon of Lower Crab Creek Coulee and the deep basin of the mighty Columbia River. Around the flank of the mountain is the Wahluke Slope—a great desert wildlife area offering tremendous views of the ribs and ridges of this immense 50-mile-long Saddle Mountain uplift crossing the Columbia Basin. From the parking area, roam at will through the area on the loop route and game trails, exploring the columnar basalt columns near cliff outcroppings, rocky ridge tops, and vast sagelands filled with the dried balsamroot leaves from last year's plants.

Frequently (especially during the long winter months) the wind howls down from the north, blasting the sheer face of the mountain with powerful force. Don't be surprised if you see hang gliders and paragliders soaring out in front of the north face of the mountain—they love the strong winds that rise up over the butte.

Heading east along the ridge, you'll find fields of flowers underfoot, especially in May. About a mile out on the ridge, you'll cross a vast flat area of what we learned to be one of the last natural areas of bunchgrass remaining undisturbed in the region. Look for great gardens of wildflowers here as well: yellow bells carpet the slope, with large clumps of balsamroot punctuating the landscape.

Look closely along the leeward side of the small side ridges and hills: You might find one or more coyote dens in the sandy soil. The wily hunters

love this region for its unlimited rodent hunting and abundance of hares, rock chucks, and even deer. Don't linger too long near any den sites you encounter— some will undoubtedly be abandoned, but some may be active and your presence could put off the parents.

After nearly 2 miles of walking, you'll have covered the best part of the ridge. Turn back whenever you like, though you can extend your hiking pleasure several more miles by continuing eastward and dropping down some 500 to 800 feet in elevation before turning and hiking back along the lower slope to return to your starting point.

A hiker roams the open ribs and gullies of eastern Saddle Mountain.

43 CRAB CREEK WILDLIFE AREA

Round trip ■	4 to 6 miles
Hiking time ■	3 to 4 hours
Difficulty ■	Moderate
Starting elevation ■	500 feet
High point ■	900 feet
Best season ■	Year-round
Maps ■	Washington State Department of Natural Resources (DNR) Priest Rapids
Contact ■	Washington Department of Fish and Wildlife
Permits/passes ■	Washington Department of Fish and Wildlife Vehicle Permit required

From Ellensburg, drive east on Interstate 90 to Vantage and across the Columbia River. Immediately after crossing the river, turn right (south) at exit 137 onto State Route 26 and continue 0.9 mile to a junction with SR 243. Turn right onto SR 243 and drive 7.4 miles before turning left onto Beverly/Crab Creek Road (just after passing under the enormous railroad trestle bridge). In a couple of miles, you enter the Crab Creek Wildlife Area near the Beverly Dunes, which are visible along the south side of the road. At 9.2 miles from SR 243, just after passing an abandoned old building on the left is a large parking area on the right at the base of Saddle Mountain. This will put you very near to the middle of the long Lower Crab Creek Wildlife Area, a good starting point for any route. Park here, cross the road, and follow a rough old jeep track to the railroad grade by the trestles.

Broad, rolling sand dunes. A wide, gurgling blue creek. Deep, emerald-green lakes. Towering mountains and vast meadows of desert wildflowers. All await you here. At 17,000 acres, the state-owned Crab Creek Wildlife Area is bigger than some federal wilderness areas in Washington State. What's more, the area is just as rich in wildlife and natural habitat as many wildernesses. Crab Creek also has the distinction of being the longest creek in the United States, and the fact that much of it is protected as wildlife habitat makes it wonderfully special.

After just 0.5 mile of hiking, you'll find the railroad grade of the old Chicago/St. Paul/Milwaukee Railroad. The two trestles near the access point for this route mark the start of a great adventure. Once on the railroad route, hike west along the old rail corridor as it passes through the marshlands of the Lower Crab Creek area. The sloughs and ponds along the creek sport lovely crops of swaying cattails and silky marsh reed grasses. These marshy bogs provide fertile habitat for a variety of animals, too. During one visit, we counted no less than five species of waterfowl, two belted kingfishers, and a

A hiker heads out into the heart of Lower Crab Creek Coulee.

squadron of great blue herons flying by. Red-winged blackbirds call from the reeds, and a few yellow-headed blackbirds are also in the area.

At about a mile out from the vehicle, drop off the rail corridor and freely roam around, over, and between lovely miniature coulees within the vast Crab Creek Coulee. Many wildlife paths weave through the area, and following these always leads to an adventure. If nothing else, they'll lead you to a cool watering hole or a fast route back to the higher slopes above the rail grade.

After exploring the southern edge of the creek basin near the rail grade, wander north across the mile-wide coulee to explore the red cliffs of the coulee. The iron-rich cliffs are remarkably beautiful—the rust-stained rock proves rich in lichen, providing a fantastic mosaic of color to view and photograph.

From about 2.5 miles out, pick a path up the modest slope—an easy stand-up scramble for the most part—and in less than a mile, you'll find a wonderful high viewpoint from where you can admire the entire sprawl of the wildlife area and, to the south of it, the long line of Saddle Mountain.

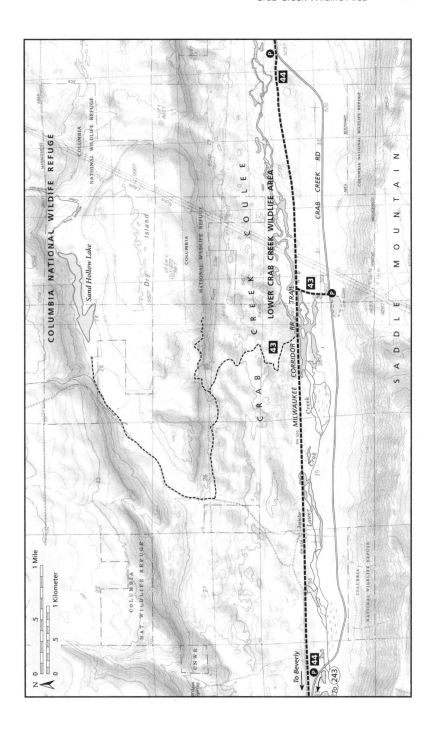

44 MILWAUKEE RAILROAD

Round trip ■	10 miles (40 miles with extended treks)
Hiking time ■	4 hours
Difficulty ■	Easy
Starting elevation ■	500 feet
High point ■	500 feet
Best season ■	Year-round
Maps ■	Washington State Department of Natural Resources (DNR) Priest Rapids
Contact ■	Washington State Department of Natural Resources
Permits/passes ■	Washington State Department of Natural Resources (DNR) free use permit required

From Ellensburg, drive east on Interstate 90 to Vantage and across the Columbia River. Immediately after crossing the river, turn right (south) at exit 137 onto State Route 26 and continue 0.9 mile to a junction with SR 243. Turn right onto SR 243 and drive 7.4 miles before turning left onto Beverly/Crab Creek Road (just after passing under the enormous railroad trestle bridge). At about 5.5 miles from SR 243, Crab Creek Road turns away from the railroad grade. Find a place to pull off the road and walk to the railroad grade and start hiking. (See page 121 for trail map.)

The old Milwaukee road railway slices eastward from the Columbia River through the heart of the Crab Creek Wildlife Area. Rambles through the open desert can be fun (see the Lower Crab Creek Wildlife Area hike and connect into it if you like), but following the old railway provides a flat, easy trail trek. The Washington State Department of Natural Resources maintains the road-to-trail conversion as a nonmotorized trail. It rolls through broad sagebrush flats, past deep, trout-rich Nunnally Lake, and through the dunes in the heart of the Crab Creek Coulee.

A bucket of rusted, unused railroad spikes along the Milwaukee Railroad trail

Heading east along the rail trail, you can walk 1 mile or 20 before turning back. The railway runs east through the heart of the Crab Creek Coulee (indeed, you can pick up the trail just outside Beverly after you turn off SR 243). From the recommended trailhead, the railway leads away from the dirt road, giving you more time to explore the quiet desert. If the mood strikes you, roam north away from the trail for greater exploration—you can wander up to the long, deep Nunnally Lake or the emerald green gems of Merry Lake and Lenice Lake, all popular trout-fishing ponds accessibly only by foot. You may follow the route west into the Lower Crab Creek area to join with that route as well.

45 | WHITE BLUFFS–NORTH SLOPE

Round trip ■	**8 miles**
Hiking time ■	4 to 5 hours
Difficulty ■	Easy
Starting elevation ■	400 feet
High point ■	700 feet
Best season ■	Year-round
Maps ■	Washington State Department of Natural Resources (DNR) Priest Rapids
Contact ■	Washington Department of Fish and Wildlife
Permits/passes ■	Washington Department of Fish and Wildlife Vehicle Permit required

From Ellensburg, drive east on Interstate 90 to Vantage and across the Columbia River. Immediately after crossing the river, turn right (south) at exit 137 onto State Route 26 and continue 0.9 mile to a junction with SR 243. Turn right onto SR 243 and drive 14.3 miles, then turn left (east) onto the Mattawa Highway/SR 24 Cutoff Road (signed as "24SW"). Drive 13.8 miles along this straight road to its junction with SR 24. Turn left onto SR 24. Just past milepost 63, turn right onto the dirt road signed "Wahluke National Wildlife Refuge" and guarded with a huge solar-powered gate system, which closes at night. Drive 4.0 miles to an intersection, turn right and head down the hill 1.3 miles to a pullout area by large trees. Park here and walk up toward the faint trail you will see on the slopes north of the parking pullout. The parking area is closed from 2 hours after dusk until 2 hours before sunrise.

The mighty Columbia River has been called the Heart of the West. Lewis and Clark and their famous Corps of Discovery journeyed along the wild waters of the Columbia nearly two hundred years ago as they sought to open the West to U.S. expansion. The river is filled with the waters from millions

Springtime thunderheads form over the Hanford Reach in the White Bluffs region.

of acres of wilderness, but humans long ago tamed this massive river—at least most of it. Purely through serendipity, the lonely Hanford Reach is the last free-flowing stretch of the Columbia River. This section was undammed simply because the sensitive nature of the work being done at the Hanford Nuclear Reservation prevented such massive projects as a dam from being completed within its borders.

The Hanford Reach can be seen from the long stretch of the White Bluffs. Wildlife makes full use of this pristine stretch of river and surrounding native lands. Look for horned lizards sunning themselves on the rocks and big rafts of waterfowl on the free-flowing river. On a recent winter day, we spotted more than a thousand Canada geese on the river, with scores of tundra swans resting on the sandy islands dotting the river.

Heading north from the parking area, you'll find a remarkable desert trek along the White Bluffs, just across the river from the still heavily restricted Hanford Nuclear Reservation managed by the U.S. Department of Energy.

The trailhead is near the historic White Bluffs Landing. A modern boat ramp now sits at the site of an old ferry that used to cross over to the town of White Bluffs—now a distant pre–World War II memory. A faint trail leads up from the parking area by the grove of cottonwood trees on the slope above the trailhead. The path is faint but grows into an established trail once above the bluffs. The route follows the crest of the bluffs above the river for nearly 4 miles.

The White Bluffs themselves are shimmering ivory-colored cliffs towering 400 feet above the river. The rolling crown of the bluffs sports a thick garden of foliage, including an array of spring- and summer-blooming desert wildflowers. With the free-flowing, untamed Columbia below, the sprawling wildflower meadows at your feet, and an array of birds and ani-

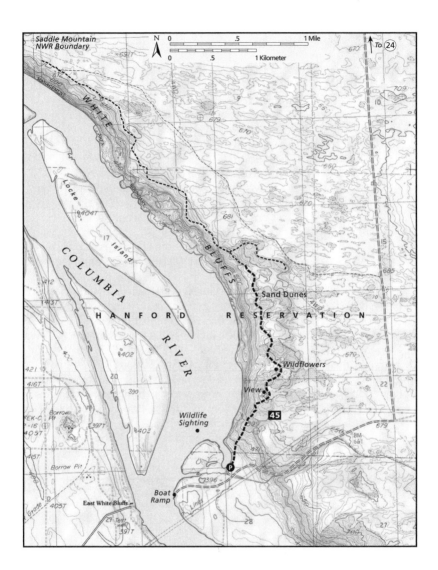

mals all around (mule deer and Rocky Mountain elk call the Bluffs home), this is as close as you'll get to seeing the Columbia River country as Lewis and Clark experienced it. To the east of the trail, take note of a series of huge sand dunes great for off-trail roaming.

At 4 miles out, you'll reach the Saddle Mountain National Wildlife Refuge. This area is adjacent to the Hanford Nuclear Reservation and is closed to the public. Heed all signs you see—the federal government doesn't take unauthorized visits to the Hanford site lightly.

46 WAHLUKE LAKE

Round trip ■ **4 miles**
Hiking time ■ 2 to 3 hours
Difficulty ■ Easy
Starting elevation ■ 725 feet
High point ■ 725 feet
Best season ■ Year-round
Maps ■ Washington State Department of Natural Resources (DNR) Priest Rapids
Contact ■ Washington Department of Fish and Wildlife
Permits/passes ■ Washington Department of Fish and Wildlife Vehicle Permit required

From Ellensburg, drive east on Interstate 90 to Vantage and across the Columbia River. Immediately after crossing the river, turn right (south) at exit 137 onto State Route 26 and continue 0.9 mile to a junction with SR 243. Turn right onto SR 243 and drive 14.3 miles, then turn left (east) onto the Mattawa Highway/SR 24 Cutoff Road (signed as "24SW"). Drive 13.8 miles along this straight road to its junction with SR 24. Turn left onto SR 24. Just past milepost 63, turn right onto the dirt road signed "Wahluke National Wildlife Refuge" and guarded with a huge solar-powered gate system, which closes at night. Drive 4 miles to an intersection, continuing straight at the four-way intersection (right leads to White Bluffs Landing). At 5.8 miles from SR 24 (1.8 miles past the intersection), pull off and park by the "closed" jeep track that heads east.

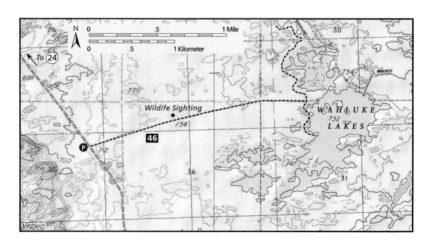

This area is a natural coulee. The sandy soil allows water to drain through soil and collect in the bottom of the coulee forming the Wahluke Branch-10 (WB-10) Wasteway. The wasteway water flows westward into the White Bluffs area. The gradual slope of this coulee has allowed the water to spread out and form several small ponds and cattail marshes. Russian olive and willow trees have been spreading rapidly, taking over some of the wetlands.

Beautiful hawk feathers discovered in the Wahluke Slope Wildlife Area

The old jeep track leads in an almost straight line through open desert prairie for nearly 1.5 miles to the area of "the lakes." This is a loosely applied term in that the lakes only fill with water following spring runoff and heavy rains. The underground water seepage, though, keeps the local flora rich and abundant. The rich plant life and periodic sources of water help keep a large population of upland game birds alive and thriving here, too. Quail, chukar, pheasant, partridge, and doves live here, meaning bird hunters also heavily use the area after mid-October.

Once in the lake basin area, wander 0.5 mile farther around the pools before heading back to the start of your route.

47 | WHITE BLUFFS–SOUTH SLOPE

Round trip ■	**10 miles**
Hiking time ■	6 hours
Difficulty ■	Moderate
Starting elevation ■	900 feet
Low point ■	370 feet
Best season ■	Year-round
Maps ■	Washington State Department of Natural Resources (DNR) Priest Rapids
Contact ■	Washington Department of Fish and Wildlife
Permits/passes ■	Washington Department of Fish and Wildlife Vehicle Permit required

From Ellensburg, drive east on Interstate 90 to Vantage and across the Columbia River. Immediately after crossing the river, turn right (south) at exit

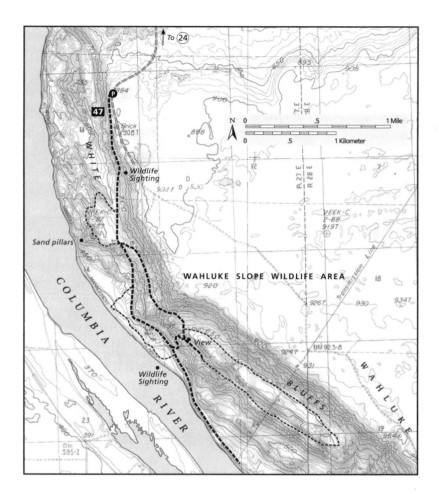

137 onto State Route 26 and continue 0.9 mile to a junction with SR 243. Turn right onto SR 243 and drive 14.3 miles, then turn left (east) onto the Mattawa Highway/SR 24 cutoff road (signed as "24SW"). Drive 13.8 miles along this straight road to its junction with SR 24. Turn left onto SR 24. Just past milepost 63, turn right onto the dirt road signed "Wahluke National Wildlife Refuge" and guarded with a huge solar-powered gate system, which closes at night. Drive 8.1 miles to the end of the road. Make use of a new circular parking area to the right of the road at a river overlook. The parking area is closed from 2 hours after dusk until 2 hours before sunrise.

The White Buffs area offers an incredible desert landscape to explore. The amazing clay/sand bluffs boast amazing patterns woven into their faces—patterns created by the network of sand and clay layers as well as the hundreds of holes that serve as nesting sites for cliff swallows and many species of raptors that come to this area in spring. Heading south, you have numerous roaming options, and going in this direction would take many visits to fully explore.

Heading south from the trailhead along the old paved roadway, you can enjoy the amazing bluffs and the wonderful river views. You'll be walking along the Hanford Reach, the last free-flowing section of the Columbia. One mile down the road, look carefully for an unsigned trail that leaves the roadway on your left (a trail leads right also for more roaming out to sandstone pillar formations overlooking the river) where the roadway passes through a flat area before it goes through a deep road cut.

Head up this trail, climbing into the hills, and you'll be greeted with some of the best steppe land roaming in the state. The trail leads along the base of the tremendous bluffs to the east and skirts the deep ravines cut

Fascinating sandstone formations along the Columbia River in the southern White Bluffs region

by erosion that lead below to the road and river. Coyote sign can be found everywhere up on these bluffs as the rodent hunters have plenty of prey to feast upon. Watch for mule deer, too, as they frequent this trail system, which allows them access from the rich prairie atop the bluffs to the water in the river below.

The trail continues to climb steeply to a high point and then generally remains along the ridge. We call this "The Great Valley" as the climb up reveals a vast broad valley that makes it easy to picture a wagon train passing through it in the year 1850 or so. It is an amazingly long valley with bluffs 400 to 500 feet high lining both sides. Hike the full length of it to really appreciate the quiet of the desert. The Great Valley rolls on like this for well over a mile.

From that point, you can find game trails leading down through the steep gullies to the river below. This drops you back on the riverside road about 2 miles from the trailhead (though you'll have covered nearly 3 miles by making the hike up the bluffs). From here, continue south along the river for 2 or 3 more miles before moving inland a bit. This lets you return to the trailhead by hiking the flatlands between the road and the river. Return the way you came.

48 McGee Ranch

Round trip	■ 5 miles
Hiking time	■ 2 to 3 hours
Difficulty	■ Easy
Starting elevation	■ 450 feet
High point	■ 450 feet
Best season	■ Year-round
Maps	■ Washington State Department of Natural Resources (DNR) Priest Rapids
Contact	■ Washington Department of Fish and Wildlife
Permits/passes	■ Washington Department of Fish and Wildlife Vehicle Permit required

From Ellensburg, drive east on I-90 to Vantage and across the Columbia River. Immediately after crossing the river, turn right (south) at exit 137 onto SR 26 and continue 0.9 mile to a junction with SR 243. Turn right onto SR 243. After 15.2 miles on SR 243, pass Mattawa Cutoff Road/24SW. At 29 miles, cross the Vernita Bridge (now on SR 24). At 1.1 miles past the rest area facilities (just over the bridge south of the Columbia River), turn right on Midway Road/Midway Substation. Drive 1.0 mile to the access road on the right (left side of Midway Road is closed to public access; Midway Road is fenced and closed at the end of public land 2.5 miles from SR 24). Park here and hike in the access or drive in 0.3 mile and park at the Y to start a big loop hike.

This region south of the Columbia River sits at the northwesternmost part of the Hanford Reach. Priest Rapids Dam blocks the flow of the river just to the northwest, around a gentle bend in the river. The McGee Ranch Unit of the Wahluke National Wildlife Refuge encompasses 9000 acres (only a portion of which is open to the public) that serve as a crucial link for wildlife movement between the Hanford Reservation and the Yakima Training Center lands. These two huge blocks of federal land are heavily restricted and completely closed to public access, but their designation as a nuclear reservation and an Army training base actually provides the highest possible level of protection from development. The McGee Ranch property benefits from that and allows the public a chance to experience the rich wildlife population of the area.

If the river level is low enough, the first part of any hike here should involve a stroll along the sandy banks of the Columbia River. You can hike 1 mile east from the trailhead parking area to the SR 24 Vernita Bridge. The sandy shore shows the vast wildlife activity of the seemingly "barren" lands: Coyote, deer, grouse, rabbit, and shorebird tracks usually cover the sand.

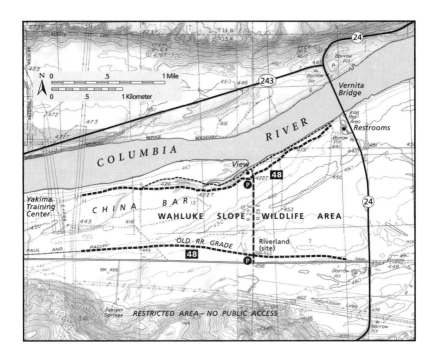

Once tiring of the river shore, head back to the trailhead area and head west. Hiking cross-country on the north side of the road that goes through the heart of this area reveals lovely grassland-filled gullies dotted with hawthorn trees and red-twigged shrubs. Meadowlarks fill the air, and rabbits fill the brush underfoot.

To the west you can see one of the U.S. Army facilities, the Yakima Training Center, on the horizon. Keep hiking toward it and in 1.5 miles reach a fence line, which signals your turn-around. Unofficial four-wheeler tracks lead to this area, too, though they are less enjoyable to hike than the recommended route (too dusty). The walk back to the trailhead creates a 3-mile loop, which coupled with the mile of river shore walking creates a relaxing 4-mile day hike.

Rocks and sand line the Columbia River at its low winter level, on the McGee Ranch unit of the Hanford Reach.

Spring flowers include some desert parsley species, balsamroot, yellow bells, and ballhead waterleaf.

49 PRIEST RAPIDS WILDLIFE AREA

Round trip ■	5 miles
Hiking time ■	2 to 3 hours
Difficulty ■	Easy
Starting elevation ■	450 feet
Low point ■	400 feet
Best season ■	Year-round
Maps ■	Washington State Department of Natural Resources (DNR) Priest Rapids
Contact ■	Washington Department of Fish and Wildlife
Permits/passes ■	Washington Department of Fish and Wildlife Vehicle Permit required

From Ellensburg, drive east on Interstate 90 to Vantage and across the Columbia River. Immediately after crossing the river, turn right (south) at

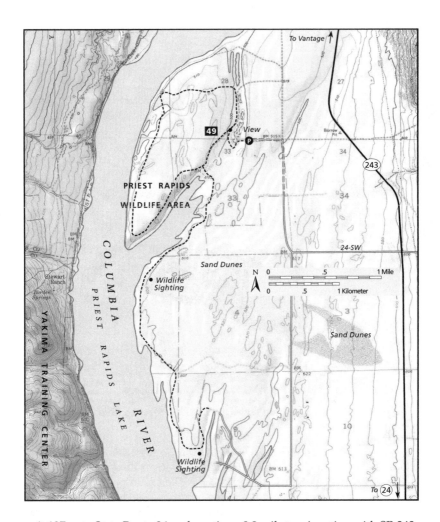

exit 137 onto State Route 26 and continue 0.9 mile to a junction with SR 243. Turn right onto SR 243 and drive 14.3 miles. Turn right (west) at Mattawa Highway/SR 24 Cutoff Road (signed as "24SW"). Drive 1 mile before turning right onto a gravel road. Continue 1 mile from 24-SW and turn left on a dirt road signed as the entrance to the Priest Rapids Wildlife Area. Continue 0.3 mile on this very rough dirt road to a nice large parking area.

From this small wildlife area, you'll enjoy views of Sentinel Gap. Along the route, you may also see bald eagles hunting over the sloughs south of the trailhead near the boat launch and red-tailed and Cooper's hawks hunting over the desert prairies.

This wildlife area in the region north of Priest Rapids Dam offers a

A huge flock of Canada geese cover a wintering feeding field at Priest Rapids Wildlife Area.

dramatic view of Sentinel Gap—the deep cut in the 1800-foot-tall Saddle Mountain Ridge through which the Columbia River flows.

From the trailhead, drop down into the often mud-packed dry slough area and roam among the old dead trees, stumps, and oddly shaped rocks that dot the mudflats. From here, head south around the slough, passing cattail marshes along the way, and continue roaming a peninsula that points off to the northwest. (Instead, you might want to hike southwest along a huge slough/backwater to the Columbia River and then hike south along the river itself.)

After reaching another slough, hike inland around it. You'll eventually come to an area of irrigated fields that are usually filled with hungry Canada geese in winter. We counted more than 700 birds here before abandoning the count. On the far eastern side of this field is a small access road that leads out. A better plan is to hike back out the 3 miles you followed on your way in. Keep an eye out for pheasants, quail, Hungarian partridge, and doves.

50 HORSETHIEF BUTTE

Round trip	■	**1 mile**
Hiking time	■	1 hour
Difficulty	■	Easy
Starting elevation	■	350 feet
High point	■	500 feet
Best season	■	Year-round
Maps	■	Washington State Department of Natural Resources (DNR) Hood River
Contact	■	Washington State Parks and Recreation
Permits/passes	■	Washington State Parks and Recreation Parking Pass required

From Yakima, drive east on Interstate 82 to exit 37, signed "US Highway 97/ Goldendale." Drive this four-lane highway to a signed right-turn only to US 97/Goldendale once you reach Toppenish. Drive south on US 97 through Goldendale until you reach a junction with State Route 14. Drive west on SR 14 for 14.7 miles and find the Horsethief Butte trailhead on your left (if

Balsamroot and many other flowers cover the top of Horsethief Butte.

coming from the west, drive 1.2 miles past the entrance to Horsethief Lake State Park). Park along the somewhat wide gravel shoulder of SR 14 on either side of the highway.

Despite the name of the butte, this is a peaceful preserve for recreationists to explore. Huge lupine and balsamroot flower displays are profuse throughout the spring, with white biscuit root, yellow bells, salt-and-pepper lomatium, and some type of wallflower species filling the carpet of color that spreads over the area. Still, all is not peaceful. There is death camas aplenty here, and tons of poison oak in the rocks of the butte. Be careful!

While this hike is short, you can combine it with other nearby hiking routes to round out a day. Or just take your time here—our valiant

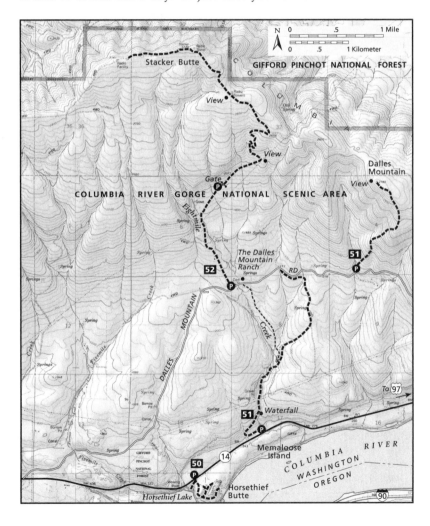

photographer spent more than 2.5 hours here and had to be dragged away kicking and screaming because there were still things to see.

The well-signed trail climbs away from the shoulder of SR 14 near the outhouse. Immediately you are greeted with stunning views west to the Columbia River and the area around Horsethief Lake. Above you, the butte is spectacular. The approach to the top winds through grassy meadows filled with flowers. Views continue to improve as you look south over the river and west to Horsethief Lake State Park's camp area. At the fork in the trail, stay left and head up the butte. As you climb, you'll find petroglyphs on the rock walls—but also lots of poison oak. Be careful.

51 THE DALLES MOUNTAIN

Round trip ■	**8 miles**
Hiking time ■	5 hours
Difficulty ■	Difficult
Starting elevation ■	350 feet
High point ■	2825 feet
Best season ■	March through November
Maps ■	Washington State Department of Natural Resources (DNR) Hood River
Contact ■	Washington State Parks and Recreation
Permits/passes ■	Washington State Parks and Recreation Parking Pass required

From Yakima, drive east on Interstate 82 to exit 37, signed "US Highway 97/Goldendale." Drive this four-lane highway to a signed right-turn-only to US 97/Goldendale once you reach Toppenish. Drive south on US 97 through Goldendale until you reach a junction with SR 14. Drive west on SR 14 for 13.9 miles and find a gated pullout/road on your right. Pull in by the "Road Closed" gate (do not block the gate!) and park on the shoulder of SR 14.

Unique views of the eastern gate of the Columbia River Gorge can be had here, but more importantly, you can immerse yourself in the natural desert world that Lewis and Clark encountered as they passed along the Columbia. This route leads hikers past a picturesque waterfall and through fields of wildflowers—including white biscuit root, yellow bells, salt-and-pepper lomatium, chokecherry and serviceberry, and a plethora of mock orange.

Horsethief Lake State Park, also known as Dalles Mountain Ranch State Park, offers great experiences in the desert country east of the Columbia River Gorge. From the trailhead, hike up the gated road, immediately

finding glorious views of a stunning waterfall. A short 0.5 mile up the road puts you right alongside the waterfall. Incredible!

As you climb, the views of Horsethief Butte and the Columbia River grow increasingly impressive. The road winds up a gully along the creek. At times, the brush alongside encroaches to the point that the road becomes a faint trail.

Near the top, keep hiking as the slope levels off east of the creek gully. About 2.5 miles into the hike, you'll hit the Dalles Mountain Road. Cross the road and find a steep trail leading the final

A large waterfall on the lower section of Eightmile Creek on The Dalles Mountain

1.5 miles to the summit (you likely will need to hike a bit east along the road to find this upper trail).

52 | COLUMBIA HILLS NATURAL AREA PRESERVE

Round trip ■	6 miles
Hiking time ■	3 to 4 hours
Difficulty ■	Difficult
Starting elevation ■	1350 feet
High point ■	3220 feet
Best season ■	March through November
Maps ■	Washington State Department of Natural Resources (DNR) Hood River
Contact ■	Washington State Department of Natural Resources
Permits/passes ■	None

From Yakima, drive east on Interstate 82 to exit 37, signed "US Highway 97/ Goldendale." Drive this four-lane highway to a signed right-turn-only to US 97/Goldendale once you reach Toppenish. Drive south on US 97 through Goldendale until you reach a junction with State Route 14. Drive west on SR

Lupine and balsamroot carpet the upper slopes of the Columbia Hills
Natural Area Preserve.

14 for 16.5 miles and turn right onto Dalles Mountain Road. Drive up this
road for 3.4 miles to the Dalles Mountain Ranch site and the old stagecoach
wagon. Begin here for a longer hike up the road to your left at the wagon (or
from here if gated), or be lazy and drive the very steep and rough 1.4 miles
up the road (through the gate) to the end of the road at the gated entrance
to the DNR lands of the Columbia Hills Natural Area Preserve. (See page
136 for trail map.)

This natural preserve managed by the Washington State Department of
Natural Resources (DNR) is a huge 6000-acre area along the top portion of
the long rolling hills and ridges known as the Columbia Hills, extending
from The Dalles Mountain area westward. Lupine and balsamroot form a
solid carpet of color underfoot in springtime, and squadrons of songbirds
flit and flutter around you, while majestic raptors—hawks, eagles, falcons,
and vultures—soar overhead.

From the upper DNR signed trailhead, hike up the old gated road, climbing 1.5 miles to the top of the butte. (If you start by the wagon at the Dallas
Mountain Ranch for the longer hike, this hike is 3 miles up.) Done early in
the day, you'll find unmatched sunrise views south into Oregon, with the
rolling hills laid out like a pastel painting. At 1.5 miles you reach the 3220-
foot summit of Stacker Butte. Here the flora is much more susceptible to the
harsher winter conditions at this higher elevation.

Enjoy the summit views, including those down into Oregon, before looping back down the slopes. You may detour out along the base of the bluffs to enjoy the warm sun radiating off the rocks, the birds (canyon wrens, meadowlarks, quails, raptors soaring and hunting), and the wildlife (marmots, mule deer, and various small mammals). From here, hike down into the gully to the west to enjoy the wonderful native oak tree stands that cluster around the Eightmile Creek drainage. Return to the road and continue down to the trailhead.

53 CATHERINE CREEK

Round trip ■	1.5 miles
Hiking time ■	1 hour
Difficulty ■	Easy
Starting elevation ■	300 feet
Low point ■	180 feet
Best season ■	March through November
Maps ■	Washington State Department of Natural Resources (DNR) Hood River
Contact ■	USFS Gifford Pinchot National Forest, Mount Adams Ranger District
Permits/passes ■	USFS Region 6 Trail Park Pass required

From Bingen, drive east 4.6 miles on State Route 14 to milepost 71 and the junction on the left with County Road 1230. Turn left onto County Road 1230 and follow it 1.4 miles to the Catherine Creek parking lot on the north side of the road. The Catherine Creek Universal Access Trail is located at the east end of the Columbia River Gorge National Scenic Area.

Catherine Creek is an area of unique natural beauty and is of great botanical significance. Over ninety species of wildflowers can be found in the area, from grass widow, which blankets the ground as early as February, to western ladies' tresses, which may bloom into July. The Catherine Creek

Death camas (Zigadenus venosus)

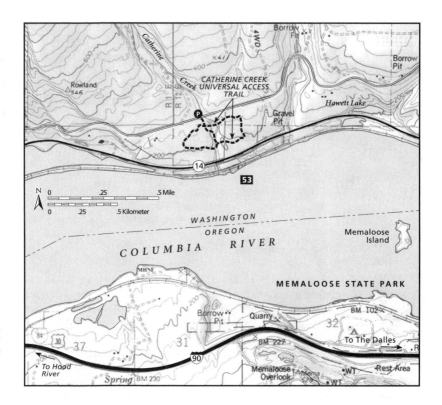

Universal Access Trail offers dramatic views of the Columbia River and Mount Hood. Weather on this south-facing drainage is much sunnier and drier than the western Gorge and can be quite windy. Dress appropriately, and be aware that you will encounter no restrooms, water, or garbage facilities.

The paved, universal access trail offers two levels of difficulty for wheel-chairs. The short 0.25-mile "easy" route will take you to a viewpoint over-looking Catherine Creek Falls. The "moderate" routes form loop opportunities up to 1.25 miles in length through open grasslands, vernal ponds, and oak woodlands.

That's right—this pretty forest area offers a unique experience in Washington: a walk in a natural hardwood deciduous forest. You'll find a lovely old oak forest stand on the slope above Catherine Creek, as well as great gardens of spring wildflowers. The trails are well maintained and easy, making this a wonderful place to bring novice hikers or other folks not used to hiking: The well-graded trails make this a literal walk in the park. At both ends of the gentle loop, enjoy great views from established viewpoints.

54 | JUNIPER DUNES WILDERNESS

Round trip ■	Up to 15 miles
Hiking time ■	3 to 6 hours or backpack
Difficulty ■	Moderate
Starting elevation ■	800 feet
High point ■	1000 feet
Best season ■	March through June or October through November
Maps ■	Washington State Department of Natural Resources (DNR) Walla Walla
Contact ■	Bureau of Land Management, Spokane
Permits/passes ■	None

From Pasco, drive east on US 12 to the junction with the Pasco–Kahlotus Highway. Turn left (north) onto the Pasco–Kahlotus Highway and drive 5.6 miles to Peterson Road (the junction is at a small crop duster airstrip and grain silo). Turn left onto an unnamed wide gravel road and continue 4 miles northeast. The road quickly turns to rough dirt as it leaves the farmlands and enters Bureau of Land Management property. At the 4-mile point, follow the signs to the right. A large parking area is 100 yards down this road. If you're driving a low-clearance passenger vehicle or the conditions are very wet, park here and walk 3.5 miles on the rough road to the wilderness boundary. If you're in a high-clearance vehicle, drive along the rough, rutted sand road to the wilderness boundary, marked by a barbed-wire fence and gate. Park near the gate.

Ask Washington hikers to describe their idea of "wilderness" and most will talk passionately about alpine lakes, towering spires of rock, glaciers, ancient forests, and deep river valleys. One of Washington's finest protected wilderness areas, though, fails to meet any of those expectations.

Deep in the heart of the dry, desert country of the lower Columbia Basin sits the Juniper Dunes Wilderness Area, the only Bureau of Land Management wilderness in the entire state. Covering just 7,140 acres, it is also the only wilderness area in the state to be completely enclosed by barbed wire—put there not to keep the animals in but to keep the motorcycles and ORVs out. Fortunately, the wire works and the deer and coyotes can leap over or under the wire as they please.

The Juniper Dunes Wilderness exists as an oasis of natural wonder just a few minutes drive from the urban sprawl of Pasco. The only trail in this wilderness is an old jeep track that slices across the southern end of the small desert preserve, but no trails are needed here. To experience the wonders of this place, simply disappear into the sand dunes and juniper groves.

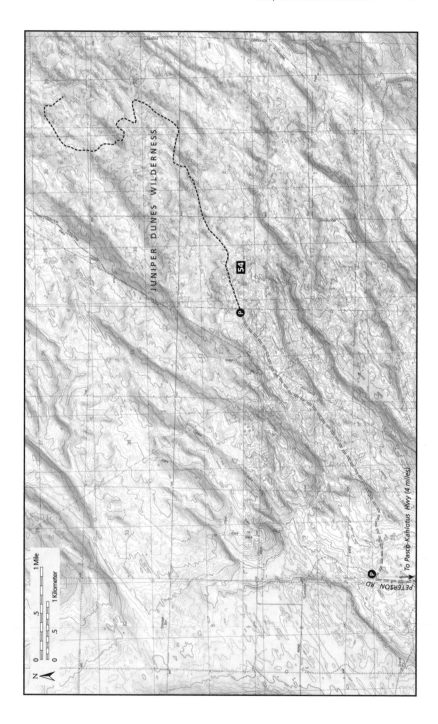

You'll find six large groves of the desert juniper trees, the largest remaining concentration of this species this far north. Between the well-spaced groves are individual trees—some of which truly could be classified as old-growth specimens. Many of the broad, fragrant trees are hundreds of years old, but this is no old growth forest. Aside from the few large groves, most of the trees exist in small clumps of no more than two or three trees scattered across the rolling hills.

A wonderful array of plant life populates these low hills, which are indeed sand dunes—but not in the "Sahara Desert" sense of the term. A few barren mounds of shifting sand are present, but most dunes are carpeted with sagebrush, wild rye grass, Indian ricegrass, an assortment of such desert flowers as phlox, larkspur, and blue-eyed Marys, and a few small species of cactus including prickly pear and Simpson's hedgehog.

A complex web of animal tracks criss-crosses the sands. As you explore the wilderness area, watch for mule deer, coyotes, foxes, rattlesnakes, deer mice, kangaroo rats, porcupines, badgers, rabbits, and skunks, among others. Red-tailed hawks, turkey vultures, prairie falcons, and golden eagles circle overhead, and great horned owls stare from the thick branches of the junipers. I can't even begin to identify the assortment of small birds that flitter around the sagebrush and juniper branches.

This small wilderness is a wildlife-lover's dream. The lack of trails means you can roam freely throughout the area, following bird songs and animal tracks. If you get lost, a hike of not more than 4.5 miles in any direction will take you to the boundary of the wilderness area, marked with a strong, steel, barbed wire fence (to keep out the motorcycle and four-wheel-drive enthusiasts who recreate on the surrounding BLM property).

Spring is the ideal time to visit as the desert bursts with new growth and increased animal activity. The junipers acquire fresh shoots of new, green needles, the desert flowers are all blooming, the mammals are scurrying around looking for mates and new homes and some fresh food, and the reptiles are still largely inactive due to the still-cold nights.

Hikers can pitch camp anywhere they please in the wilderness, but the lack of any water source means folks will have to pack in all the water they need for their stay. In the spring, that's not too hard, but by July, when daytime temperatures can reach and exceed 100 degrees F., it means carrying several gallons of water on your back. If you go, take plenty of water,

Whipped by wind, desert parsley leaves patterns in the sands of Juniper Dunes.

a good pair of binoculars, and a camera. You'll want to record this unique jewel of a wilderness area.

55 McNary National Wildlife Refuge

Round trip ■	**2 miles**
Hiking time ■	1 hour
Difficulty ■	Easy
Starting elevation ■	350 feet
High point ■	350 feet
Best season ■	November through March
Maps ■	Washington State Department of Natural Resources (DNR) Walla Walla
Contact ■	U.S. Fish and Wildlife Service–McNary National Wildlife Refuge
Permits/passes ■	None

From Pasco, drive east on US 12, crossing the Snake River. About 1.5 miles past the Snake River Bridge, turn left onto Maple Street and drive 0.3 mile

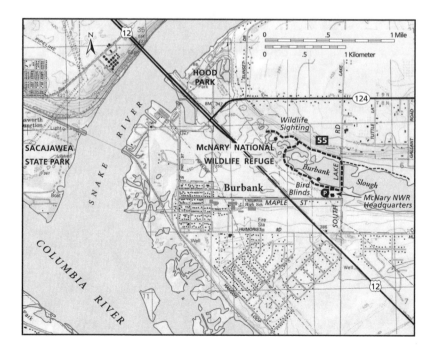

before turning left into the parking lot of the McNary National Wildlife Refuge Headquarters and Environmental Education Center.

The McNary National Wildlife Refuge is primarily a waterfowl preserve. The refuge encompasses many flooded fields, sloughs, and inlets along the Columbia River. It also sprawls across farmlands that provide winter forage for migratory birds. This area draws thousands of ducks, geese, and swans each year, usually beginning in November. Look for tundra swans, redheads, cinnamon teal, green-winged teals, mergansers of all kinds, buffleheads, Canada geese, mallards, pintails, and the ever-present coots.

Even when the migratory waterfowl are gone, the area is worth a visit. With desert on one side and the rich riparian area of the Columbia River on the other, an odd mix of birds and animals congregates at the refuge. Meadowlarks, red-winged blackbirds, and an array of swallows flit around the reeds near the water. Quails, pheasants, and mourning doves duck under the sagebrush and desert plants. Mule deer wander throughout the area, but you'll also find hares, badgers, beavers, muskrats, and more.

The route you'll follow is a self-guided nature trail that begins at the refuge's environmental education center and winds around part of the Burbank Slough. Interpretive signs and a photo/bird watching blind are located along the trail. The blind, found less than 0.25 mile out, and the trail to it are paved and accessible to wheelchairs. Beyond that, the trail narrows and turns to dirt. The path wanders out to impressive viewpoints and many sheltered locations that allow you to photograph birds more easily.

The loop is closed by hiking South Lake Road from the north side of

Sunrise by Burbank Slough in the McNary National Wildlife Refuge

the slough back to the education center. Off-trail rambles can be enjoyed by walking across the road to the east side into rolling refuge lands, but be aware that this part of the refuge is open to hunting, so it should be visited by casual walkers from mid-October through January.

Spend some time visiting the refuge's education center, which alone is well worth the visit.

56 WALLULA HABITAT MANAGEMENT UNIT

Round trip ■ **6 miles**
Hiking time ■ 3 hours
Difficulty ■ Easy
Starting elevation ■ 350 feet
High point ■ 350 feet
Best season ■ November through March
Maps ■ Washington State Department of Natural Resources (DNR) Walla Walla
Contact ■ U.S. Department of Fish and Wildlife (least through U.S. Army Corps of Engineers)
Permits/passes ■ None

From Pasco, drive east on US 12, crossing the Snake River, and continue east nearly to a junction with State Route 730 (found just before crossing the Walla Walla River). Turn left onto a gravel road signed "Wallula Habitat Management Unit." Drive 0.4 mile on the gravel road (stay left at the Y junction you encounter almost immediately) to a nice pullout parking area. A nice trail leads down toward slough areas from here. Hike both east and west from this location.

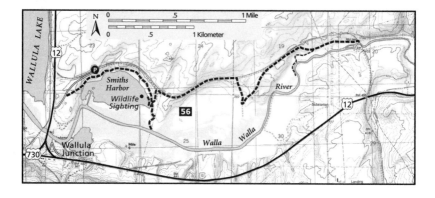

A tundra swan stretches its wings in one of the pools at the Wallula Habitat Management Unit.

This is a lonely area of the Walla Walla River Delta, where the Walla Walla River empties into the Columbia River. The waters here are flat and slow moving, creating great habitat for a number of birds and animals, both in and out of the water. However, beyond the rich riparian world at the rivers' edges, the desert rolls on. So fish and frogs, waterfowl and beavers live as neighbors with desert-dwelling rattlesnakes, horned lizards, scorpions, and kangaroo rats. All in all, this is a novel world to explore.

Find the trail leading east and set off to explore. Within 0.5 mile you'll find a viewpoint overlooking Smiths Harbor—a body of water that looks like a lovely lake but is actually just part of the slow-moving Walla Walla River Delta. Here birdlife is buzzing! Birds range from raptors to game birds to songbirds—kingfishers, herons, geese, flickers, sage sparrows, quails, and more.

From here the trail rolls along the area between the gravel road and the harbor for another mile before reaching the eastern end of the water and meeting another road that comes down from the main access road (this road is closed until March 15 each year). Hike down the road about 0.5 mile to reach the Walla Walla River and more rich riparian habitat surrounding it.

Hike back up the road or angle northeast and hike cross-country another 1.5 miles just off the main access road to find a faint game trail to follow. You'll reach another road heading toward the river about 3 miles from your starting point. The way passes the winding Walla Walla River, and if you reach a railroad grade turning south to cross the river, you are about at the eastern end of the public lands of the National Wildlife Refuge site.

57 ┊ TWIN SISTERS ROCK

Round trip	■	1 mile
Hiking time	■	1 hour
Difficulty	■	Easy
Starting elevation	■	300 feet
High point	■	500 feet
Best season	■	Year-round
Maps	■	Washington State Department of Natural Resources (DNR) Walla Walla
Contact	■	Walla Walla County Department of Public Works
Permits/passes	■	None

From Pasco, drive east on US 12, crossing the Snake River, and continue east to a junction with State Route 730 (found just after crossing the Walla Walla River. Turn right onto SR 730 and continue 2 miles to find the signed pullout

Twin Sisters Rock towers above the surrounding sand- and sage-covered terrain.

parking area at the base of Twin Sisters on the left.

Twin Sisters are two pillars of basalt that jut from the cliffs along Wallula Gap overlooking the Columbia River. Geologists say the rock formation is the result of erosion from a great flood near the end of the last Ice Age, about 12,000 to 15,000 years ago. A Cayuse legend states that the natural monument was formed when Coyote, an animal spirit, fell in love with three sisters, then became jealous of them and turned two into stone. The third was turned into a cave, says the legend. Regardless of the reason the pillars were formed, the trail here—though short—provides some remarkable adventures. From the area at the base of the Twin Sisters Rock to the highland area rocks to the south, you'll enjoy amazing views of the Wallula Gap on the Columbia River.

Yes, this is a short hike, but it offers a lot in that short distance. This trail offers a great study of the geology of the Columbia Basin, as well as an introduction to the desert flora—which is easy to see here as the plethora of desert blooms push right up against the trail (and the access road).

From the trailhead, an old-fashioned stairlike stile gets you over the fence at the trailhead. The trail leads up a steep gully to a junction. Going left at the junction takes you up to the base of Twin Sisters—be careful of the loose rock here. Going straight takes you back behind to the east side of Twin Sisters and great views of them. Small sand dunes nestle along the base of the pillars. About 0.5 mile out, you'll find a fence and marker of private land behind it. *Don't cross the fence.* Hike to the highland just south of Twin Sisters and enjoy the stellar view of Wallula Gap.

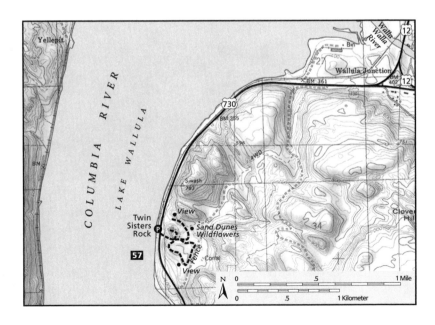

58 ┆ CHAMNA NATURAL PRESERVE

Round trip ▪ **3 miles**
Hiking time ▪ 2 hours
Difficulty ▪ Easy
Starting elevation ▪ 350 feet
High point ▪ 350 feet
Best season ▪ Year-round
Maps ▪ Washington State Department of
Natural Resources (DNR) Richland
Contact ▪ Tapteal Greenway Association
Permits/passes ▪ None

From Yakima, drive east on Interstate 82 toward the Tri-Cities area and take exit 102 toward Pasco/Richland. Drive this freeway to exit 4 (signed "Hwy 240/Vantage") and loop around the off-ramp, go over the overpass, and turn right at the first light. After turning at this light, continue about 0.5 mile and turn right at the road signed "Chamna Nature Preserve." Continue over the freeway, and turn right onto Lacy Road (signed for the natural preserve as well). Go 0.25 mile and turn right into the signed preserve (across the road from the gravel pit/plant). Continue 0.3 mile into the preserve to the large parking area.

The Chamna Natural Preserve is a new parkland near the confluence of

Open meadows and riparian zones in the Chamna Natural Preserve

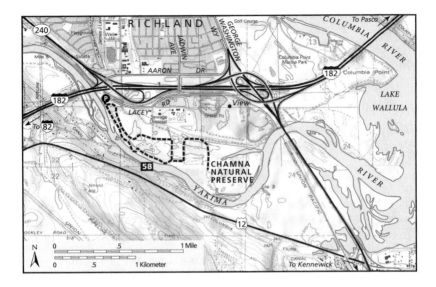

the Yakima and Columbia Rivers and offers hiking through a multitude of habitats ranging from grasslands to riparian wooded areas. It is tucked away on the north side of about 2 miles of the Yakima River at the Yakima Delta, with the river on one side and freeways on the other. Still, the wildlife will tell you it's all okay and they love it here—they appreciate the work being done to preserve the area!

Time your visit correctly and you'll find yourself hiking through a corridor lined with 10-foot-tall walls of fragrant wild roses all in bloom. These usually bloom late in spring (mid-May). If the roses aren't in bloom, never fear. You'll be treated to great numbers of red-tailed hawks overhead. Perhaps the mourning doves will be calling from the rose brambles, or countless other birds will be flitting and fluttering throughout the area.

The trail leads back along the Yakima River. This early stretch of the trail features the great wall of wild roses. With the flowers in bloom and the spring birdsong in full volume, this is a magical trail. Listen especially for warblers and white-crowned sparrows.

We flushed multiple groups of mourning doves when we hiked back from the Columbia River through the inland areas of grass and sage. These open prairie lands are prime hunting ground for the resident red-tailed hawks.

Hikers can wander along 2 to 3 miles of trails lining the two rivers and the lands between.

Note: Until 1997, this area was a convenient illegal dumping ground for thoughtless locals, as well as an unofficial racetrack for off-road vehicle enthusiasts. After that time, huge boulders were put in place to keep vehicles out, and a major cleanup and restoration were initiated. Work is still underway, but the former dump is now becoming a desert paradise.

59 | RATTLESNAKE SLOPE WILDLIFE AREA

Round trip	■	**5 miles**
Hiking time	■	2 to 3 hours
Difficulty	■	Moderate
Starting elevation	■	400 feet
High point	■	2000 feet
Best season	■	Year-round
Maps	■	Washington State Department of Natural Resources (DNR) Richland
Contact	■	Washington Department of Fish and Wildlife
Permits/passes	■	Washington Department of Fish and Wildlife Vehicle Permit required

From Yakima, drive east on Interstate 82 to exit 96 for Benton City. After exiting, turn left and drive through Benton City. Continue north on State Route 225. At 7.3 miles from I-82, find a fenced parking area on the left (west) side of the highway.

Upland birds love this sprawling desert prairie. The ground-hugging birds sprint among the tufts of plants. They take refuge, and find dinner, in such glorious wildflowers as balsamroot, large-headed clover, wild onion, and canyon-bottom communities of beautiful orange globe mallow. Of course, where upland birds (pheasants, quail, and partridge) are found, coyotes are sure to be present. Hike a short distance in any direction and

Signposts mark the main entrance to the Rattlesnake Slope Wildlife Area.

you'll find coyote signs. Tracks and scat can be found all over the place, as well as holes freshly dug by rodents as "safe houses," some of which have been enlarged by coyotes breaking into those sanctuaries. You might also find badger burrows in the hillsides of the small side canyons.

This region has vast areas of native bunchgrass, and local land managers have seeded more than 1000 acres of the wildlife area with sagebrush to try to reestablish the native ground cover, which had suffered from many successive years of uncontrolled fires.

From the parking area, hike due west into the main canyon gully, gaining elevation steadily. In the first 2 miles of trekking through the open country, you'll gain nearly 1200 feet in elevation. As you reach the top of the ridge, take note of the black volcanic rock formations along the spine, then angle off to the south to find the bottom of a second canyon/gully with another well-trod trail. Drop down along this trail to about 3.5 miles, then turn east to close a loop of nearly 5 miles.

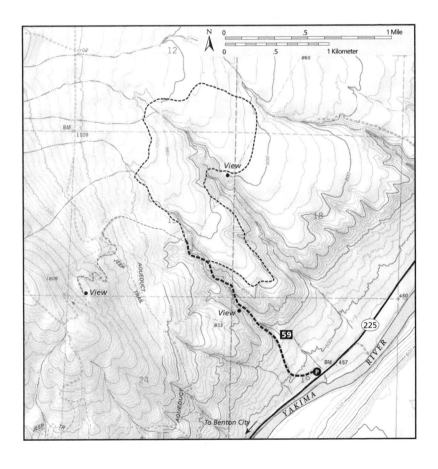

60 ┆ Horse Heaven Hills

Round trip ■	**5 to 6 miles**
Hiking time ■	3 hours
Difficulty ■	Moderate
Starting elevation ■	2300 feet
Low point ■	2000 feet
Best season ■	April through June and October through November
Maps ■	Washington State Department of Natural Resources (DNR) Richland
Contact ■	Bureau of Land Management, Spokane
Permits/passes ■	None

From Yakima, drive east on Interstate 82 to exit 96 for Benton City. After exiting, turn right and head out Webber Canyon Road through the tiny community of Kiona. At 0.6 mile from the freeway, turn right on McBee Road and continue up this good gravel road 2.4 miles to the top of the ridge. Find a side jeep track heading up the ridge. Park here at a small gravel area.

The long, rough ridge of the Horse Heaven Hills stretches for miles above the Yakima River Valley. The spiny ridge is a true desert treasure—barren of trees and scoured endlessly by winds sweeping in from the Columbia River Basin, the Horse Heaven Hills are nonetheless well named. In years gone by, wild mustangs enjoyed the bounty of this rich desert ridgeline—the hills, lacking trees, shade, and water, sport a luxurious blanket of desert grasses and wildflowers on which horses love to graze. The wild horses are long gone, but the local population of mule deer still finds heaven in the rich hillside meadows, as do an assortment of birds and animals. How rich is the foliage? Our wild plant expert identified the following in one short visit: lupine,

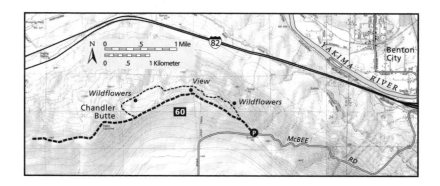

Hooker's balsamroot, Douglas's brodiaea, Cusick's sunflower, nine-leaf desert parsley, larkspur, Cusick's shooting star, yellow bells, and many species of milk vetch and locoweed.

From the ridge-top parking area, begin a sweeping hike down the slopes of the flower-filled hills on the north side of the ridge crest. This north slope is all part of the BLM land and nice to hike when the wind is ripping in from the south. The bulk of the ridge provides some protection from the wind.

After hiking down the slope and exploring a few of the many gullies that line the slope (check these out since many boast badger burrows), hike west on a traverse of the slope for a couple of miles. Go as far as you like. Eventually you'll want to angle back to the ridge top and then turn back to your start—a good turnaround point is 2046-foot-high Chandler Butte about 3 miles from the start of your journey. Follow the ridgeline back to your starting point. During the entire outing, you'll find fabulous views overlooking the Yakima Valley from Benton City back toward Prosser, below to the north, and out on farmland from the ridge southward.

61 ❘ CHIEF JOSEPH WILDLIFE AREA– GRANDE RONDE RIVER

Round trip ■	**4 miles (6 miles to the highlands)**
Hiking time ■	3 hours
Difficulty ■	Moderate
Starting elevation ■	850 feet
High point ■	850 feet (2000 feet to the highlands)
Best season ■	April through June
Maps ■	Washington State Department of Natural Resources (DNR) Clarkston
Contact ■	Washington Department of Fish and Wildlife
Permits/passes ■	Washington Department of Fish and Wildlife Vehicle Permit required

From SR 129 in Asotin, south of Lewiston, drive south on Snake River Road. At 15 miles, the road turns to good gravel. At 22 miles, veer away from the Snake River to head up into the Grande Ronde River Canyon, and at 25.2 miles from the SR 129 junction in Asotin cross the Grande Ronde Bridge. Continue 0.6 mile to the first access road to your left.

The wildlife viewing throughout the Grande Ronde country is stunning. At times, wild turkeys can be seen flying (a rarity!) from one side of the canyon to the other, and they always seem to be roaming the highlands. Hungarian partridge, ruffed and blue grouse, partridge, and quail all can be found scurrying through the brush on quiet spring days. Bighorn

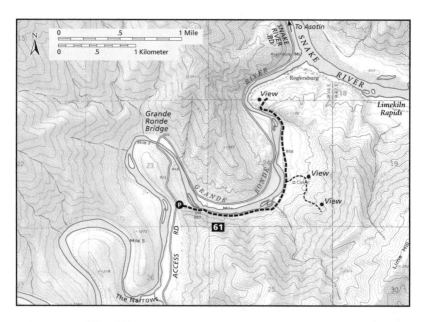

The fascinating walls of the Grande Ronde Canyon in the Chief Joseph Wildlife Area

sheep can be viewed on the canyon cliffs above the river, too, if you are fortunate.

Hike down the old road to the banks of the river and continue alongside

the lush riparian world for nearly a mile. As the river starts to bend northward, look for a rough route (an old jeep track) that heads south into the highlands. As you climb this side path, note how the terrain changes to a rocky
canyon cliff environment still dotted with small stands of oak and aspen. Up
higher, the balsamroot, lupine, serviceberry, and bluebells bloom in spring.
Remember to stick to the old roads rather than wandering cross-country because this is prime rattlesnake country: The wide trail of the roadway makes
sighting vipers easier than if you were crashing through the brush.

The highlands side trip achieves stunning views of the river canyon, but
the nearly flat river walk provides plenty of scenery to keep you engrossed.
Keep an eye and ear alert and you might encounter grosbeaks, warblers,
chickadees, and many other singing birds active in the rich riverside foliage.
You can continue along the river shore for a good 2 miles before turning
back at a fence near the Grande Ronde's junction with the Snake River. The
side road up the bluffs above the river adds another 2 miles (1 up, 1 down)
to the journey.

62 CHIEF JOSEPH WILDLIFE AREA–GREEN GULCH

Round trip ■	**4 to 6 miles**
Hiking time ■	3 to 4 hours
Difficulty ■	Moderate
Starting elevation ■	1300 feet
High point ■	2800 feet
Best season ■	April through June
Maps ■	Washington State Department of Natural Resources (DNR) Clarkston
Contact ■	Washington Department of Fish and Wildlife
Permits/passes ■	Washington Department of Fish and Wildlife Vehicle Permit required

From SR 129 in Asotin, drive south on Snake River Road. At 15 miles, the road
turns to good gravel. At 22 miles, veer away from the Snake River to head up
into the Grande Ronde River Canyon, and at 25.2 miles from the SR 129 junction in Asotin cross the Grande Ronde Bridge. At 3 miles from the bridge, reach
the parking area signed for Chief Joseph/Asotin Wildlife Area. The parking
area is adjacent to an old abandoned farmhouse. To begin, hike up the road
100 yards and find the gated road just prior to reaching the bridge over Joseph
Creek. It is well signed as "Public Access for Hunting/Fishing."

This corner of the state is a very wild land and makes you feel very small
in God's creation. This is one of the most remote parts of Washington, with

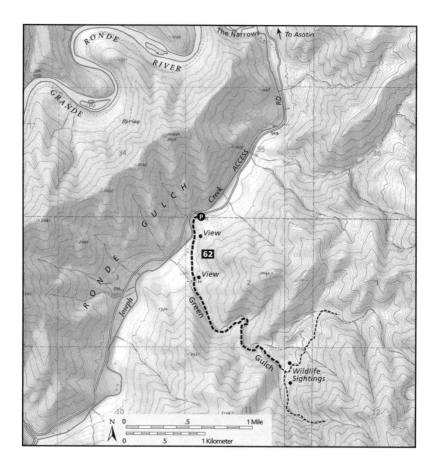

a small human population in the immediate area but a huge population of wildlife and birds. What's more, as you hike through Washington's desert, you'll be just 3 or 4 miles from Oregon and 8 to 10 miles from Idaho—but as the saying goes, you can't get there from here. The other states are isolated by rushing rivers that lack bridges. You must make long detours around this area to get to the other states. That increases the isolation of this stunning natural area.

This is a great hike to explore the highland areas above the Grande Ronde. Before you set out on the main route, take a moment and hike across the road from the parking area to investigate the lush Joseph Creek area. This bird-rich creek basin is worth spending a moment—or more. Once you've seen, heard, and photographed the birds along the picturesque creek, head up the main road about 100 yards farther to the signed (and gated) access road found just before the creek. The road is signed "Public Access: Fishing

A horned lark rests on a rock one frosty winter morning.

and Hunting." This is the Green Gulch area. The road/trail heads up into the steepening terrain to the southeast of the Grande Ronde.

Hike along the road, keeping an eye out for wild turkeys (thick in this area). At about 2 miles, you'll find the two-track trail narrowing to a single path. Look here for a pair of side gullies. These secondary gulches can easily be explored via the well-trod game trails zigzagging up them.

Spring is a prime time to visit as the views down to Joseph Creek and its lush green riparian vegetation sets off perfectly the fascinating green canyon walls of this Grande Ronde gulch.

63 | MARMES POND/LYONS FERRY PARK

Round trip ■	4 miles
Hiking time ■	3 hours
Difficulty ■	Moderate
Starting elevation ■	600 feet
High point ■	750 feet
Best season ■	November through March
Maps ■	Washington State Department of Natural Resources (DNR) Connell
Contact ■	U.S. Army Corps of Engineers
Permits/passes ■	None

From Dayton, drive US 12 north 14 miles. Turn left on State Route 261 and continue through the tiny community of Starbuck (sorry, the only coffee here is usually day-old Hills Brothers at the small cafe). You'll pass Lyons Ferry Park at 14.7 miles but keep going. About 200 yards past the entrance to the

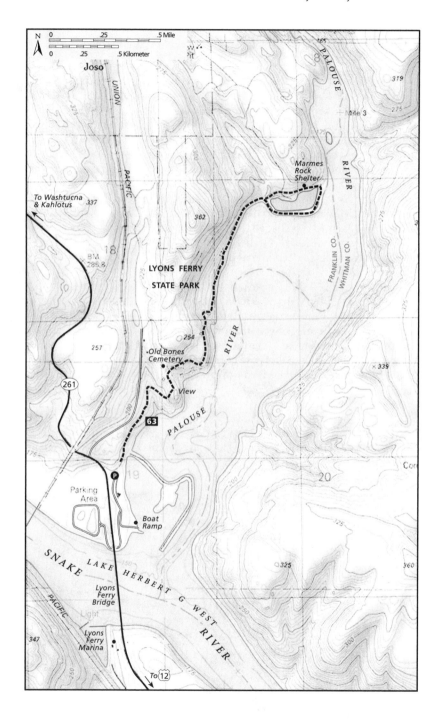

N

0   .25   .5 Mile
0   .25   .5 Kilometer

Joso

PALOUSE

Mile 3

UNION

PACIFIC

RIVER

319

275

Marmes
Rock
Shelter

To Washtucna
& Kahlotus   337

362

LYONS FERRY

STATE PARK

FRANKLIN CO.
WHITMAN CO.

BM
285.8

18

254

RIVER

×339

257

Old Bones
Cemetery

261

View

63   PALOUSE

19

20

Cor

P

Parking
Area

Boat
Ramp

325

360

SNAKE

LAKE

HERBERT G

WEST

Lyons
Ferry
Bridge

Light

RIVER

PACIFIC

347

Lyons
Ferry
Marina

To 12

park, turn right onto a small gravel roadway and enter a gravel parking lot near the end of a spit at the mouth of the Palouse River.

Marmes Pond is a man-made pool on the edge of the Palouse River. The "pond" was actually meant to be a dry hole, but things didn't work out as planned. The pond was formed when an archeologist from Washington State University found an old rock shelter and human bones at a dig site along the shores of the lower Palouse River—the bones, dubbed the "Marmes Man," were dated to more than 10,000 years old—much older than any other remains found in the region. Before a full dig could be organized and carried out, the Corps of Engineers completed work on Little Goose Dam on the Snake River, just downstream on the mouth of the Palouse. As the impoundment waters backed up behind the dam, they pushed their way up the Palouse. In a last-ditch effort to buy some time to protect the Marmes dig site, engineers tossed up an earthen dike around the dig, but water oozed through, flooding the dig site and creating a pond over what could have been one of the most promising archeological finds in Washington.

The trailhead is located near where the gravel road enters the parking lot. The paved path climbs a bit more than 0.75 mile to a covered overlook area at the crest of the ridge above the mouth of the Palouse. The views up the Palouse River Canyon from here are outstanding, and you can also peer down the Snake River toward the mouth of the Tucannon River. Waterfowl fill the air and waterways here in the winter months (December through March, typically). Birds of prey—especially red-tailed hawks and kestrels—fill the air year-round as they feed on small rodents and snakes.

From the overlook, hikers can ramble cross-country around the ridge top (beware of poison oak, which is common in the area) or follow a faint path up into the Palouse Canyon. The path descends from the ridge and angles down to the shoreline of the Palouse River. At times, the trail is steep and narrow. Be careful, especially along the edge of the river, as the banks can slide and fall away unexpectedly.

About 2 miles from your vehicle, you'll find yourself at Marmes Pond and the dig site. Nothing is left of the dig, but if you have a fishing rod, drop a line in the pond—the folks from the Lyons Ferry

One of many yellow-bellied marmots in the rocks around Lyons Ferry–Marmes Pond

Fish Hatchery stock the pond periodically, and anglers can often pull big rainbow trout from the green waters of the pond.

The trail from the ridge to the pond provides outstanding views of the lower Palouse River canyon and introduces you to many of the local inhabitants of the region. Most visitors here meet at least a few of the locals, including swallows, mule deer, coyotes, ground squirrels, raptors (including golden eagles, rough-legged hawks, northern harriers, Swainson's hawks, kestrels, ravens, and red-tailed hawks), bull snakes, rattlesnakes, lizards, scorpions, and porcupines.

64 PALOUSE FALLS

Round trip ■ **2 to 3 miles**
Hiking time ■ Up to 3 hours
Difficulty ■ Moderate
Starting elevation ■ 923 feet
Low point ■ 630 feet
Best season ■ March through June
Maps ■ Washington State Department of Natural Resources (DNR) Connell
Contact ■ Washington State Parks and Recreation
Permits/passes ■ Washington State Parks and Recreation Parking Pass required

From Dayton, drive US 12 north for 14 miles. Turn left on State Route 261 and continue through the tiny community of Starbuck (sorry, the only coffee here is usually day-old Hills Brothers at the small cafe). You'll also pass Lyons Ferry Park at 14.7 miles. At 20.5 miles from US 12, turn right onto Palouse Falls Road signed "Palouse Falls State Park—2." Drive down the hill 2.4 miles to enter the park and to park.

Its size and splendor make Palouse Falls one of the most scenic and impressive waterfalls in all of Washington, but its location adds even more magic and wonder to its image. Nestled in a deep coulee, the Palouse River creeps mostly unseen through the scablands north of the Snake River. It is only when you are right at the edge of the river's chasm that you can see and appreciate the deep cut the river makes through the basalt highlands. The same holds true for the falls, which starts in a deep cut and falls into a deeper hole. The falls can't be seen until you are nearly on top of it, but then—*wow!* A broad, broken plateau of black basalt stretches out to the horizon as you approach the entrance to the state park, when suddenly—*boom!*—there they are: the thundering waters of Palouse Falls pounding 198 feet into a circular bowl carved out of the cinder-black rock. Winter and spring are the prime

Views down the Palouse River Canyon from above Palouse Falls

times to see the falls. In the dead of winter, the jagged cliffs around the falls are lined with shimmering bands of ice, while in spring, the runoff from snowmelt in the high country has the falls running full bore as a thundering spectacle.

Palouse Falls is a photographer's delight. Sunlight streams over the complex canyon walls, birds flitter around the cliffs, picking insects out of the air, and wildflowers color the sandy benches between rimrock bluffs.

From the parking area, a paved trail winds around the overlook area—this is where 98 percent of visitors stay, as it provides wonderful views of the falls with little or no effort.

The local wildlife also hang out here. A large community of yellow-bellied marmots lives in burrows dug just across the safety fence that keeps human visitors from plunging into the deep pool. Resident reptiles also appreciate the smooth sunbaked surface of the paved path on cool days. We've frequently seen bull snakes and the occasional rattler sunning themselves on this path—scuff your boots every other step to warn the serpents before you reach them and they'll quickly and quietly slither off the path.

Once you've enjoyed the views from the easy-access trail, head north on the well-marked dirt trail leading out of the parking lot. In spring and early summer, this path is lined with a veritable rainbow of color. The local wildflower bonanza includes balsamroot, bluebells, yellow bells, buckwheat, three species of desert parsley, lupine, locoweed, vetch, and death camas.

The trail winds through the upper plateau area, skirts an old, seldom-used but still active railroad track, then drops into a small cirque filled with massive sagebrush. Before descending to the banks of the Palouse River above the falls, the trail weaves around—and under—some sage towering 8 to 10 feet. The river then drops through a series of step rapids before reaching the head of the falls (out of sight from this point).

Many trails lace around the upper canyon area for the hiking from here, but they are narrow and have a great deal of exposure (steep cliffs). Don't explore past the head of the falls: There is no safe way to descend to the bottom of the falls, despite the presence of trails that appear to lead that way.

As you return to the parking area, take a moment to notice the nearby railroad tracks. Because trains have to stay on fairly flat tracks (can't have a lot of severe ups and downs, anyway), the rail route was carved into the plateau to avoid the bluffs and ravines. The tracks essentially follow an open-topped tunnel through the basalt plateau. That's amazing engineering in an amazing landscape.

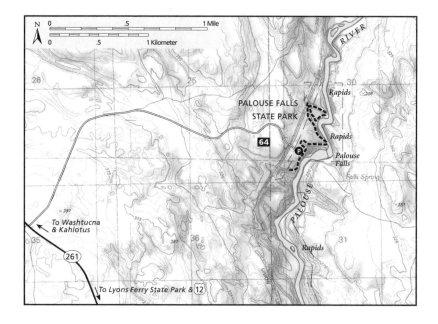

65 KAMIAK BUTTE

Round trip ■	3.5 miles
Hiking time ■	2 to 3 hours
Difficulty ■	Moderate
Starting elevation ■	2700 feet
High point ■	3600 feet
Best season ■	March through November (closed during high-fire danger)
Maps ■	Washington State Department of Natural Resources (DNR) Pullman
Contact ■	Whitman County Parks
Permits/passes ■	None

From Colfax, drive east on State Route 272 to Palouse and to a junction with SR 27. Turn south onto SR 27 and drive 3.2 miles south before turning west onto

Clear Creek Road (well signed for "Kamiak Butte County Park"). Drive Clear Creek Road for 0.5 mile and turn left on Fugate Road. Drive another 0.5 mile (1 mile total from SR 27) and turn left into Kamiak Butte County Park. Drive all the way to the wooded park at the end of the road and an upper trailhead area by the signboard, trailhead, and campground area.

Kamiak Butte stands like an island in the rolling wheat fields of the Palouse country—not merely a physical island of rock jutting up above the fertile

The typical rolling hills of the Palouse, seen from the summit of Kamiak Butte

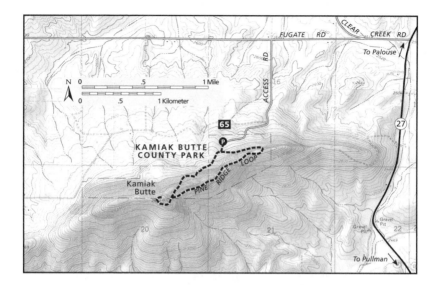

soils of the Palouse hills but also an "ecosystem island." The dry butte supports a rich sage desert ecosystem on its southeastern face, with a lush forest—ponderosa pine, Douglas fir, grand fir, even some cedar—on its north face. This combination of vegetation provides excellent habitat for an array of birds and animals, and the high top of the butte offers outstanding views of the sprawling Palouse country of southeast Washington (and Idaho).

The Pine Ridge Loop, 3.5 miles in length, offers the best variety of desert terrain and ecosystems. Under the forest floor lies a lush carpet of moss and vegetation more typical of the Cascades. Found here as well are amazing flower species for eastern Washington: Calypso orchids, starflower, trillium, bluebells, strawberry, fairy bells, false Solomon's seal, and glacier lilies line the trail.

After about 1.5 miles, the trail reaches the 3644-foot summit of the butte and a brand new world. Suddenly the forest falls away, and you walk into a windblasted, rocky, desert terrain. You'll find only a few pine trees dotting the open meadows that sport flora more typical of the Columbia Basin: paintbrush, three species of desert parsley, desert shooting star, desert bluebells, yellow bells, prairie star flower, balsamroot, serviceberry, lupine, larkspur, grass widows, and more.

The trail rolls more than 0.5 mile across the long summit ridge of the butte, with stunning views across the Palouse. From here, you can see hundreds of miles in all directions across thousands of square miles of rolling hills.

Continue hiking to the east end of the butte, passing through very wide open meadows on the south-facing slope, then plunge down quickly into the deep forest of the northern slope again to return to the trailhead.

66 ¦ WASHTUCNA COULEE
(KAHLOTUS RAILROAD GRADE)

Round trip ■	**8 miles (13-mile option)**
Hiking time ■	3 to 4 hours
Difficulty ■	Moderate
Starting elevation ■	870 feet
High point ■	900 feet
Best season ■	March through June
Maps ■	Washington State Department of Natural Resources (DNR) Connell
Contact ■	Washington State Parks and Recreation
Permits/passes ■	None

From Kahlotus, drive south on the Pasco–Kahlotus Highway to 0.4 mile south of State Route 260. Find a pullout on the railroad side of the roadway. Park there and scramble down to the railroad grade. The tunnel heading to Devils Canyon is just 200 yards to the south. Alternatively, hike the other way into the Washtucna Coulee lands, skirting what is known as Lake Kahlotus (now a dry lakebed).

A hike is also accessible by driving 3.7 miles east of Kahlotus on SR 260 (or 4.3 miles west of the SR261/SR 260 junction) to Fry Road, turning right, and parking. This makes a nice 8-mile round trip from Fry Road to the tunnel and back.

The broad, deep chasm of Washtucna Coulee cuts through the

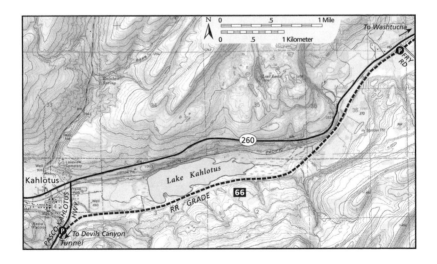

sagebrush flats of the Snake River plateau country, providing a wonderful exposé of the power of the Great Missoula Floods that carved Washington's coulees after the last great Ice Age. As spectacular as Washtucna Coulee is, the most majestic view of this route is found by peering down Devils Canyon. Here, you'll witness the full splendor of the incredible geologic history of this region.

Following the railroad grade from the parking area, stroll through a wildflower garden filled with fragrant sagebrush, buttercups, sage violets, and vast expanses of desert parsley. Just a few hundred yards south, the rail route leads into a cool, dark tunnel that pierces a bluff before leading into the upper reach of Devils Canyon.

From the tunnel, the trail rolls down Devils Canyon, but that route is a bit tricky as several important trestles are out of service and some additional tunnels are blocked or closed. Go through the tunnel, enjoy the outstanding views, then head back to the trailhead and hike in the opposite direction, following Washtucna Coulee toward the town of Washtucna.

The Kahlotus Railroad Grade enters a tunnel in Washtucna Coulee.

This coulee is not as deeply cut as the massive trenches of Moses Coulee or Grand Coulee, but the sheer rock walls and solid rock footing provide ample evidence of the awesome power of the Great Missoula Floods, which carved the coulees. Those flood waters rushed through the landscape, cutting channels as the deluge flowed through. Some of the water lingered. As you explore up the trail, you'll pass the now dry basin of ancient Lake Kahlotus. In very wet years, a bit of water still pools in the low parts of the basin, but generally this prehistoric lake is bone dry. At 4 miles from the parking area, you'll find yourself at Fry Road (alternative access point). Turn around and head back to complete the 8-mile hike.

To experience all this area has to offer, plan your hike for late in the afternoon. That way, as you trek along this route, you'll be able to enjoy the vast open views across miles of farmland, listening to the call of coyotes as sun sets. Take another run through the tunnel to peer down Devils Canyon in the twilight as the evening shadows highlight the truly graphic nature of the landscape. Sharp angles, cuts, and bluffs mark the canyon, and the setting sun throws those features into stark relief. Make sure you bring your camera.

If you have two vehicles available, you could park a vehicle in Kahlotus and enjoy a one-way, 13-mile hike from the tunnel back to the town of Washtucna.

67 SNAKE RIVER/COLUMBIA PLATEAU TRAIL

Round trip	■	**6 to 8 miles**
Hiking time	■	4 hours
Difficulty	■	Moderate
Starting elevation	■	600 feet
High point	■	750 feet
Best season	■	November through March
Maps	■	Washington State Department of Natural Resources (DNR) Walla Walla
Contact	■	Washington State Parks and Recreation
Permits/passes	■	Washington State Parks and Recreation Parking Pass required

From US 12 near Pasco, take the Kahlotus exit. Drive the Pasco–Kahlotus Highway about 24 miles before turning right onto Snake River Road. Drive down the steep, winding Snake River Road through McCoy Canyon. At 28.8 miles, stay straight at the junction to reach the end of the road (5 miles from Pasco–Kahlotus Road). Park by the railroad grade trail or down by the river at the Snake River junction. No facilities are available here.

The 134-mile-long Columbia Plateau Trail (also called the Pasco/Fish

Hiking along the Snake River on a portion of the Columbia Plateau Trail

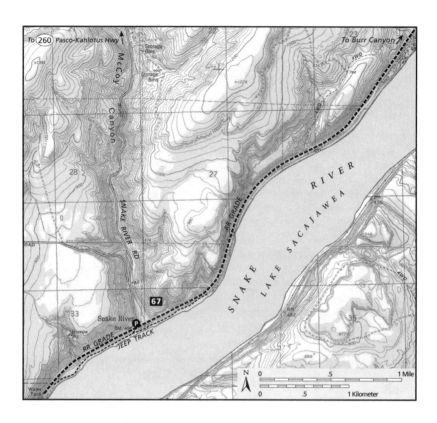

Lake Trail) followed the old, historic route of the Spokane–Portland–Seattle Railroad from Pasco to Spokane. The trail today is a fabulous way to experience the human and natural history of this unique landscape. The trail pierces the basalt scablands of the lower Snake River country and crosses the rimrock country of the Columbia River Plateau. It tracks through coulees cut by the Great Missoula Floods of 16,000 years ago.

Settlers first used the route in the 1850s when wagon train master John Mullan surveyed a wagon road roughly following the same track we hike today. A half century after the first wagons rolled along the route, the surveyors for the railroad plotted the course that's still used—but not by trains—today. The section described here goes through some of the most rugged, scenic country along the entire route.

Leaving the parking area, hike upriver (northeast) to enjoy incredible views up the Snake River. The scenery is almost beyond belief. Desert country? No! You're traveling through dry environments, but this is a rich ecosystem, teeming with wildlife, large and small. Mule deer the size of small elk range throughout the area. Coyotes as big as timber wolves prowl the canyons. Even a few cougars prowl the canyons, keeping the deer population from exploding out of control. Raptors soar on the thermals rising over this sun-drenched canyon, while swallows and sparrows flit and flutter around the cliffs. On the ground at your feet, Hungarian partridge, chukar, and quail dart through the brush.

The trail follows the old railroad bed, but along this 4-mile stretch, a good part of the old dirt wagon road parallels the railbed, and that old dirt track is easier to hike—it lacks the rough crushed rock ballast that covers the railway.

Hiking east along the north shore of the Snake River provides ample opportunities to enjoy the sparkling waters of the river and the plethora of birds and other animals that are at home in the area. It also immerses you in the human history of the region. You'll be thrilled with the old telegraph poles that dot the route—some with old glass and ceramic insulators in place and wires strung between them.

The side canyons and sagebrush forests along the walls create interesting patterns around you, especially if you are hiking here early in the morning or late in the afternoon when the low angle of the sun casts the interesting topography into sharp relief and heavy shadows.

Hikers can travel as far up the Snake River as they like, but a good turnaround point is the mouth of Burr Canyon, where the trail crosses the Burr Canyon Road.

68 ▌ BIG FLAT HABITAT MANAGEMENT UNIT

Round trip ■	6 to 7 miles
Hiking time ■	3 to 4 hours
Difficulty ■	Easy
Starting elevation ■	500 feet
High point ■	500 feet
Best season ■	Year-round
Maps ■	Washington State Department of Natural Resources (DNR) Walla Walla
Contact ■	U.S. Army Corps of Engineers
Permits/passes ■	None

From US 12 near Pasco, take the Kahlotus exit. Drive the Pasco–Kahlotus Road about 12.7 miles to a sharp left in the road. Leave the main road here by driving straight ahead onto a gravel-dirt road signed "Big Flat Habitat Management Unit." Drive down this sometimes steep road (Herman Road) 1.5 miles to the parking area. Walk past the gate and start hiking along the Snake River and flats ahead.

This area was trammeled after the construction of the Ice Harbor Dam,

Male and female Goldeneyes in the slack waters of the Snake River

but since 1997 the heart of this remote wildlife area has been restored to native health. The Corps of Engineers has hosted revegetation plantings to restore the native steppe plants to improve the wildlife habitat (and therefore wildlife populations). The route through the area takes advantage of the restoration efforts, exploring the rich foliage and wildlife habitat of the area along the pretty stretch of the Snake River—a section of Lake Sacajawea, the impoundment behind the Ice Harbor Dam. The first 2 miles of hiking along

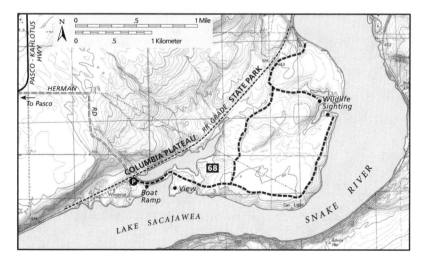

the road (closed to vehicles) lead directly to the top of the bluff overlooking the area. Wonderful views!

Dalton Lake at the trailhead is a popular fishing spot, often crowded with families. Once away from the trailhead, you'll find solitary hiking. At about 0.5 mile from the trailhead, a side road leads to the left. Pass by it for now, but keep it in mind for later exploration.

Continue along the road as it follows the river. At about 2 miles, you'll reach the end of the road at a point overlooking a small cove along the riverbank. Great views abound—waterfowl often seek refuge in this sheltered spot, and deer frequently water along the shoreline here, too.

Backtrack along the road to that sidetrack. If you prefer to keep your outing to 4 miles, head back to your vehicle, but to stretch your trek another 2 or 3 miles, head up that side track to access the heart of this wild area. The road/path winds around small rocky bluffs above the river. When you reach a junction in a mile or so, keep right to find a viewpoint looking back down on the river.

Facing page: Basalt cliffs reflect in a small pond, Escure Ranch BLM land, Towell Falls hike.

SPOKANE

S pokane is the capital city of what is known regionally as the Inland Empire. This region encompasses the upper Columbia River drainage of Washington, especially the lands from the Cascades to the Rockies and from the Palouse country north to Canada. Spokane marks the heart of this region, which includes broad sweeps of desert prairie, dry desert forests, dry country lakes, and deep rimrock coulees.

The Inland Empire boasts some of the richest wildlife habitat in the state, and contains a greater diversity of life than nearly any other part of the United States of America. You'll find virtually all the species of animals that roam and fly in other parts of eastern Washington, but here in the northern desert you'll also find moose wading among the marshes and low scrub forests. Endangered lynx prowl the dry pine forests and highland deserts along the Canadian border.

The Spokane area also presents a wonderful geologic history. The great basalt lava flows of southeast Washington stretched north into this area. The conical knob of Steptoe Butte is the uppermost summit cone of an old quartzite mountain that was all but inundated by the lava flows. The floods that carved the coulee country to the west at the end of the Ice Age also washed over the northeast corner of the state, leaving large out-of-place rocks (erratics) scattered here and there around the region.

Several Native American tribes lived in the Inland Empire, dating back more than 10,000 years, and European-American settlers discovered the fertile soils and rich natural resources of the area in the mid-1800s. Several old wagon roads and railways slice through the landscape. Reminders of the timber industry can be seen here and there in the form of old timber flumes and mill ponds. The lands of the upper Inland Empire—the region surrounding Spokane—treated settlers harshly, however. Summertime temperatures frequently top 100 degrees F., and winter temperatures plummet below zero. Little rain falls in the summer, but snow often clogs roads and trails in winter. All in all, this was a tough environment in which to carve out a homestead—as evidenced by the many old, abandoned log cabins that dot the high desert—but it's a wonderful natural world to explore on foot.

Views across a marshy area of Crab Creek enroute to Frog Lake

69 ┊ FROG LAKE/CRAB CREEK/ MARSH LOOP TRAILS

Round trip	■	3+ miles
Hiking time	■	2 to 3 hours
Difficulty	■	Easy
Starting elevation	■	950 feet
High point	■	1000 feet
Best season	■	Year-round
Maps	■	Washington State Department of Natural Resources (DNR) Priest Rapids
Contact	■	U.S. Fish and Wildlife Service, Columbia National Wildlife Refuge
Permits/passes	■	Washington Department of Fish and Wildlife Vehicle Permit required

From Vantage, drive east on Interstate 90; crossing the Columbia River and leaving the freeway at exit 137 (State Route 26). Drive SR 26 for 25.3 miles before turning left onto SR 262 toward Potholes State Park. Continue 17.7 miles from SR 26, and at the far eastern end of the O'Sullivan Dam, turn right into the Columbia National Wildlife Refuge entrance signed for Soda Lake Campground and Othello (this is directly across the road from a massive public fishing boat launch site). Drive into the refuge and continue past the turn to Soda Lake at 1.1 miles. Turn right at 2.2 miles, and at 2.8 miles reach the northern Crab Creek trailhead. At a junction just past the Crab Creek trailhead, keep left on the main road (don't go straight). In another mile (3.9 miles total from the O'Sullivan Road entrance) is the Frog Lake/Marsh Lake trailhead area. The parking area is on the right (west) side of the road, and the trio of trails begins on the east side of the road.

By late spring, this area becomes very hot and dry, yet every valley bottom is covered with lush green vegetation and at least a small body of water —be it a creek, a lake, or a largish bog/mosquito hatchery. While the small waters are rich with aquatic life, the desert begins 1 or 2 feet above the waterline, with prickly pear cactus, sagebrush, cheatgrass, lots of dusty bare ground, and rattlesnakes. In winter, bitter cold weather settles in, and a cold silence envelops the land—until the birds wake up. Then you'll be blasted awake by the call of the 100,000 ducks and geese that stop in this refuge during the annual migration. Most notable of the migratory birds are the sandhill cranes that stop over in March each year.

Five species of snakes are found within the refuge, including the western rattlesnake, which is fairly common. Visitors should be alert for rattlesnakes but must remember that they, like all other species of wildlife on the refuge, are protected. Rattlesnakes might be found anywhere on the refuge

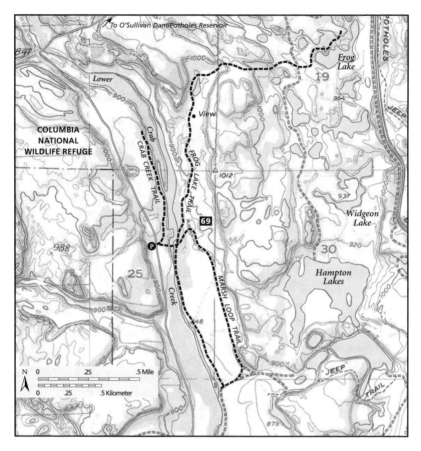

during warm weather but are most abundant in rocky areas and in heavy vegetation.

This trail crosses the creek and, staying left, slowly climbs out of the coulee that harbors Crab Creek. Views across the creek and the mesalike areas across the coulee are grand with billowing sage. White-crowned sparrows and red-winged blackbirds fill the bushes here.

Frog Lake is reached in about 1 mile. The small pond is a pretty little pool supporting a large population of birds and amphibians. Keep going on the trail and loop around a low butte behind the lake—or go off-trail and carefully climb the low butte to enjoy views of the entire refuge. The trail loops around the butte and returns to the trailhead in about 3 miles.

Don't stop there. The 1-mile Crab Creek Trail takes off just to the left of the signposts and follows the west side of the creek. It comes out a mile to the north at a north trailhead access to the same trail. The riparian habitat of the creek hosts hordes of birds and small mammals.

Don't stop yet. The Marsh Loop Trail is another 1-mile loop trail that heads out from the same junction as the Frog Lake Trail once across the creek. This is a nature loop trail and great for wildlife viewing and birding.

70 | CHUKAR LAKE/BLYTHE LAKE

Round trip ■	**4 miles**
Hiking time ■	2 to 3 hours
Difficulty ■	Moderate
Starting elevation ■	900 feet
High point ■	1000 feet
Best season ■	Year-round
Maps ■	Washington State Department of Natural Resources (DNR) Priest Rapids
Contact ■	U.S. Fish and Wildlife Service, Columbia National Wildlife Refuge
Permits/passes ■	Washington Department of Fish and Wildlife Vehicle Permit required

From Vantage, drive east on Interstate 90, crossing the Columbia River and leaving the freeway at exit 137 (State Route 26). Drive SR 26 for 25.3 miles before turning left onto SR 262 toward Potholes State Park. The road continues north and bends east, becoming O'Sullivan Dam Road. At 14 miles from SR 26, turn right onto a gravel road (signed "Public Fishing Access and Blythe/Chukar Lakes") across from the Mar Don Resort. Drive 1.3 miles to

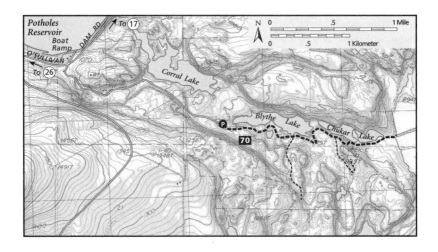

Stunning overview of Chukar Lake on a frosty morning

enter the Columbia National Wildlife Refuge (brochures and maps available at reader board here) and continue to the road end at 1.7 miles.

The channeled scablands region west of the lakes fills the scenic views here, creating a wonderful mosaic, especially in the twilight hours. The low angle of light casts the textured landscape into stark relief, creating complex patterns of shade and light. This glorious scenic landscape is made richer yet thanks to the plethora of wildlife thriving in the area. On any given day, you might see one or more of the following: coyotes, rabbits, hawks, deer, reptiles (rattlesnakes, bull snakes), and birds! birds! birds! (sandhill cranes, owls, cliff swallows, violet green swallows, American kestrels, northern harriers, and red-tailed hawks).

Start hiking up the abandoned jeep track past Blythe Lake to enter the marvelous coulee country. The sagebrush growing along the track provides a silver-green stage for the birds that flit through the area. Hike the jeep track to its end, where you'll find views north across Blythe Lake to the stark basalt cliffs beyond.

Climb to the ridge above the coulee and follow it parallel to the shore of Blythe Lake to reach Chukar Lake about 1.5 miles from the trailhead area. Drop down the slopes to the lakeshore and pick up the gravel road that rolls in from the southeast. This road cuts through vast marshy areas of prime waterfowl habitat, all a part of Marsh Units 1 and 2 of the Columbia National Wildlife Refuge.

After another mile hiking along the road, turn back and climb to the top of the plateau areas above the coulee. You might consider heading cross-country here—or anywhere along the route that strikes your fancy, for that matter—to explore the impressive coulee formations about 0.5 mile to the west. Once your urge to ramble is gone, head back to Blythe Lake and your vehicle.

71 ┆ Goose Lake Plateau

Round trip ■	7 to 8 miles
Hiking time ■	4 to 5 hours
Difficulty ■	Moderate
Starting elevation ■	900 feet
High point ■	1000 feet
Best season ■	Year-round
Maps ■	Washington State Department of Natural Resources (DNR) Priest Rapids
Contact ■	U.S. Fish and Wildlife Service, Columbia National Wildlife Refuge
Permits/passes ■	Washington Department of Fish and Wildlife Vehicle Permit required

From Vantage, drive east on Interstate 90, crossing the Columbia River and leaving the freeway at exit 137 (State Route 26). Drive SR 26 for 25.3 miles before turning left onto SR 262 toward Potholes State Park. Continue 17.7 miles from SR 26. At the far eastern end of the O'Sullivan Dam, turn right into the Columbia National Wildlife Refuge entrance signed to Soda Lake Campground and Othello (directly across the road from the massive public fishing boat launch site). Drive into the refuge, and continue past the turn to Soda Lake at 1.1 miles. Turn right at 2.2 miles, and at 2.8 miles reach the northern Crab Creek trailhead. At a junction just

A hiker roams the vast grass-lands of the Goose Lake Plateau.

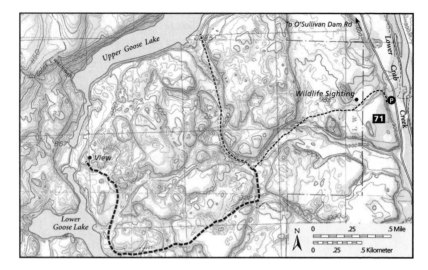

past the Crab Creek trailhead, keep left on the main road (don't go straight). In another mile (3.9 miles total from the O'Sullivan Road entrance) is the Frog Lake/Marsh Lake trailhead area. The parking area is on the right (west) side of road— this trail begins to the west, behind the parking area (the trails across the road are for the Frog Lake/Marsh Loop routes).

This area is part of eastern Washington's channeled scabland, created by glacial floodwaters of the Pleistocene epoch. It is mostly rolling countryside with basalt outcroppings forming cliffs, mesas, box canyons, and potholes. Many of the canyons and potholes are filled with water that has seeped from the Potholes Reservoir north of this unit. A long history of frequent range fires has turned almost all of this area into grassland, comprised mostly of Sandberg bluegrass and cheatgrass.

Step onto the trail to the west of the parking area and you'll peer out onto a series of boot-built trails heading toward the cliffs and a single trail angling up the steep face of the cliffs. Pick the most trammeled path to the cliff, then hike up the single path to the top to find awe-inspiring views near and far. Miles of open grassy terrain stretch out before you. Head southwest around and through wildflower prairie areas surrounded by massive basalt pillars of the scabland. After going between two of the basalt bumps, continue southwest, following the game trail you've been on. It soon enters a narrow canyon area between two broad 50-foot-high plateaus. Hike through this narrow area for 0.5 mile, and you'll come to a broad open junction with gullies heading off in four directions.

Angle up the old jeep road to the right/north. At 2.5 miles total from the trailhead, you will come to the upper plateau view down to Upper Goose Lake. Backtrack, and at the junction go south and shortly veer right/west on another old jeep track. Go 1 mile more and you'll be at Lower Goose Lake.

To prove how rich in hiking routes this area is, you can hike down another old jeep road to the southeast from this junction and hit the main gravel road that heads south of the trailhead area toward Othello. Hike back up the road 1.5 miles to loop back to the trailhead.

72 ■ DESERT WILDLIFE AREA

Round trip ■	6 miles
Hiking time ■	3 to 4 hours
Difficulty ■	Moderate
Starting elevation ■	1100 feet
High point ■	1150 feet
Best season ■	October through March
Maps ■	Washington State Department of Natural Resources (DNR) Moses Lake
Contact ■	Washington Department of Fish and Wildlife
Permits/passes ■	Washington Department of Fish and Wildlife Vehicle Permit required

From Moses Lake, drive west on Interstate 90 and leave the freeway at exit 164/Dodson Road. Turn south onto Dodson Road. Drive 3.4 miles and turn left into the large gravel, public access parking lot area signed "Public Hunting/Fishing."

The Desert Wildlife Area encompasses 35,100 acres. This was a true

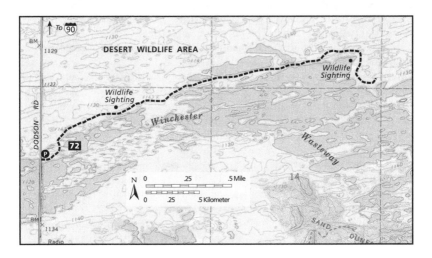

One of the many marshes and ponds along the Winchester Wasteway in the Desert Wildlife Area

desert prior to the coming of the Columbia Basin Irrigation Project. Black sands (ground-up basalt) formed sand dunes, which were very actively moving until recent times. The natural basin now serves as a collector for irrigation water from upslope farmlands. Most of this water is collected in the Winchester and Frenchman Hills Wasteways. The bulk of the land that comprises the Desert Wildlife Area borders both sides of the Winchester Wasteway—the main channel brings water from the Soap Lake area to the north down to the Potholes area basin and its surrounding farmland. You'll find a multitude of hunter/fisher trails that lead all along the north side of the wasteway and the numerous ponds/lakes/seeps around the wasteway. Each body of water has its own special appeal, each boasting a unique population of plants and animals. Hawks are commonly seen soaring overhead, giving testimony to the plethora of small birds, mammals, and reptiles in the area. The foliage includes pretty stands of hawthorn and Russian olive trees along the waterways.

From the parking area, head out along the north side of the wasteway. As you hike, you'll see huge sand dunes to the southeast—across the water.

About 2 miles out from the trailhead, you'll have curved around the north side of the lakes basin and, still following the waterline, you'll turn south. Continue south and keep following the shore. The best scenery and wildlife viewing are seen in the first 3 miles of walking, so turn back at your leisure beyond that point.

73 Potholes Wildlife Area–North

Round trip ■	8 miles
Hiking time ■	3 to 4 hours
Difficulty ■	Easy
Starting elevation ■	1050 feet
High point ■	1050 feet
Best season ■	October through March
Maps ■	Washington State Department of Natural Resources (DNR) Moses Lake
Contact ■	Washington Department of Fish and Wildlife
Permits/passes ■	Washington Department of Fish and Wildlife Vehicle Permit required

From Moses Lake, drive west on Interstate 90 and leave the freeway at exit 169/Hiawatha Road. Turn left at the overpass, and on the south side of the freeway, following signs pointing to "Sanitary Landfill," turn left onto the freeway frontage road. Drive 1 mile and turn right at C-NE Road (also signed "Sanitary Landfill"). Drive C-NE Road for 0.2 mile and, just after passing the landfill transfer station, park at the gated road turn-around area marking the entrance to this northwest corner of the Potholes Wildlife Area.

This is a great getaway since the trailhead is just a couple minutes off I-90 and offers access to tremendous roaming options in the northernmost reaches of the Potholes Wildlife Area. In this northern section of the wildlife area, the Potholes Reservoir is mostly just small lagoonlike curves of shallow water surrounded by rich habitat for wildlife (thanks to the huge stands of trees around the waterways).

The Potholes Wildlife Area covers 32,500 acres, with 20,000 acres of surface water when the reservoir is full of snowmelt each spring. That means several thousand acres of water cover the natural sand dune area, creating hundreds of small islands and seasonally flooded areas that are popular homes for a variety of birds, including pelicans and egrets, and other animals. The marshy areas in the seasonal flood plain sport huge fields of cattail and bulrush, which in turn support great populations of

Proof of the volcanic past in the Potholes region

birds and animals. The western part of the Potholes area still has many active sand dunes, especially east of the Winchester and Frenchman Hills Wasteways.

The first 1.5 miles of the hike rolls along the ruler-straight (closed) road heading due south. Views are lovely across the great sand basin in front of you. You slowly drop in elevation as you walk, entering richer wildlife habitat with each step. Quails, pheasants, hawks, and coyotes are often spotted in the first mile of this desert walk.

Pass the first road to the right (it enters private land in less than 0.5 mile, where it is closed to public access). At the next Y, take the road to the right. For the next 2.5 miles, stroll along the western side of the Potholes lakes, where you'll find many opportunities to roam over to the water.

Keep an eye on the lake, as the waterways draw a variety of birds: look for white pelicans, great white egrets, Canada geese, and an array of ducks. About 4 miles from the trailhead you reach the end of the gated road. This is a good turnaround point.

74 POTHOLES WILDLIFE AREA–DUNES RAMBLE

Round trip ■	4 miles
Hiking time ■	2 to 3 hours
Difficulty ■	Easy
Starting elevation ■	1100 feet
High point ■	1100 feet
Best season ■	Year-round
Maps ■	Washington State Department of Natural Resources (DNR) Moses Lake
Contact ■	Washington Department of Fish and Wildlife
Permits/passes ■	Washington Department of Fish and Wildlife Vehicle Permit required

From Moses Lake, drive west on Interstate 90 and leave the freeway at exit 169/Hiawatha Road. Turn left at the overpass. On the south side of the freeway, turn left onto the freeway frontage road following signs pointing to "Sanitary Landfill." Drive 2.5 miles and turn right at the gravel road marked with a brown Washington Department of Fish and Wildlife "Public Fishing" sign. Drive 2.6 miles on this gravel road as it passes under some power lines. At the Y turn right. Drive this gravel road 1.1 miles, and at the next Y turn left. Drive this last gravel road a final 1.2 miles to the end of the road at a large turnaround and parking area.

This is desert hiking at its best—a lovely trail (a fisher trail turned into a great hiking trail) that bobs up and down over little dunes for miles. As you walk through the sand dune environment, enjoy expansive views to the south overlooking the heart of the Potholes area—miles and miles of water surrounded by miles and miles of sand dunes.

The trail leads due south out of the turnaround area along the top of the dune on which you parked. As you begin your walk, you'll immediately enter a garden of wildflowers—wallflower (yellow), yellow bells, and fern-leaf desert parsley cover the ground and are especially lovely when seen beneath the willow trees along the water.

At about 1.5 miles out, follow the trail down to the edge of the water. If you are an angler, bring a rod and reel and you might catch crappie, bluegill, bass, and/or perch in the murky waters. Indeed, you can often catch fish

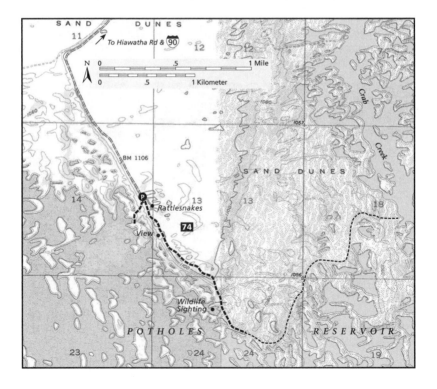

Hiking in the Potholes area along rolling sand dunes

with your hands—the panfish love the sun-warmed shallows and frequently get trapped in isolated pools as the reservoir levels drop. During low water, you might see fish skeletons scattered across the sands—the local raptors and coyotes make quick work of the trapped fish.

From this fishy area, head east for another mile or more and encounter dunes that roll on seemingly endlessly. Turn around after playing in the sand dunes for a while.

75 GLOYD SEEPS–NORTH

Round trip	5+ miles
Hiking time	3 hours
Difficulty	Easy
Starting elevation	1200 feet
High point	1200 feet
Best season	Year-round
Maps	Washington State Department of Natural Resources (DNR) Moses Lake
Contact	Washington Department of Fish and Wildlife
Permits/passes	Washington Department of Fish and Wildlife Vehicle Permit required

From Interstate 90 in Moses Lake, take exit 179 and head north on State Route 17 toward Othello. Drive 3.8 miles north on SR 17 and take the Stratford Road exit. Turn right and drive north on Stratford Road for 16.4 miles before turning left on Road 20NE. Drive 5 miles on Road 20NE, then turn left on Road E-NE. Follow this gravel road 1 mile. At a sharp right turn in the road (road becoming 19NE), find the large parking area on the left side of the road.

The Gloyd Seeps Wildlife Area is a narrow band of habitat—it never exceeds 2 miles in width at any point, but it is very long from north to south, providing plenty of hiking opportunities. Look for the usual birds (ducks and waterfowl along the waterways, quail and pheasant in the brush, red-winged blackbirds and swallows everywhere else). You might also find horned lizards, jackrabbits, and coyotes throughout the area.

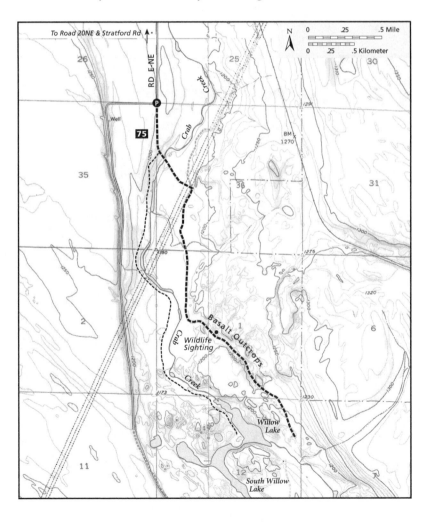

Begin your hike by walking past the gate on the road. Hiking options abound. The most direct and very enjoyable route follows an old four-wheel-drive road (closed to vehicles) southeast from the parking area. This leads you through some of the best habitat that you will find anywhere for sharp-tailed grouse, meadowlarks, bluebirds, and partridges. The way passes under some power lines. These broad, open sagelands are dotted with miniature basalt coulees that are worth exploring. Eventually the road takes you almost 3 miles to beautiful Willow Lake and South Willow Lake. Here geese and swans winter.

From Willow Lake, you again have options: Keep hiking southeast another mile or so, or head off cross-country to make the return trip to the parking area more like a loop. Hiking along the eastern side of the broad area takes you along many natural rock sculptures and desert meadowlands.

76 GLOYD SEEPS-SOUTH

Round trip ■	3.5 miles
Hiking time ■	2 to 3 hours
Difficulty ■	Easy
Starting elevation ■	1200 feet
High point ■	1200 feet
Best season ■	Year-round
Maps ■	Washington State Department of Natural Resources (DNR) Moses Lake
Contact ■	Washington Department of Fish and Wildlife
Permits/passes ■	Washington Department of Fish and Wildlife Vehicle Permit required

From Interstate 90 in Moses Lake, take exit 179 and head north on State Route 17 toward Othello. Drive 3.8 miles north on SR 17 and take the Stratford Road exit. Turn right and drive north on Stratford Road. At 12.4 miles from SR 17, turn left on Road 16. Drive this dirt road 3.2 miles, turn right (going straight here is a private drive), take the left fork at a Y—this last stretch can be very muddy and undrivable in winter—and drive to the turnaround parking area at the end of the road, 4.1 miles total from Stratford Road.

Come spring, this area explodes in color. Wildlife dots the landscape, but the bright and gaudy plumage of migrating birds (waterfowl and land dwellers) colors the sky, the bushes, and the water. Yellow-headed blackbirds, numerous warbler species, flycatchers, and, of course, meadowlarks galore flock here every spring to feast on the emerging bugs. Waterfowl also use the area as they migrate north. In short, this is a must-see site for anyone who considers birding part of their outdoor life.

Hike out along the closed jeep track from the parking area, passing alongside a pond to quickly find a network of trails that lead along the eastern side of Crab Creek. You can scramble around and over wonderful basalt "blobs," getting in some nice bouldering practice. If rock-hopping isn't your bag, you can still enjoy the mosaic patterns of lichen and moss growth on the blobs. The wildflowers erupt in a tremendous bloom come spring, thanks to the ready availability of water to keep the fragile plants fresh and lively.

After hiking 1 mile, you'll find well-positioned hunting/photography blinds along the creek/lake. In autumn, these are usually occupied by duck hunters but are available to anyone on a first-come, first-served basis. The blinds make great locations from which to view or photograph the local birds.

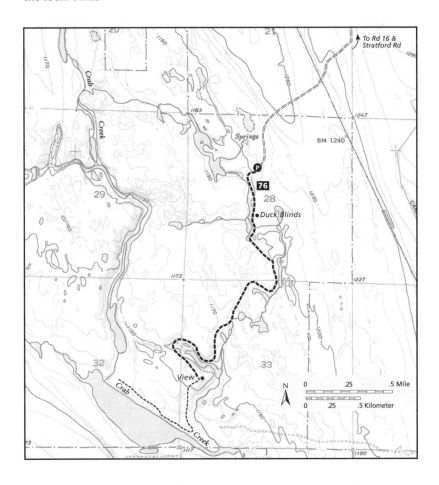

A marshy section of Crab Creek as it passes through the Gloyd Seeps Wildlife Area

Continue hiking south along Crab Creek, picking your path from among the network of hunter tracks and game trails. You can push on another 2 to 3 miles before turning back.

11 COLUMBIA PLATEAU–AMBER LAKE

Round trip ■	**Up to 23 miles**
Hiking time ■	As long as you want
Difficulty ■	Moderate
Starting elevation ■	2300 feet
Low point ■	2100 feet
Best season ■	Year-round
Maps ■	Washington State Department of Natural Resources (DNR) Rosalia
Contact ■	Washington State Parks and Recreation
Permits/passes ■	Washington State Parks and Recreation Parking Pass required

From Vantage, drive east on Interstate 90 to exit 257, signed "Tyler/Cheney." After exiting, turn right and drive 9 miles on State Route 904. Turn right

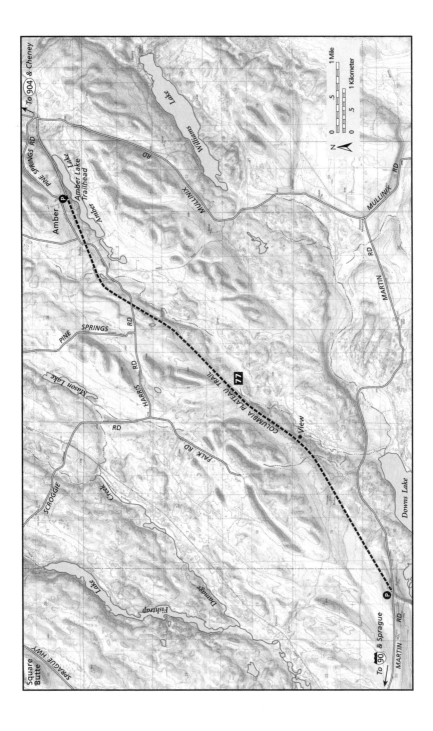

onto Mullinix Road. Drive Mullinix Road 9.3 miles, and turn right onto Pine Springs Road. Drive 1.4 miles on Pine Springs Road and turn left on Houck Avenue. Head downhill, veer right after crossing the railroad grade, and follow the signs 1000 feet to the huge parking lot. This is the preferrred access, although the route also can be accessed from its southern end via the Martin Road trailhead. To reach this alternative, turn onto Pine Springs Road and continue south on Mullinix Road to the point where the road crosses the trail at the well-marked Martin Road trailhead.

This 23-mile scenic corridor currently passes through the heart of the wildlife-rich Turnbull National Wildlife Refuge. The route offers opportunities to see interpretive panels, numerous wildlife species, and associated scenic landscapes. Trail signage indicates key features along the trail, as well as mile markers with numbers referencing the distance from Portland, Oregon, as established by the Spokane–Portland–Seattle Railroad in the early 1900s.

The old railroad right-of-way slices through the heart of one of the richest wildlife areas in Washington. From the trailhead, amble to the south and enjoy the desert scenery on both sides of the trail. Because the route is smooth and level, you can cover many more miles than you might expect.

Big sky dominates the Columbia Plateau Trail past Amber Lake.

The trail angles past Amber Lake—stay on the trail, because moose are sometimes seen lumbering through the area near the lake—and cuts through the high desert sagelands to the southeast. Bald eagles can frequently be seen overhead as they soar aloft while searching area lakes for fish. Mule deer also frequent the area.

In 7 miles, you'll reach another trailhead at Martin Road. Turn around here or continue as far as you like, for a total mileage of up to 23 miles (one-way).

Note: This trail is open to bicycle traffic, so stay alert when walking here.

78 LAKEVIEW RANCH

Round trip	■	4 miles
Hiking time	■	3 hours
Difficulty	■	Moderate
Starting elevation	■	2300 feet
Low point	■	2100 feet
Best season	■	Year-round
Maps	■	Washington State Department of Natural Resources (DNR) Moses Lake
Contact	■	Bureau of Land Management, Spokane
Permits/passes	■	None

From Vantage, drive east on Interstate 90 to exit 206, signed "State Route 21–Lind/Odessa." After exiting, turn left and drive 18.1 miles north on SR 21 to Odessa. In town, turn right at the junction with SR 28. In 0.1 mile, turn left and follow the signs to "Hwy 21–Wilber." Continue on SR 21 for 2.8 miles. Turn left onto Lakeview Ranch Loop Road, which is signed with a BLM brown binoculars "wildlife viewing" sign. Take this good gravel road 5.2 miles and pull into the well-signed Lakeview Ranch BLM area

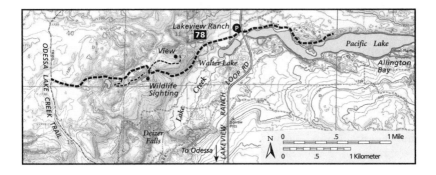

Surprise in the desert: west of the Lakeview Ranch area, a stunning lake suddenly appears surrounded by basalt cliffs.

on the left side of the road. Drive between the two barns and park in the parking area.

This old ranch, complete with abandoned farmhouse and outbuildings, has been shed of its domestic livestock in favor of turning the land over to the abundant wildlife that thrives here. Jackrabbits (both white-tailed and black-tailed) bound through the sagebrush, mule deer browse among the wildflower prairies, and coyotes prowl the coulees and canyons (seeking those bounding jacks, no doubt).

The trailhead area offers reader-board kiosks with full information on the area, as well as maps of the ranch. There are many route options, including some scrambling possibilities. We offer a basic route here, but using the information available at the kiosks, you can modify and personalize your outing. Information on wildlife is also available, and occasional the BLM asks visitors to help biologists by keeping an eye out for specific species that biologists track to monitor the health of their populations.

From behind the buildings, the old jeep track heads off into the open lands to the southwest. Angle down into the broad coulee full of sage and prairie grasses. As you roam (you actually are going flat here) into the coulee, the rugged basalt cliffs rise up on your right, providing opportunities for some great photography.

About 1.2 miles into the hike you'll come to a scenic junction at the end of the road. To the north is a huge lake surrounded by coulee cliffs. Another lake sits 0.15 mile to the south. You have many options to choose from, but the best bet is to head west, following the trail sign. The rough path soon turns into a proper hiking trail that heads up onto a bench above the lake and continues another 1.5 miles past 2 more small lakes and eventually intersects with the Odessa–Lake Creek Trail (see Hike 80). Continue or turn back here, for a total 4- to 5-mile trek.

79 BOBS LAKES

Round trip	■	**3 miles**
Hiking time	■	2 hours
Difficulty	■	Moderate
Starting elevation	■	1840 feet
Low point	■	1450 feet
Best season	■	Year-round
Maps	■	Washington State Department of Natural Resources (DNR) Moses Lake
Contact	■	Bureau of Land Management, Spokane
Permits/passes	■	None

From Vantage, drive east on Interstate 90 to exit 206, signed "State Route 21-Lind/Odessa." After exiting, turn left and drive 18.1 miles north on SR 21 into Odessa. In town, turn right at the junction with SR 28. In 0.1 mile, turn left and follow the signs to "Hwy 21–Wilber." Continue on SR 21 for 2.8 miles. Turn left onto Lakeview Ranch Loop Road, which is signed with a BLM brown binoculars "wildlife viewing" sign. Take this good gravel road 3.4 miles before turning left onto the jeep track where Lakeview Ranch Road takes a sharp right. Park here and start the hike down the jeep track past the "Road Closed" BLM signs.

Winter, while frequently bitterly cold here, offers unique hiking opportunities. Dress warmly and you'll enjoy exploring the snow-dappled

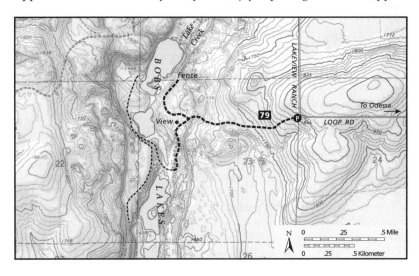

sagelands. This area serves as a winter stopping area for trumpeter swans, cranes, geese, mergansers, goldeneyes, canvasbacks, and other migrating waterfowl. Deer fill the coulee here, and during winter, when the lake levels are low, the many species of wildlife that roam through the area leave their tracks for you to enjoy—giving you the chance to experience the animals even if you never see them. Don't know how to find and read tracks? No worries! The soft mud of the low-water lake basins captures perfect imprints of passing animals, including birds.

This hike rolls down a wonderful old two-track trail (old jeep road) to lead you into the upland steppes of the Odessa Coulee. The path provides easy hiking with stunning views every step of the way. The 1.5-mile stretch to Bobs Lakes cuts through a prairie grass environment rather than pure sageland, offering a refreshing change of scenery from the typical desert walk.

When you come to a fence—here or anywhere—don't climb over, under, or through it. Any fences you encounter along this route mark the boundary between open public lands and adjacent private property, and trespassing on private property is frowned upon in this locale.

The trail switches back and forth steeply as it descends through the coulee cliffs to reach the bottom of the canyon near Bobs Lakes—a series of shallow lakes if there is water in them, mud holes if there is no water. The trail deposits you between the two largest lakes, so go both north and south to enjoy roaming around each lake as much as you wish. You can also scramble up the slopes above the lake in a few places to gain a better view of the area—this is the best way to spot critters that might be lurking near the lakes.

Note: Poison ivy thrives along the west shores of the lakes: Take care!

80 | ODESSA–LAKE CREEK TRAIL

Round trip ■	**Up to 26 miles**
Hiking time ■	6+ hours
Difficulty ■	Moderate
Starting elevation ■	1500 feet
High point ■	1840 feet
Best season ■	Year-round
Maps ■	Washington State Department of Natural Resources (DNR) Moses Lake
Contact ■	Bureau of Land Management, Spokane
Permits/passes ■	None

From Vantage, drive east on Interstate 90 to exit 206, signed "State Route 21–Lind/Odessa." After exiting, turn left and drive 18.1 miles north on

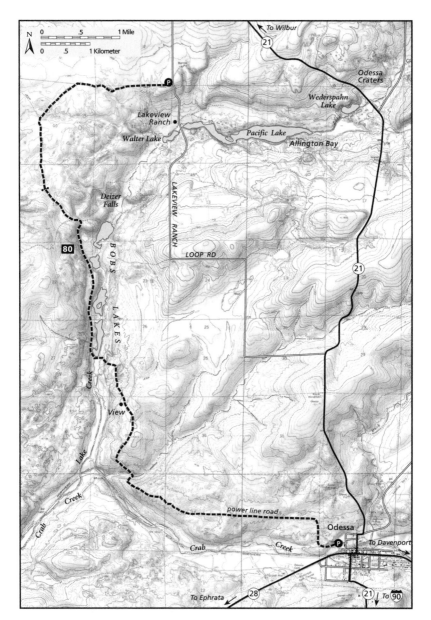

SR 21 into Odessa. In town, turn left at the junction with SR 28. In one block, turn right onto Birch Street, which is well signed for "Odessa–Lake Creek Trail." Drive over the train tracks and in 0.1 mile turn left following the signed route to the trailhead (this is Alice Street). Pass between

A trail marker along the Odessa–Lake Creek Trail

two trucking company buildings on a gravel road and continue beyond, following signs for 0.3 mile to the trailhead, veering to the left the last 100 feet to the parking area.

With about 13 miles of one-way mileage, this route stands out as one of the longest shrub–steppe hikes in Washington. You could arrange a vehicle shuttle to enjoy the entire distance one-way, or you could do a daylong round-trip hike of 26 miles. The trail is smooth and mostly level the entire way. You also could load your backpacking gear, hike 13 miles, and spend a night at the established campground at Pacific Lake.

The trail leaving the south trailhead is a lovely dirt path winding through basalt hills, piles of crumpled rock, and gullies. After about 0.5 mile, it merges with an old road. Head west on this road as it passes under a series of power lines. At about 2 miles, the trail angles north through a gate on an old jeep track. Here you'll start to find great views over the rugged Lake Creek drainage area: a lovely little canyon/gully in this channeled scablands terrain. You eventually wind down basalt cliffs, and at 6 miles from the trailhead you'll cross Lake Creek at the south end of Bobs Lakes. The lakes are frequently dry, and you can roam across the muddy flats to enjoy the animal tracks imprinted in the mud.

From the west side of the lakes, head north again, winding up the basalt rocks. Once on top of the highlands again, head straight north, once again on an old road. At about 10 miles from the start, you get to the gates that begin the start of the ORV-accessible portion of the trail (that is, the northernmost 3 miles of road) before you eventually curve to the right and come out just north of Lakeview Ranch and Pacific Lake. If you like, you can join with the Lakeview Ranch route here and expand your outing by linking that hike (Hike 78) with this one. The campground at Pacific Lake and the Lakeview Ranch trailhead area is 0.5 mile south of where you come out to the road.

81 ODESSA CRATERS

Round trip ■	**2 miles**
Hiking time ■	1 to 2 hours
Difficulty ■	Easy
Starting elevation ■	1700 feet
High point ■	1700 feet
Best season ■	Year-round
Maps ■	Washington State Department of Natural Resources (DNR) Moses Lake
Contact ■	Bureau of Land Management, Spokane
Permits/passes ■	None

From Vantage, drive east on Interstate 90 to exit 206, signed "State Route 21-Lind/Odessa." After exiting, turn left and drive 18.1 miles north on SR

View into the huge Amphitheater Crater

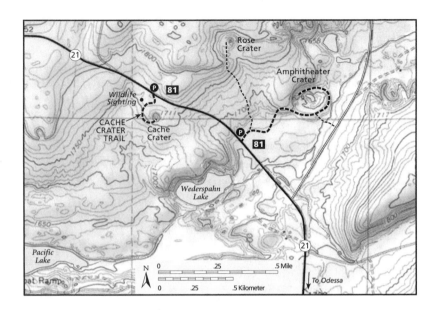

21 into Odessa. Continue 6.7 miles past Odessa on SR 21 to a parking area signed for "Odessa Craters."

This area north of Odessa is dotted with geological oddities: craters left in the aftermath of the Great Missoula Floods. The craters range in appearance from a simple deep hole in the ground to a vast depression a quarter mile around—looking almost look like a meteor might have glanced across the steppe landscape. New parking areas with trail signage guiding folks to these craters make it easy to enjoy them.

For the first stretch of your legs, hike 0.5 mile northeast from the parking area to the Amphitheater Crater—one of the bigger pits to explore. There is a faint trail in places and game trails in other areas—even a little bit of flagging in winter of 2003. Return to your vehicle but keep walking northwest for a 0.5-mile loop to Rose Crater. As you explore the lands around the holes, enjoy the rich sagebrush ecosystems and the presence of some beautiful birds. This area boasts a sizeable population of horned larks.

After enjoying nearly a mile of walking around the Rose and Amphitheater Craters, drive your vehicle northwest another 0.3 mile on SR 21 and turn left into the parking access for the Cache Crater Trail (we spotted a herd of seven mule deer here during our research visit).

Cache Crater Trail winds 0.2 mile to a deep pit of a crater. Though the distance is short, the beauty is great. Enjoy the wildflowers and the wildlife. In addition to the deer, you'll likely see quail along the path, and hawks high above.

82 ESCURE RANCH

Round trip ■	**8+ miles**
Hiking time ■	4 to 5 hours
Difficulty ■	Moderate
Starting elevation ■	1400 feet
High point ■	1650 feet
Best season ■	Year-round
Maps ■	Washington State Department of Natural Resources (DNR) Rosalia
Contact ■	Bureau of Land Management, Spokane
Permits/passes ■	None

From Vantage, drive east on Interstate 90 toward Spokane and take exit 245 for Sprague. Turn right off the freeway and drive 8.1 miles south on State Road 23, passing through the town of Sprague, to Lamont Road. Turn right on Lamont Road and continue 2.6 miles until the road veers left and turns into Revere Road. After 8.3 miles (0.2 mile after crossing the Milwaukee Corridor railroad grade) turn right on Jordon–Knott Road. Drive 2.2 miles on Jordon–Knott Road and turn right into the Rock Creek Management Area (BLM). Cross over the cattle guard and drive 2.5 miles to road's end to park by Rock Creek and the Escure Ranch site.

An old wooden stable, crowned by a rusted sheet-iron roof, stands at the trailhead on Escure Ranch. Several other old buildings

An old seeder rests on a fence line just outside of the Escure Ranch farm site.

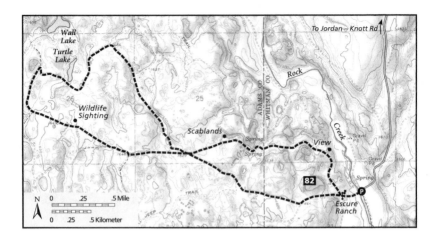

remain among the collection of barns and outbuildings that mark the historic headquarters of the now-defunct ranch. Corrals and fences divide the grounds of the headquarters into a patchwork of small yards. This wonderful old ranch setting creates an Old West feel that lingers throughout a hike. Beyond the buildings, you'll find black basalt mesas dotting the landscape around lakes, and many of these sheer-sided buttes can be seen reflected in the lake waters.

The hike begins at the old wooden bridge crossing the huge flow of Rock Creek. Views up and down the creek from the vantage point of the bridge are stunning. After hiking the road through the ranch buildings, the road branches out at the gate (keep the gates closed, please). Both forks of the road/trail merge again at about 1.5 miles into the trek, but the right-hand road leading north proves the more scenic.

In about 0.5 mile after cresting a hill, the path bends to the west for the start of a magical mile of hiking through miniscule canyons surrounded by basalt mesas and cliffs, all reflecting in the numerous small lakes and ponds and marshes through here. It is awesome!

Next you'll move out into a broad prairielike region. At about 1.5 miles from where the trails merge, you'll reach a Y junction with a road coming in from the north and another from the south. Keep hiking straight along the south trail, passing more and more flowers. Pass another jeep track on the left, and at the second trail on the left, follow it to hike west, then south for as much as 2 more miles, where you'll reach the western boundary of the BLM land.

Retrace your steps back to the Y junction and head north on the right branch. At any trail split over the next 3 miles, always stay right to complete a loop that takes you up past the lovely Turtle Lake area. When you reach the road you came in on, follow it the 2.5 miles back to the ranch house area and the trailhead.

83 ¦ Breeden Road/Wall Lake

Round trip ■	**8 to 10 miles**
Hiking time ■	4 to 5 hours
Difficulty ■	Moderate
Starting elevation ■	1700 feet
Low point ■	1600 feet
Best season ■	Year-round
Maps ■	Washington State Department of Natural Resources (DNR) Rosalia
Contact ■	Bureau of Land Management, Spokane
Permits/passes ■	None

From Vantage, drive east on Interstate 90 toward Spokane and take exit 245 for Sprague. Turn right off the freeway and drive 8.1 miles south on State Road 23, passing through the town of Sprague, to Lamont Road. Turn right on Lamont Road and continue 2.6 miles until the road veers left and turns into Revere Road. After 8.3 miles (0.2 mile after crossing the Milwaukee Corridor railroad grade) turn right on Jordon–Knott Road. Drive 1.4 miles on Jordon–Knott Road to reach the northern boundary and access to the BLM land at Breeden Road. Park here (the road is technically open to vehicles for

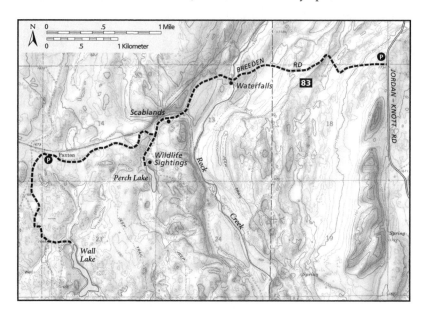

Cascading rapids on Rock Creek along Breeden Road

another couple of miles, but it is very rough, and in places very muddy and wet, making the route difficult even for a four-wheel-drive high-clearance vehicle).

With a collection of lakes, lots of vegetation, and a location nestled in the desert smack dab in the middle of the great Pacific Flyway (the route use by migratory waterfowl), it's not hard to guess where the ducks and geese are going to stop. This area draws waterfowl like a magnet, with the first great flocks arriving in mid-October and continuing through January.

This hike follows the far northern boundary of this BLM land. As you hike, you'll slowly drop over the first mile to a stunning "meadow" area bounded by scraggly trees. At 1.4 miles, just before reaching Rock Creek, you'll notice a jeep track that leads off to the south. This track is closed to vehicles and provides another option for a side hike to extend your mileage if you desire a longer trek. The side trail loops out for a brief jaunt into the heart of the BLM land's northern area before rejoining Jordon–Knott Road. Hike this and the road back for a 6-mile loop.

Rather than taking the side trail, however, we recommend you continue on the main road/trail. At 1.6 miles, you'll cross the beautiful Rock Creek. Rock Creek enters the BLM land here under the Breeden Bridge in a fury of rapids and stair-step waterfalls.

At about 2.6 miles from the trailhead, you reach another jeep track (closed to vehicles) leaving to the south. Hike this side trail for another 0.5 mile to reach lovely Wall Lake. Turn around and head home.

84 ¦ TOWELL FALLS

Round trip ■	**6+ miles**
Hiking time ■	3 hours
Difficulty ■	Easy
Starting elevation ■	1400 feet
High point ■	1450 feet
Best season ■	Year-round
Maps ■	Washington State Department of Natural Resources (DNR) Rosalia
Contact ■	Bureau of Land Management, Spokane
Permits/passes ■	None

From Vantage, drive east on Interstate 90 toward Spokane and take exit 245 for Sprague. Turn right off the freeway and drive 8.1 miles south on State

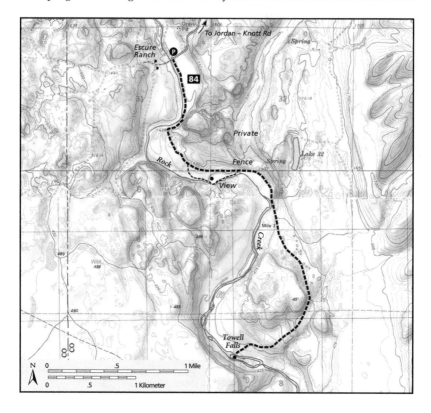

Rock Creek flows strongly in early spring.

Road 23, passing through the town of Sprague, to Lamont Road. Turn right on Lamont Road and continue 2.6 miles until the road veers left and turns into Revere Road. After 8.3 miles (0.2 mile after crossing the Milwaukee Corridor railroad grade) turn right on Jordon–Knott Road. Drive 2.2 miles on Jordon–Knott Road before turning right into the Rock Creek Management Area (BLM). Cross over the cattle guard and drive 2.5 miles to the end of the road and parking area by Rock Creek and the Escure Ranch site. The gate out to the trail/old road is by the BLM signboard and is signed "Towell Falls—3 miles."

The rewards of this wonderful hike are pretty straightforward. You get to wander a great jeep road for 3 miles to a glorious desert waterfall. You'll have the opportunity to enjoy a side trip to the banks of picturesque Rock Creek. You'll also find amazing views of basalt mesas rising 150 to 200 feet above the surrounding landscape. In short, this is a desert journey with incredible water works.

From the trailhead, head south along the road. The first 0.5 mile is flat across a refreshing bunchgrass/cheatgrass meadow with Rock Creek gurgling along just 100 feet to the west. As you hike, enjoy great views of the Escure Ranch buildings across the creek. The cliffs ahead of you are amazing, and you'll soon roll around them.

Just as you pass around the cliffs, a small desert tarn punctuates the landscape and reflects the rising mesa before you perfectly. At 1 mile, the trail passes a fenced area and then angles off to the east. From here you may roam freely toward Rock Creek—don't go in the other direction since it is private land.

Continuing along the trail, you'll find a sharp southern turn takes you down to the banks of Rock Creek. The last 1.5 miles to Towell Falls angle away from the creek and wind around a low hill of sorts before dropping down alongside the creek. Towell Falls is a lovely 12- to 15-foot drop in the creek and really stands out in this desert scene.

85 PACKER CREEK

Round trip ■	**4 miles**
Hiking time ■	2 to 3 hours
Difficulty ■	Moderate
Starting elevation ■	1700 feet
High point ■	1800 feet
Best season ■	Year-round
Maps ■	Washington State Department of Natural Resources (DNR) Rosalia
Contact ■	Bureau of Land Management, Spokane
Permits/passes ■	None

From Vantage, drive east on Interstate 90 toward Spokane and take exit 245 for Sprague. Turn right off the freeway and drive south 17.8 miles on SR 23. At 0.6 mile past Wagner Road, turn right into small parking area at a gated road.

Coal-black basalt bluffs and towering colonnades stand over the Packer Creek property. An intermittent lake nestled in the base of a coulee at the east side of the tract dries out in late summer, but throughout the winter and spring it provides a good home to waterfowl. Ducks and blue herons routinely fly around the lake and nearby marshy ponds, while other birds inhabit a grove of old poplars near a small spring along the valley floor in the western part of the tract. Orioles build nests on the branches, and woodpeckers bore holes in the tree trunks. On the ground along the dirt banks at the edge of the coulees, look for badgers, small rodents, and other burrowing animals.

At 1652 acres, this area—at first glance—seems a little small for wild land hiking. However, once you step into the desert, you'll find you can roam over *all* the 1652 acres of this desert playland.

Hiking southwest on the old road leading from the trailhead area takes you into the heart of the land. At about 0.5 mile you'll reach Packer Creek. You'll also bump into a pocket of private land tucked into the BLM parcel (a private residence is situated on the private land parcel—respect the landowner's privacy, please). The road turns sharply away from the private property.

After rolling east along the property line, the trail turns south. In about a mile you'll reach the area dotted with lovely basalt pinnacles. The road goes all the way to the boundary with the Milwaukee Railroad Corridor. The railroad corridor is the southern boundary of the BLM land, so walk west along the rail line 0.5 mile and then head off northward, back toward the private residence to loop back up to that road and hike out.

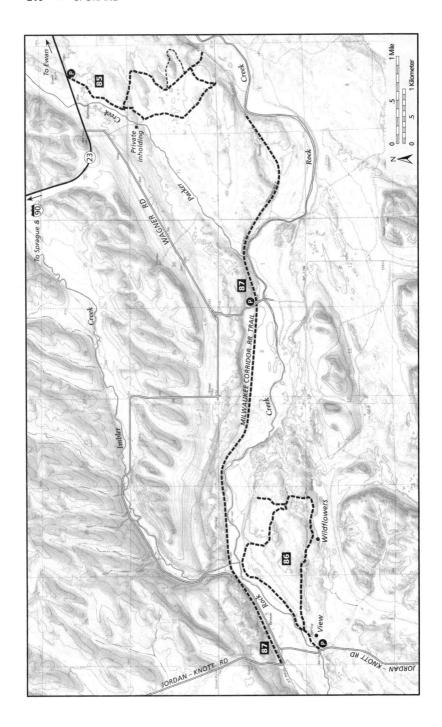

86 ROCK CREEK WILDLIFE AREA

Round trip ▪	**6 miles**
Hiking time ▪	3 hours
Difficulty ▪	Moderate
Starting elevation ▪	1600 feet
High point ▪	1700 feet
Best season ▪	Year-round
Maps ▪	Washington State Department of Natural Resources (DNR) Rosalia
Contact ▪	Washington Department of Fish and Wildlife
Permits/passes ▪	Washington Department of Fish and Wildlife Vehicle Permit required

From Vantage, drive east on Interstate 90 toward Spokane and take exit 245 for Sprague. Turn right off the freeway and drive 8.1 miles south on State Route 23, passing through the town of Sprague, to Lamont Road. Turn right on Lamont Road and continue 2.6 miles until the road veers left and turns into Revere Road. After 8.3 miles (0.2 mile after crossing the Milwaukee Corridor railroad grade) turn right on Jordon–Knott Road. Drive 0.3 mile on Jordon–Knott Road. Just before the bridge over Rock Creek, park in the area to the left. Hike over the bridge to the south side of Rock Creek to start hiking.

Just when you thought you were stuck in the middle of endless cultivated farmland, you find this nugget of wild perfection! This wonderful refuge in a farm-rich region offers great habitat to wildlife and wonderful hiking to hikers. The entire south side of Rock Creek is part of the protected (and unnamed) wildlife

Winter gives clear views of nesting birds in the desert. Here, a flycatcher nest hangs from a hawthorn tree in the Rock Creek Wildlife Area.

area. Because no name is posted for the public land unit here, we dubbed it the Revere–Rock Creek Wildlife Area.

A wonderful old jeep track follows along the south bank of Rock Creek, weaving through public wildlife lands and offering a great riparian desert walk. Follow the road for the entire 3 miles, or extend your trek by making side excursions out along the fishing and game trails that criss-cross the lands above the creek.

As you follow the road, you'll enter several areas with good brush cover—this is prime habitat for the local population of upland game birds, especially quail and huns (Hungarian partridge).

To create a loop outing, follow the jeep track about 0.3 mile, then look for a track that veers off to the right away from Rock Creek. Take this as it climbs up into highland areas. Once above the creek basin, the track swings out around a pretty series of ponds, seeps, and springs set among some starkly beautiful rocky pinnacles at 2 miles. From there, veer left and start winding down toward the creek once more. After about a mile of wandering through the area, you'll be back down at Rock Creek, which you can then follow back to the trailhead.

87 ¦ ROCK CREEK/MILWAUKEE RAILROAD CORRIDOR

Round trip ■	**12 miles**
Hiking time ■	5 to 6 hours
Difficulty ■	Easy
Starting elevation ■	1600 feet
High point ■	1600 feet
Best season ■	Year-round
Maps ■	Washington State Department of Natural Resources (DNR) Rosalia
Contact ■	Washington State Department of Natural Resources
Permits/passes ■	Washington State Department of Natural Resources (DNR) free use permit required

From Vantage, drive east on Interstate 90 toward Spokane and take exit 245 for Sprague. Turn right off the freeway and drive 8.1 miles south on State Route 23, passing through the town of Sprague. At 17.1 miles from I-90, turn right on Wagner Road. Drive 2.5 miles and veer left at the Y and head downhill 0.6 mile to the Milwaukee Corridor railroad trail crossing and access. (See page 210 for trail map.)

This section of the old Milwaukee Railroad right-of-way offers a unique

Actually a weed of sorts, teasel (Dipsacus fullonum) *lines parts of the Milwaukee Railroad Corridor in the Packer Creek–Rock Creek areas.*

perspective on the desert environment. The trail rolls through some largely untouched sections of desert ecology, providing close-up experiences with the natural plants and animals that thrive in this hostile environment. At other times, the route passes through cultivated farmlands, offering visitors a chance to see the hard work and commitments needed on the part of the farmer to scratch a living from these dry lands. Because the trail passes through private property, it is important that trail users stay on the rail–trail corridor. Do not leave the trail on this hike at any point. Be a good steward by respecting the landowners.

The hike east on this route is great as it heads up to SR 23 about 6 miles away. At least five places within the first few miles are on a grade that runs right up to a bench overlooking Rock Creek for great views. Keep an eye out for kingfishers and eagles. Along the trail, watch for deer, porcupines, skunks (!), and squirrels.

Note: At dozens of places, hikers (and mountain bikers) can jump on the 143-mile rail–trail and enjoy a day in the desert. This is one of the more unique sections. Hikers should consider their maps and look into further explorations on this wonderful trail corridor through the desert county.

88 TWIN LAKES

Round trip	■	**2 to 6 miles**
Hiking time	■	1 to 4 hours
Difficulty	■	Moderate
Starting elevation	■	1875 feet
High point	■	2200 feet
Best season	■	Year-round
Maps	■	Washington State Department of Natural Resources (DNR) Coulee Dam
Contact	■	Bureau of Land Management, Spokane office
Permits/passes	■	Washington Department of Fish and Wildlife Vehicle Permit required

From Vantage, drive east on Interstate 90 to exit 231 for Tokia. After exiting, turn north (left) over the freeway, and at 0.2 mile continue straight at the stop sign. This is now Danekas Road. Drive Danekas Road 1.4 miles and turn right on Hills Road (also known as Harrington–Tokia Road). Pass the Rocky Ford Wildlife Area access after 6.2 miles and enter Harrington at 18.0 miles. At 18.5 miles, in Harrington, turn left onto State Route 23 and continue 0.25 mile to a junction with SR 28. Turn left, and in 0.2 mile turn right on Coffee Pot Road. Drive Coffee Pot Road 14.1 miles and turn right on Highland Road. Drive 1.4 miles and turn right on Twin Lakes Road/Wildlife Area access road. Drive 1.9 miles before pulling off to the left to park, just before the road drops down steeply to the lakes. Hike this steep, rough section rather than trying to drive it.

Arrowleaf balsamroot covers the basalt cliffs surrounding Twin Lakes.

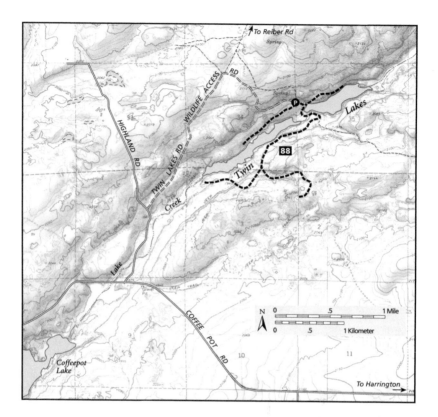

This is a prime example of a desert hiking area that offers many hours of slow wandering and contemplation of the unique environment, even though the mileage isn't as great as some other areas. You'll find exciting geological formations and history as you explore the huge canyon/coulee that holds the Twin Lakes.

Starting on the north side of the lake at the parking spot, hike down the road just 0.15 mile. At that point, rather than hike all the way straight down to the lake, turn west on the closed jeep track that follows along the rimrock bluff on the wall of the coulee. This offers views up to the top of the basalt cliffs of the canyon and down to the lush western Twin Lake. Here balsam-root and desert parsleys cover the spring landscape, joined by occasional groupings of yellow bells and desert bluebells. Raptors float high overhead on the thermals that spin up off the sun-heated rocks.

Hike along the coulee wall for a little over 1 mile (*Note:* The jeep track peters out after 0.5 mile or so—just keep hiking cross-country along the slope). As you follow the natural contours of the slope, you'll slowly descend until you are close to the lake elevation, but the route around the lower end of the lake isn't easily hikeable. Turn back here and curve back along your path to the main road. Backtracking actually proves beneficial here, as it provides a different look at the canyon. Heading east, the rock forms and coulee walls are seen from a new angle, with different shadow lines and textures. You'll also enjoy views of both lakes when heading back to the main trail/road.

Once on the main road/trail below the parking area, turn and descend to the lake basin and follow the road between the two lakes. Just after crossing between the lakes, look for another old track heading to the right. This leads along the southern side of the western lake. This great lakeshore stroll covers another 0.25 mile. Continue on the path as it climbs nearly 200 feet up the slope above the lake. You'll find a network of game trails through the rocks and sage up the bluff. Ramble around at will, then return to the lakes and explore their shorelines as you take it easy before heading for home.

89 FLORENCE LAKE

Round trip ■	**4.5 miles**
Hiking time ■	2 hours
Difficulty ■	Moderate
Starting elevation ■	2200 feet
High point ■	2250 feet
Best season ■	Year-round
Maps ■	Washington State Department of Natural Resources (DNR) Coulee Dam
Contact ■	Washington Department of Fish and Wildlife
Permits/passes ■	Washington Department of Fish and Wildlife Vehicle Permit required

From Vantage, drive east on Interstate 90 to exit 231 for Tokia. After exiting, turn north (left) over the freeway. At 0.2 mile, continue straight at the stop sign. This is now Danekas Road. Drive Danekas Road 1.4 miles, and turn right on Hills Road (also known as the Harrington–Tokia Road). Pass the Rocky Ford Wildlife Area access after 6.2 miles, and enter Harrington at 18 miles. At 18.5 miles, in Harrington, turn left onto State Route 23 and continue 0.25 mile to a junction with SR 28. Turn left, and in 0.2 mile turn right on Coffee Pot Road. Drive Coffee Pot Road for 6.1 miles and turn right on Lamp Road. Drive this good gravel road 4 miles and then turn left on Seven Springs Road. You'll come to a number of gravel roads merging at 0.2 mile—go straight here. At 5 miles from Coffee Pot Road, find a map signpost at Grant Road (another option for a good road hike into the region). At 7.4 miles from Coffee Pot Road (1.4 miles past signed Reiber Road), pull off to the right side of the road by a fence gate. Park here. Walk through the gate and hike along the south side of the marshes that adjoin the fence.

Wherever you find water in the desert, you'll find wildlife, and this route offers further proof of that. With many small pools, puddles, and marshes formed by a series of seeps oozing from the ground, this part of the Swanson Lakes Wildlife Area is rich in wildlife. One of the pools of water here is ringed with cattails and a host of robust trees, mostly Russian olive and hawthorn. These trees provide wonderful cover for a host of critters. Along the route, we spotted in the trees no less than six hawk nests and what looked like the nest of a great-horned owl. The water supports plenty of plant life, which in turn feeds armies of small birds and mammals. These in turn bring out the predators. The residents of those nests in the trees are usually seen soaring overhead—the hawks (both red-tailed and rough-legged) are the most numerous raptors, but you can also sometimes spot northern harriers, Cooper's hawks, and kestrels. Competing with the raptors for a share of the area's mice, rabbits, and voles are coyotes. Look for tracks in the mud near the waterways.

Start hiking along an old jeep track. The first 0.25 mile passes a series of small ponds fed by year-round seeps (very low-flow natural springs). Lots of wildlife can be seen along here. You'll find the jeep track disappearing (according to maps, it runs all the way to the lake). Nature has recalled the roadway. Never fear, however. Just keep hiking up the draw, heading northeast and you'll reach

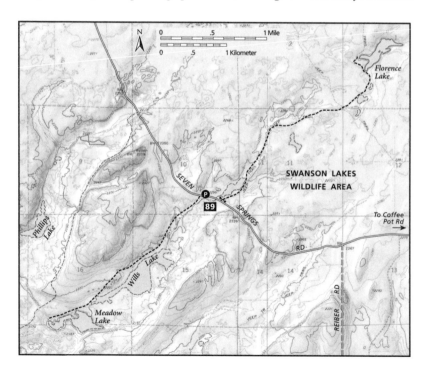

the lake after walking about 2.2 miles.

The route up the draw pierces prime upland bird habitat, so be prepared for unexpected appearances of game birds. Pheasants especially like to hold tight to a hiding place under a bush until you nearly step on them, then explode in a burst of feathers and raucous calls from under your feet. The unwary who first experience this often get such a blast of adrenaline that they won't sleep for a week!

As you approach the shores of Florence Lake, watch the shoreline for waterfowl. Ducks and geese stop here during their annual migrations, and some

One of many small, marshy ponds seen while hiking the land's contours to reach Florence Lake

actually winter here (they end their southern migration here since there is good feed among the farm fields outside the wildlife area and good cover and protected habitat on the lake). That means winter, despite the chill (okay, frigid blast), is a splendid time to visit the region.

90 | REIBER ROAD LOOP

Round trip ■	9 miles
Hiking time ■	5 hours
Difficulty ■	Moderate
Starting elevation ■	2100 feet
High point ■	2200 feet
Best season ■	Year-round
Maps ■	Washington State Department of Natural Resources (DNR) Coulee Dam
Contact ■	Washington Department of Fish and Wildlife
Permits/passes ■	Washington Department of Fish and Wildlife Vehicle Permit required

From Vantage, drive east on Interstate 90 to exit 231 for Tokia. After exiting, turn north (left) over the freeway. At 0.2 mile continue straight at the stop sign.

This is now Danekas Road. Drive Danekas Road 1.4 miles, and turn right on Hills Road (also known as the Harrington–Tokia Road). Pass the Rocky Ford Wildlife Area access after 6.2 miles, and enter Harrington at 18 miles. At 18.5 miles, in Harrington, turn left onto State Route 23 and continue 0.25 mile to a junction with SR 28. Turn left, and in 0.2 mile turn right on Coffee Pot Road. Drive Coffee Pot Road for 6.1 miles and turn right on Lamp Road. Drive this good gravel road 4 miles, then turn left on Seven Springs Road. You'll come to a number of gravel roads merging at 0.2 mile—go straight here. At 5 miles from Coffee Pot Road find a map signpost at Grant Road (another option for a good road hike into the region). At 6 miles from Coffee Pot Road (1 mile past the Washington Department of Fish and Wildlife map signpost), turn left on Reiber Road, signed "Public Lane Access Route." Drive this rough road 1.2 miles to the end of the road and parking area. Check the signpost at the trailhead to view the map showing the closed roads to hike for the 9-mile loop hike. Start hiking on the road behind the signpost.

This hike is best enjoyed early in the day. Late in the year (or early in the new year), start hiking shortly after sunrise to enjoy the cold beauty of the winter morning—the golden sunshine on the rocks, trees, and desert plants creates glorious patterns and colors along this desert trek. If you're lucky, a

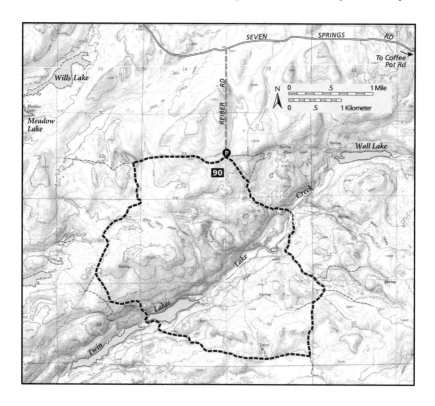

morning frost will have cast a mantle of crystal white over the sagelands so that the sun sparkles magically off the icy landscape.

Heading west through the fence behind the sign-in reader board, jump onto the first leg of the loop, which rolls due west for about 1.5 miles. The rich foliage along this stretch shelters a strong population of Hungarian partridges. This first section of the loop is fairly flat and level. At about 1.5 miles, look for a path that heads to the left (south). The trail winds down and around the rocky landscape and past a lovely small lake (seasonal).

About 0.5 mile past the lake, go left. After crossing open desert prairie, cross the main road that enters the Twin Lakes region. Across this road, to the west, is another jeep track that takes you down to the crossing between the two Twin Lakes.

Keeping going past the road for Twin Lake (see Hike 88). For the next 2 miles, pass through very isolated areas dotted with marshes and small ponds. Waterfowl and mule deer thrive around these wet areas. After another 2 miles, turn left and begin the 2.5 miles northward to close the loop.

91 SWANSON LAKES

Round trip ■	3 to 4 miles
Hiking time ■	2+ hours
Difficulty ■	Easy
Starting elevation ■	2250 feet
High point ■	2250 feet
Best season ■	Year-round
Maps ■	Washington State Department of Natural Resources (DNR) Coulee Dam
Contact ■	Washington Department of Fish and Wildlife
Permits/passes ■	Washington Department of Fish and Wildlife Vehicle Permit required

From Vantage, drive east on Interstate 90 to exit 231 for Tokia. After exiting, turn north (left) over the freeway. At 0.2 mile, continue straight at the stop sign. This is now Danekas Road. Drive Danekas Road 1.4 miles, and turn right on Hills Road (also known as the Harrington–Tokia Road). Pass the Rocky Ford Wildlife Area access after 6.2 miles, and enter Harrington at 18 miles. At 18.5 miles, in Harrington, turn left onto State Route 23 and continue 0.25 mile to a junction with SR 28. Turn left, and in 0.2 mile turn right on Coffee Pot Road. Drive Coffee Pot Road for 6.1 miles, and turn right on Lamp Road. Drive this good gravel road 4 miles, then turn left on Seven Springs Road. You'll come to a number of gravel roads merg-

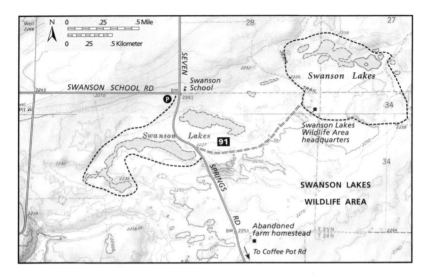

ing at 0.2 mile—go straight here. At 5 miles from Coffee Pot Road, find a map signpost at Grant Road (another option for a good road hike into the region). At 10 miles from Coffee Pot Road (4 miles past signed Reiber Road), reach the intersection with Swanson School Road. Find the parking area here.

The Swanson Lake Wildlife Area is a magical desert oasis. Between gorgeous expanses of sageland, you'll find fantastic pools of water, sparkling like gems on the desert floor. These jewels not only reflect the glorious beauty surrounding them, but they also draw in another type of beauty: a bounty of wildlife. The bright lakes are made all the more picturesque thanks to the brilliantly colored plumage of the ducks, geese, and shorebirds that occupy the lakes basin. Deer, coyotes, badgers, rabbits, and other small mammals patrol the desert around the lakes. Wildflowers

An abandoned farm house sits just south of the Swanson Lakes area.

turn the fertile, moist soils around the lakes and seeps into fragrant displays of color each spring.

You'll find many options for roaming along the northern edge of the huge Swanson Lakes Wildlife Area. Swanson Lakes is made up of two lakes, one on each side of Seven Springs Road. From the parking area, stroll southwest along the shore of the westernmost of the lakes. Hike a mile along the shore of the lake before turning back—you can't loop entirely around the lake because of a small tract of private property on the far shore. On your return, feel free to wander away from the anglers' trails that you followed on your way out. Roam cross-country through the open country around the lake back to the area near the start.

Walk back to the start of the route, cross the road, and head out along the shore for 0.5 mile or so before turning back and returning to the trailhead/parking area. Follow the dirt road to the wildlife area's headquarters buildings. The buildings are at least a mile in behind the lakes, and by walking the road you can enjoy the local desert scenery, the information board halfway in, and great views of the Swanson Lakes. Look for ducks, geese, and swans—both tundra swans and trumpeter swans use the lake as a refuge. The entire region around the lakes is a great place to roam, with its flat, open prairie lands and wonderful views to the horizon.

92 ┊ WILSON CREEK

Round trip ■	2 to 4 miles
Hiking time ■	2+ hours
Difficulty ■	Easy
Starting elevation ■	2000 feet
High point ■	2100 feet
Best season ■	Year-round
Maps ■	Washington State Department of Natural Resources (DNR) Coulee Dam
Contact ■	Bureau of Land Management, Spokane
Permits/passes ■	None

From Spokane, drive west on US 2 past the town of Wilbur, then turn south onto Govan Road. Drive through the old, tiny community of Govan (take note of the abandoned schoolhouse in the field outside of town) and out Govan Road for 5.4 miles. Turn right onto Lewis Bridge Road and drive 1.0 mile, then turn left onto Union Valley Road. Drive Union Valley Road 0.5 mile and pull into the small pullout parking area by the fence/gated area with the Wilson Creek reader board. Cross the gate and start hiking.

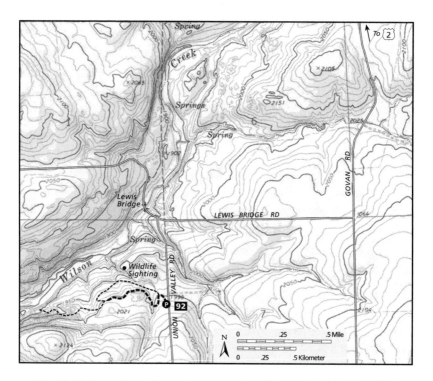

The BLM showed good sense in preserving this wonderful, if small, slice of desert paradise. Wilson Creek flows south of Govan (past an old turn-of-the-nineteenth-century schoolhouse in Govan). From the south access trailhead, you'll find a lovely trail, great wildflowers, wonderful views up and down the Wilson Creek coulee, and an incredible vantage from which to view wildlife: owls, prairie falcons, northern harriers, red-tailed and rough-legged hawks, warblers, white-crowned and golden-crowned sparrows, horned larks, meadowlarks, mountain bluebirds—it pays to visit in different seasons!

Your route follows a marked trail for more than a mile, with nicely informative interpretive signs along the way. From the end of the marked trail, continue southwest off-trail along the base of the coulee cliffs. You can push on another 0.5 mile or so, making sure you take time to hike down to the banks of beautiful Wilson Creek, a desert waterway with abundant birds and wildlife along its shores. Because the southern area is just 1 square mile in size, after your rambling walk of about 1.5 miles, you'll have reached the western boundary of the BLM lands—turn back when you hit the fence line.

For additional hiking, head back to Goven Road. At 2.1 miles north of Lewis Bridge Road, turn off to reach the northern section of the BLM lands

Sunrise along Wilson Creek

on the west side of Govan Road. The old road/trail leads in to the desert area, providing good access to interesting bumps and knobs of basalt. You can enjoy a mile or more rambling through the wildflower fields here.

93 ROCKY FORD–CRAB CREEK

Round trip ■ **6 miles**
Hiking time ■ 3 hours
Difficulty ■ Moderate
Starting elevation ■ 1800 feet
High point ■ 1900 feet
Best season ■ September through March
Maps ■ Washington State Department of Natural Resources (DNR) Ritzville
Contact ■ Bureau of Land Management, Spokane
Permits/passes ■ None

From Vantage, drive east on Interstate 90 and leave the freeway at exit 231 for Tokia. Turn north (left) over the freeway. At 0.2 mile, continue straight at the stop sign. This is now Danekas Road. Drive Danekas Road 1.4 miles

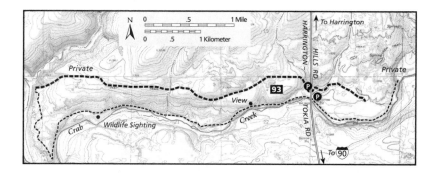

and turn right on Hills Road (also known as the Harrington–Tokia Road). Head north over the tracks. In 6.1 miles, just after crossing a bridge over Crab Creek, turn right into the large BLM parking area by the bridge.

Enjoy a great dip in the otherwise flat landscape where yet another upper portion of Crab Creek flows through. You can hike in both directions from the parking area trailhead to get the most out of your visit. Crab Creek is lined with lush growth in places, making it difficult to get down along the water's edge safely in late spring when the foliage is fully leafed out. This is great wildlife habitat but hiking through is difficult. In places, the creek seems to tunnel beneath a canopy of brush and tree boughs. Fortunately, you can skirt the outer edges of these thickets, enjoying the birds and other critters from the outside looking in. Deer and coyote track often crisscross in soft sand and muddy areas near the creek. Violet-green swallows and cliff swallows seem to be everywhere. Hawks perch in the tall hawthorn trees or soar in the sky. Herons line the banks of Crab Creek. All in all, this is a lovely oasis to explore.

To head west, drop down and walk under the bridge to hike the old path/road. Once down in the creek basin and pointing west, you'll find a network of game trails meandering roughly parallel to the creek for more than 3 miles. Because the spring foliage tends to be very thick, this route is best enjoyed in late autumn and winter.

If you want more time in the area, return to the parking area and continue east. You'll find similar experiences along the creek heading east for at least a mile before Crab Creek angles north and enters private land.

Crab Creek flows through the Rocky Ford BLM area.

94 ┊ Hog Lake

Round trip ■	**5 miles**
Hiking time ■	3 hours
Difficulty ■	Moderate
Starting elevation ■	2200 feet
High point ■	2300 feet
Best season ■	April through July
Maps ■	Washington State Department of Natural Resources (DNR) Rosalia
Contact ■	Bureau of Land Management, Spokane
Permits/passes ■	Washington Department of Fish and Wildlife Vehicle Permit required

From Spokane, drive west on Interstate 90, leaving the freeway at exit 254 (Fishtrap/Sprague Highway). Turn south (left). At 0.8 mile from I-90, turn left onto the first gravel road (across from gravel road signed "Lake Valley Loop"). Drive this good gravel road 0.5 mile, crossing Jack Brown Road

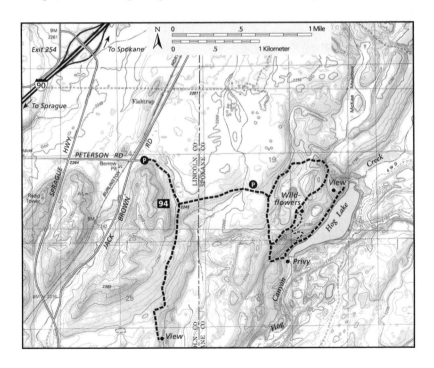

Ponderosa pines reflected in Hog Lake

before entering the BLM lands at the cattle guard (signed "Entering Public Lands"). This is a seasonal road that is usually only open from December 1 through March 31 (gated during spring/summer and fire season). Park here to hike in on the road if the gate is closed. If the gate is open, drive 1.2 miles to the actual trailhead.

Waterfowl and upland bird hunters take advantage of this area in late autumn and winter, but hikers can take advantage of the seasonal road closure (usually closed March through November) to enjoy solitary rambles on the old road. Spring is the best time to visit as you'll likely find the local desert full of migratory songbirds and the lake alive with nesting waterfowl. You might also happen across coyotes, badgers, deer, and snakes.

To access the upper portion of a 1.3-mile loop above Hog Lake, hike 1.2 miles along the main road to a trailhead/horse unloading area. After enjoying the loop in the northern highlands above the lake, drop down the short trail to the lakeshore to experience the views there. The access to Hog Lake itself is found down the steep hill about 0.2 mile from the trailhead parking area along the southern side of the upper loop. A nice fisher's trail leads along the north shore of Hog Lake to wind around the shore for great reflection views, photo opportunities, and wildlife.

Spring brings flower blooms to this glorious desert country. Yellow bells, desert bluebells, sagebrush buttercups, and even some hedgehog cactus blanket the desert here. This is a fascinating transition area as the Columbia

Basin slowly gives way to the dry pine country found farther east. As the land climbs in elevation, it draws more rainfall, and thus sports more and more woodland stands of ponderosa pine trees. Just 10 miles west of here you will find no trees, but there are trees here. Those small groves of pine bring fascinating life to the otherwise desert landscape. An astounding array of birds, especially, take advantage of them. We noted one tree about a mile into the route that sported more than sixty violet-green swallows lined up on its branches to warm in the sun.

95 FISHTRAP LAKE–NORTH

Round trip ■	4 to 10 miles
Hiking time ■	3 to 5 hours
Difficulty ■	Moderate
Starting elevation ■	2100 feet
Low point ■	1974 feet
Best season ■	April through July or September through December
Maps ■	Washington State Department of Natural Resources (DNR) Rosalia
Contact ■	Bureau of Land Management, Spokane
Permits/passes ■	Washington Department of Fish and Wildlife Vehicle Permit required

From Spokane, drive west on Interstate 90 and leave the freeway at exit 254 (Fishtrap/Sprague Highway). Turn south. At 2.4 miles from I-90, turn left on Fishtrap Road. Drive 0.7 mile and pull off on the right at the access trailhead area. Hike the jeep track leading off toward Fishtrap Lake, being certain to skirt the private home on your left as you pass it. Once past the homesite, all the land to the lakeshore from here on will be BLM public land.

The Fishtrap area is part of the Channeled Scablands of eastern Washington. The deep coulees and canyons were carved by the Great Missoula Floods following the last Ice Age tens of thousands of years ago. The combination of rich desert prairies and lakes have provided a plethora of resources for Native Americans over the last several thousand years. Native tribes utilized the plants and animals of this area for food, medicine, and building materials. Today, the Bureau of Land Management works with the Washington Department of Fish and Wildlife to manage the area for wildlife habitat, as well as for recreational opportunities.

Rattlesnakes abound throughout this area so consider hiking here early

Ponderosas pines dot the landscape above Fishtrap Lake.

in spring (March and April) before the snakes come out of their winter dens. You'll find early spring mornings cold at times, the warm mid-day temperatures bring out flower blooms by early April. What's more, spring drives the yellow-bellied marmots out of their dens in search of fresh grass and wildflowers to munch on. These in turn bring out the raptors—hawks, vultures, and occasionally eagles.

You'll find the trailhead on the main road, which leads to the resort area of Fishtrap. The trailhead is found about a mile before reaching the resort. The hiking route follows a gated jeep track, which surreptitiously bypasses the adjacent private land before proceeding out through the heart of this lovely BLM land. As you hike along the track, you'll pass many wetlands and marshes, which are filled with waterfowl throughout winter and spring. The rocky canyon cliffs are topped with huge ponderosa pines in this wonderful transition ecosystem between the desert steppe lands and pine forests.

The trails never provide direct access to Fishtrap Lake, but from the north highlands just above it, you'll have ample opportunity to ramble down to the lake following game and fisherman trails.

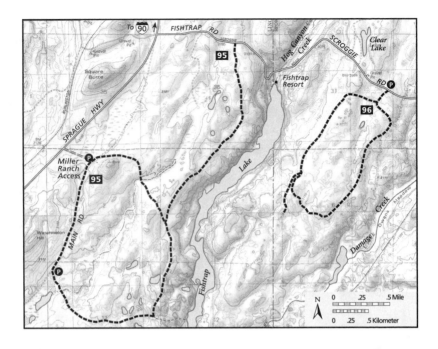

96 ¦ FISHTRAP LAKE–SCROGGIE LOOP

Round trip ■	**3+ miles**
Hiking time ■	2 to 3 hours
Difficulty ■	Moderate
Starting elevation ■	2100 feet
Low point ■	1974 feet
Best season ■	April through July or September through December
Maps ■	Washington State Department of Natural Resources (DNR) Rosalia
Contact ■	Bureau of Land Management, Spokane
Permits/passes ■	Washington Department of Fish and Wildlife Vehicle Permit required

From Spokane, drive west on Interstate 90, leaving the freeway at exit 254 (Fishtrap/Sprague Highway). Turn south. At 2.4 miles from I-90, turn left on Fishtrap Road. Drive 1.2 miles. After entering the resort area by the lake, turn left onto Scroggie Road—a nice gravel road leading across the end of

Violet-green swallows sun on a branch near Fishtrap Lake.

the lake area. Drive 1.4 miles up Scroggie Road on the south side of Fishtrap Lake and pull off to the right at the signed parking area for access to the highland BLM lands.

The BLM only recently added this land parcel to the original Fishtrap Lake public land tract on the north side of the lake. To protect adjacent private land interests, fences have been placed along the south and west sides of this parcel to prevent you from wandering off the public lands. As you wander through the desert, you'll stumble across a small pond, which hosts an array of ducks and other waterfowl.

Hike out along the wide trail track, going left at the intersection with the loop. In just a mile you'll find a small duck pond set among the sage. Enjoy the scenery around the pond before turning north to follow the trail as it loops around the public land tract. As you near the fence line, the path turns east again. As you get to this area, step off the trail and wander over to the rim of the hill to peer down on Fishtrap Lake.

Hike in an almost straight line along the main trail back to the trailhead, keeping your eyes peeled—this part of the BLM tract is prime habitat for wild turkeys.

97 TURNBULL NATIONAL WILDLIFE REFUGE

Round trip ■	**1 to 6 miles**
Hiking time ■	1 to 3 hours
Difficulty ■	Moderate
Starting elevation ■	2300 feet
High point ■	2300 feet
Best season ■	March through October
Maps ■	Washington State Department of Natural Resources (DNR) Rosalia
Contact ■	U.S. Fish and Wildlife Service, Turnbull National Wildlife Refuge
Permits/passes ■	U.S. Fish and Wildlife Service day-use permit required

From Spokane, drive west on Interstate 90, leaving the freeway at exit 257 (Tyler/Cheney). Turn south after exiting the freeway and drive 10.3 miles on

Winslow Pool in the Turnbull National Wildlife Refuge

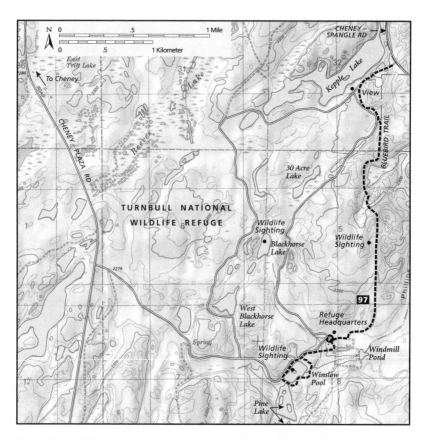

State Route 904 before turning right onto Cheney–Plaza Road just past the "Turnbull NWR" sign. Drive 4.1 miles on Cheney–Plaza Road before turning left into the refuge's main visitor entrance. Drive the good gravel road 1.3 miles in and pay your use fee at the fee station. Continue to the main headquarters to obtain maps of all the hiking areas.

Covering more than16,000 acres, the Turnbull Wildlife Refuge serves as a wildlife sanctuary to hundreds of bird species, including twenty-seven species of ducks. Mammals thrive here as well, taking advantage of the vast undisturbed habitat (only 2200 acres of the refuge are open to the public). Most visitors never leave their vehicles, taking advantage instead of the great views along the 5.5-mile auto-tour route on a well-graded gravel road. That means hikers can find solitude as they explore the wonderful wildlife habitat of the area.

From the trailhead, head out on a wonderful trail that runs out along Winslow Pool to Pine Lakes. These pools are often full of ducks, geese, and swans in all seasons. The trail also provides easy access to an assortment of blinds—camouflaged huts that allow visitors to sit in hiding while viewing waterfowl up close.

The trail continues to loop out around the far shore of Winslow Pool, then along a dike between Pine Lakes and Winslow Pool. On the south shores of these pools stands a massive stand of ponderosa pines, providing homes to brown creepers and many woodpecker species.

If you want more hiking, head out on the Bluebird Trail, a 4-mile round trip beginning from a trailhead found behind the headquarters. The trail leads north to Kepple Lake.

98 BOYER PARK BLUFFS

Round trip ■	4 miles
Hiking time ■	2 hours
Difficulty ■	Difficult
Starting elevation ■	650 feet
High point ■	2200 feet
Best season ■	Year-round
Maps ■	Washington State Department of Natural Resources (DNR) Pullman
Contact ■	U.S. Army Corps of Engineers
Permits/passes ■	None

From Colfax, drive west on US 26 for 10 miles (or from the west drive US 26 for 41 miles east of Washtucna). Turn south on the road to Lower Granite Dam. After 4.1 miles veer right onto Almota Road, continue another 9.1

A calm morning along the Snake River at Boyer Park

miles, then turn right at a well-signed intersection with SR 194 (coming in from Pullman). Continue down the winding grade with stunning views of the Palouse country and the Snake River Canyon. Reach Boyer Park at 17 miles total from US 26. Park in the lot near the boat launch facilities. You'll find the riverside trail leading away in either direction from the parking area. Hike the riverside paved trail along the Snake River in both directions from the boat launching site area.

Boyer Park, nestled along the banks of the Snake River, offers great hiking in the transition zone between the river and the sageland country above. The established trail provides a great outing in and of itself, but adventurous

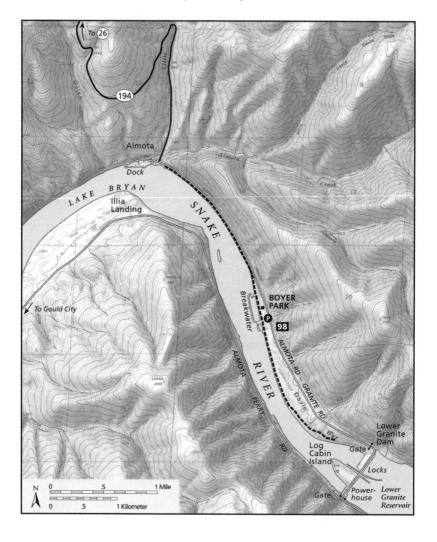

hikers can cross the road and ramble cross-country onto the slopes above the river, heading up to rimrock bluffs at the top of the canyon wall. It's excellent rattlesnake country up there (!), but it's also great habitat for mule deer and rocket-fast chukar—the upland game bird with a unique defense against predators (including human hunters): They like to run up steep slopes until they feel the predator is too close, then they take wing and zoom downslope at amazing speeds. They're beautiful birds if you can get close enough to see them.

Found near Lower Granite Dam on the Snake River's northern shore, Boyer Park is primarily a day-use park for boaters (thanks to a well-maintained boat launch) and sun worshippers, who lie out on the manicured grass lawns near the boat launch.

Hikers can quickly leave the sedentary recreationists behind by heading out on the 2-mile paved trail that follows the shoreline back to where the road comes down off the Palouse highlands. This is a great 4-mile round trip stroll, offering amazing views of the river reflecting the cliff walls on the other side.

99 ┊ TUCANNON RIVER CANYON (CAMP WOOTEN)

Round trip ■	**4 to 6 miles**
Hiking time ■	2 to 4 hours
Difficulty ■	Moderate
Starting elevation ■	650 feet
High point ■	1287 feet
Best season ■	Year-round
Maps ■	Washington State Department of Natural Resources (DNR) Clarkston
Contact ■	Washington Department of Fish and Wildlife
Permits/passes ■	Washington Department of Fish and Wildlife Vehicle Permit required

From Dayton, drive north on US 12 for 12.5 miles. Turn right onto Tucannon River Road. Drive Tucannon River Road (Forest Road 47) for 28 miles to Camp Wooten. Park near the gated entrance to Camp Wooten.

Alternatively, drive approximately 23 miles out Tucannon River Road to the Watson Lake area where you'll find a parking area used by fishers. Park here. Get across the river here (there will be high water in early spring, but it's doable by foot) and roam the northeast side of the Tucannon River in the Wooten Wildlife Area.

The Tucannon River Canyon is a transition zone, from the sagelands of the

Sulphur-yellow lupine covers the dry slopes of the Tucannon River Canyon.

lower river to the dry pine forests of the Blue Mountains at the upper end of the canyon. The Tucannon is a blue-ribbon trout stream popular with anglers of all kinds. Humans, of course, fish here, but so do kingfishers, bald eagles, falcons, raccoons, black bears, and river otters. The area around the Wooten Wildlife Area straddles the prime transition zone, with high, dry bluffs and desert prairies bounded by ponderosa pine forests. Camp Wooten is a popular recreation camp used by local 4-H and other youth groups.

Hike out along the river, exploring a mile or so southeast along the riparian enviornment. After enjoying the river basin, walk back to the main

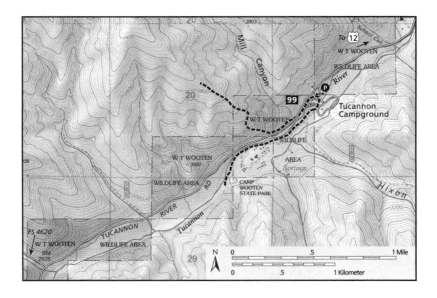

road and scramble up on the bank to the west of the road. Directly opposite the main body of Camp Wooten, you'll find a rough trail that slices almost straight up the dry, rocky slope. The trail leads more than a mile up the slope, gaining nearly 400 feet, to reach a large wooden cross that was placed here by camp-goers in the 1950s as a memorial monument to all the campers who have enjoyed the camp.

100   MOUTH OF THE TUCANNON

Round trip ■	**4 miles**
Hiking time ■	3 hours
Difficulty ■	Moderate
Starting elevation ■	650 feet
High point ■	1000 feet
Best season ■	Year-round
Maps ■	Washington State Department of Natural Resources (DNR) Connell
Contact ■	U.S. Army Corps of Engineers
Permits/passes ■	None

From Dayton, drive US 12 north 14 miles and turn left on State Route 261. Continue 7 miles to the town of Starbuck. Note: Despite the name of this

100-year-old town, the only coffee you'll find is bitter Hills Brothers brewed in the local roadside cafe.) Continue northwest. At 10.1 miles from US 12 (just past 10-mile road signpost), pull off to the right at the gated road. Park here, but do not block the gate.

The Tucannon River—one of the richest trout streams in Washington—flows out of the Wenaha–Tucannon Wilderness Area in heart of the Blue Mountains and rolls out the wildlife-rich Tucannon canyon before emptying into the broad waters of the Snake River near Lyons Ferry. The mouth of the Tucannon is a wonderfully rich wildlife delta, and the highlands above the river provide stunning views of both river canyons, as well as wildlife viewing along the high sagelands.

From the parking area, head up the dirt jeep road as it skirts between the marshy area along the Tucannon River and the canyon wall. After a mile or so of cutting through the reeds in the river lowlands, the road climbs a small bluff looking down on the reed-choked mouth of the Tucannon. Watch the waters from the road (about 30 feet above the waterline), and you'll soon notice the water's slow churning. These mudflats, covered in just a few feet of water, are home to a huge population of carp. Fish up to 4 feet long and 30 pounds thrash and churn the water from May through August during their long breeding period. During the winter months, ducks and geese fill these flats to take advantage of the rich feed on the mudflats and the shelter provided by the surrounding reeds.

The road ends at about 1.5 miles, after dropping back down to the waterline. From there, though, you can go cross-country. Hike up through the

Fascinating basalt cliffs surround the mouth of the Tucannon River Canyon near where it meets the Snake River.

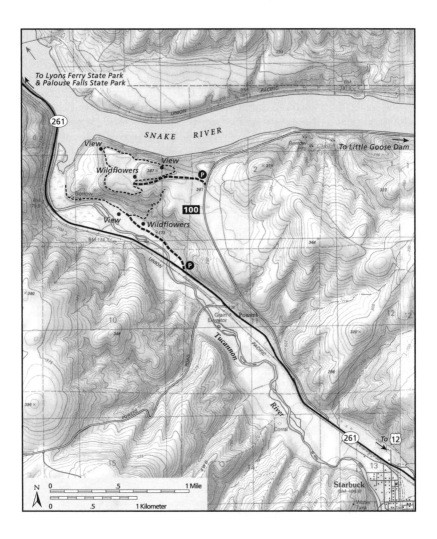

sagelands, heading directly away from the river to get a few hundred feet above the waterline. Look to the north, and you'll see Lyons Ferry and the mouth of the Palouse River a few miles away. Heading southeast, you can loop up through the highland and get above the road/trail you hiked in on. Explore the sagelands at your leisure, watching for rattlesnakes (this is prime snake country) and mule deer (which grow to the size of elk in this rich environment) before dropping back down onto the road to return to your vehicle.

APPENDIX A: CAMPING INFORMATION

To find public campgrounds near your hiking destination, please contact the following agencies. If no official campgrounds exist, the agencies will be able to provide you with current rules and regulations about dispersed camping on their lands. Generally, dispersed camping (camping outside "official" campsites) is only allowed on some state lands, and each land management agency maintains its own rules and regulations for specific sites. Call ahead to get the latest information.

USDA Forest Service—Pacific Northwest Region
PO Box 3623
333 SW First Avenue
Portland, OR 97208-3623
(503) 808-2468
www.fs.fed.us/r6/

U.S. Bureau of Land Management
333 SW First Avenue
Portland, OR 97204
(503) 808-6002
www.or.blm.gov/

U.S. Army Corps of Engineers
Walla Walla District
201 North Third Avenue
Walla Walla, WA 99362
(509) 527-7131
www.nww.usace.army.mil/html/offices/op/t/navdata/default.html

Washington State Parks and Recreation Commission
7150 Cleanwater Lane
P.O. Box 42650
Olympia, WA 98504-2650
(360) 902-8844
infocent@parks.wa.gov
www.parks.wa.gov

Washington Department of Fish and Wildlife
Natural Resources Building
1111 Washington Street SE
Olympia, WA 98501
(360) 902-2200
wdfw.wa.gov/

Washington State Department of Natural Resources
P.O. Box 47001
Olympia, WA 98504-7001
(360) 902-1004
www.dnr.wa.gov/base/recreation.html

Jeep tracks closed to vehicles are generally well-marked but do still get driven on at times. Remember, showing love and care for these lands helps keep them well-managed for everyone, including the wildlife.

APPENDIX B: CONTACT INFORMATION

U.S. FISH AND WILDLIFE SERVICE (USFWS)
Pacific Region
911 NE 11th Ave
Portland, OR 97232
(503) 231-6828
pacific.fws.gov

USFWS, Columbia National Wildlife Refuge
735 East Main Street
Othello, Washington 99344
(509) 488-2668
pacific.fws.gov/refuges/field/wa_columbia.htm

USFWS, McNary National Wildlife Refuge
64 Maple St
Burbank, Washington 99323
(509) 547-4942
midcolumbiariver.fws.gov/mcnarypage.htm

USFWS, Mid-Columbia River National Wildlife Refuges
2805 St Andrews Loop
Pasco, WA 99301
(509) 545-8588
midcolumbiariver.fws.gov

USFWS, Turnbull National Wildlife Refuge
26010 S Smith Rd
Cheney, WA 99004
(509) 235-4723
turnbull.fws.gov

U.S. FOREST SERVICE, GIFFORD PINCHOT NATIONAL FOREST
Mount Adams Ranger District
2455 Hwy 141
Trout Lake, WA 98650
(509) 395-3400
www.fs.fed.us/gpnf

WASHINGTON DEPARTMENT OF FISH AND WILDLIFE (WDFW)
WDFW Headquarters
Natural Resources Building
1111 Washington St SE
Olympia, WA 98501
(360) 902-2200
wdfw.wa.gov/

WDFW, Eastern Washington—Region 1
8702 North Division St
Spokane, Washington 99218
(509) 456-4082

WDFW, Northcentral Washington—Region 2
1550 Alder St NW
Ephrata, Washington 98823–9699
(509) 754-4624

WDFW, Southcentral Washington—Region 3
1701 S 24th Ave
Yakima, Washington 98902–5720
(509) 575-2740

WASHINGTON STATE DEPARTMENT OF NATURAL RESOURCES (DNR)
Washington State DNR Headquarters
Natural Resources Building
1111 Washington St SE
Olympia, WA 98501
(360) 902-1000
www.dnr.wa.gov

Washington State DNR, Northeast Region
225 S Silke Rd
Colville, WA 99114–0190
(509) 684-7474

Washington State DNR, Southeast Region
713 Bowers Rd
Ellensburg, WA 98926–9301
(509) 925-8510

Washington State DNR, Central Region
1405 Rush Rd
Chehalis, WA 98532–8763
(360) 748-2383

WASHINGTON STATE PARKS AND RECREATION

Information Center
7150 Cleanwater Lane
P.O. Box 42650
Olympia, WA 98504–2650
(360) 902-8844
www.parks.wa.gov

WHITMAN COUNTY PARKS

Facilities Management
(509) 397-6238
www.whitmancounty.org/Parks/Index_Pages/Kamiak.htm

APPENDIX C: ADDITIONAL RESOURCES

Audubon Society/Central Basin: *www.cbas.org*

Audubon Society/Palouse: *www.palouseaudubon.org*

BLM Spokane District Office: *www.or.blm.gov/Spokane/index.htm*

BLM Watchable Wildlife and Wildflowers: *www.or.blm.gov/watchable/index. htm*

Central Washington Native Plants: *www.cwnp.org/index.html*

East Benton County Historical Museum: *www.owt.com/ebchs*

Grand Coulee Dam: *users.owt.com/chubbard/gcdam/index.html*

Hanford Reach "Save the Reach": *www.hanfordreach.org*

Ice Age Floods Institute: *www.iceagefloodsinstitute.org/index.htm*

National Weather Service–Spokane Office: *www.wrh.noaa.gov/Spokane*

National Wildlife Refuges/Pacific Region Office: *www.r1.fws.gov/visitor/ washington.html#*

Pacific Northwest Flowers—Columbia & Great Basins: *ghs.gresham.k12. or.us/science/ps/nature/basin/basinid.htm*

The Nature Conservancy: *nature.org*

U.S. Army Corps of Engineers/Walla Walla District: *www.nww.usace.army. mil/corpsoutdoors*

U.S. Fish & Wildlife Service: *www.fws.gov*

USGS/Butterflies of Washington: *www.npsc.nbs.gov/resource/distr/lepid/ bflyusa/wa/toc.htm*

Washington Department of Fish and Wildlife: *www.wa.gov/wdfw*

Washington Department of Fish and Wildlife–Wildlife Areas and viewing points: *www.wa.gov/wdfw/lands/wildarea.htm*

Washington Native Plant Society: *www.wnps.org*

Washington Native Plant Society/Columbia Basin Chapter: *www.wnps.org/ cbasin/events.html*

Washington Native Plant Society/Wenatchee Chapter: *www.geocities.com/ RainForest/2745*

Washington Ornithological Society: *www.wos.org*

Washington State Department of Natural Resources: *www.dnr.wa.gov/base/ dnrhome.html*

Washington State Historical Society: *www.wshs.org*

Washington State Parks and Recreation: *www.parks.wa.gov*

Washington State Railroads Historical Society Museum: *www.wsrhs.org*

Western Rattlesnake Natural History: *www.uoregon.edu/~titus/herp/ viridishistory.htm*

INDEX

A

Ainsley Canyon, 46, 47
Amber Lake, 191, 192, 194
Amphitheater Crater, 201, 202
Ancient Lake, 78, 80, 81

B

Babcock Bench, 64, 78
Badger Mountain, 101, 102, 103, 104
Baldy Butte, 75
Banks Lake, 83, 88, 89, 94
Bear Canyon, 59, 60
Bear Creek, 60
Beezley Hills Preserve, 25, 107, 108
Big Burn Canyon, 56
Big Flat Habitat Management Unit, 172
Billy Clapp Lake, 95, 96, 98
Black Canyon, 48, 50
Blythe Lake, 179
Bobs Lake, 197
Boyer Park, 234
Boylston Mountains, 73
Boylston Tunnel, 70, 73
Breeden Road, 205, 206
Burbank Slough, 146
Burr Canyon, 172

C

Cache Crater, 202
Camp Delaney, 90
Camp Wooten, 236
Catherine Creek, 140
Catherine Creek Falls, 141
Chamna Natural Preserve, 151
Chandler Butte, 156
Chester Butte Wildlife Area, 111, 112
Chief Joseph Wildlife Area, 156, 157, 158
Chukar Lake, 179, 180
Cleman Mountain, 55, 57, 59
Colockum Wildlife Area, 66
Columbia Hills Natural Area Preserve, 138, 139

Columbia National Wildlife Refuge, 177, 180
Columbia Plateau Trail, 170, 192, 194
Columbia River, 64, 65, 67, 69, 113, 123, 129, 148, 152
Columbia River, dams, 32
Columbia River Gorge National Scenic Area, 137, 140
Cowiche Canyon, 75
Cowiche Canyon Conservancy, 76
Crab Creek Road, 119
Crab Creek Wildlife Area, 119, 122
Crab Creek, northern, 176, 177, 181, 191, 192, 224, 225

D

Dalles Mountain (State Park), 30, 137, 138, 139
Dalton Lake, 174
dams, 32
Dayton, 236
Deep Lake, 92
Desert Wildlife Area, 183, 184
Devils Canyon, 168
Doris, 72
Douglas Creek Canyon, 99, 101, 102, 103
Dry Falls, 89
Dry Falls Lakes, 89
Duffy Creek, 103, 104, 105
Duffy Creek Canyon, 104
Durr Road, 38, 39, 40
Dusty Hill Falls, 109
Dusty Lake, 80
Dutch Henry Draw, 109

E

Eightmile Creek, 138, 140
Escure Ranch, 174, 203

F

Fishtrap Lake, 228, 229, 230, 231
Florence Lake, 216, 218

Four Corners Sopher Flat, 102
Frenchman Coulee, 81, 82
Frenchman Hills, 186
Frog Lake, 176, 177, 182

G

Ginkgo Petrified Forest State Park,
   61, 63, 66
Gloyd Seeps Wildlife Area, 188, 189,
   190, 192
Goose Lake Plateau, 181
Goose Lake, lower, 184
Goose Lake, upper, 182
Govan, 223
Govedare, David, 65
Grand Coulee, 89, 92, 94, 98, 109, 169
Grand Coulee Dam, 83, 98
Grande Ronde River, 156, 157, 158
Grant County, 87
Great Missoula Floods, 83, 89, 169,
   171, 228
Green Gulch, 158

H

Hanford Nuclear Reservation, 116,
   124, 125
Hanford Reach, 116, 117, 124, 129, 131,
   132, 134
Hardy Canyon, 54
Hog Lake, 226, 227
Horse Heaven Hills, 155
Horsethief Butte, 135
Horsethief Lake State Park, 136

I

Iron Horse State Park, 69

J

John Wayne Trail, 69, 72
Joseph Creek, 158
Juniper Dunes Wilderness Area, 142,
   144

K

Kahlotus Railroad Grade, 168, 169
Kamiak Butte, 166
Kelley Hollow, 43, 44

Kepple Lake, 234
Kittitas Valley, 48, 50, 53

L

L.T. Murray State Wildlife Recreation
   Area, 16, 35, 37, 41, 44, 46, 48, 54, 57
Lake Kahlotus, 169
Lake Sacajawea, 173
Lakeview Ranch, 195, 196, 201
Lenore Lake Caves, 92, 93
Lewis and Clark, 123
Lower Crab Creek Coulee, 118, 120,
   122
Lower Granite Dam, 236
Lyons Ferry Park, 160, 162, 239, 240

M

Manastash Ridge, 53
Manastash Road, 51, 52
maps, 24
Marmes Man, 162
Marmes Pond, 160, 162
McCarteney Creek, 110
McGee Ranch, 130, 132
McNary National Wildlife Refuge,
   145, 146
Milwaukee Railroad, 122, 209, 212,
   213
Milwaukee–Chicago–St. Paul Rail-
   road, 73
Monument Coulee, 89
Moses Coulee, 101, 109, 110, 169
Moses Lake, 107
Mullan, John, 171

N

Naches River Valley, 58
Northrup Canyon Natural Area, 87,
   88
Nunnally Lake, 122

O

O'Sullivan Dam, 179
Oak Creek State Wildlife Area, 54, 57
Odessa Coulee, 198
Odessa Craters, 201
Odessa–Lake Creek, 196, 198, 200

Old Vantage Highway, 67
Old Wagon Road Trail, 87

P

Pacific Lake, 200
Packer Creek, 209
Palouse Falls, 163, 164
Palouse River, 162, 164
paragliders, 75
Park Lake, 91
Pegg Canyon, 101
Permits, 18
Pine Lakes, 233
Pine Ridge, 167
Pinto Dam, 97
Potholes State Park, 179, 181
Potholes Wildlife Area, 185, 186, 187, 188
Priest Rapids Dam, 131, 132
Priest Rapids Wildlife Area, 132, 134

Q

Quilomene Wildlife Area, 67
Quincy Wildlife Area, 78, 80,

R

Rattlesnake Slope Wildlife Area, 153
rattlesnakes, 22
Reiber Road, 218
Richard King Mellon Foundation, 104
Robinson Canyon, 46
Robinson Creek, 47
Rock Creek, 204, 206, 208, 211, 212, 213
Rock Creek Management Unit, 203, 208
Rock Island Creek, 105
Rocky Coulee, 67
Rocky Ford, 224, 225
Rose Crater, 202
Roza Creek, 41
Rye, 73

S

Saddle Mountain, 117, 118, 119
Saddle Mountain Wildlife Refuge, 116, 125
Sagebrush Flats, 112

Scroggie Road, 230
Selah Butte, 73, 75
Sentinel Gap, 133
Shell Rock, 50
Smiths Harbor, 148
Snake River, 149, 156, 158, 164, 170, 171, 173, 234, 239
Snake River, dams, 32
Spokane, 176
Spokane–Portland–Seattle Railroad, 171, 194
Stacker Butte, 139
Starbuck, 160
Steamboat Rock, 83, 88
Summer Falls, 98
Sun Lakes State Park, 89, 92
Swakane Canyon, 113
Swanson Lakes, 220, 221
Swanson Lakes Wildlife Area, 217, 221

T

ten essentials, 26
The Nature Conservancy, 107
Thorp, 50, 52
ticks, 23
Towell Falls, 174, 207
Trail Lake, 94
Trail Lake Coulee, 76, 94, 96
Tucannon River, 236, 237, 238, 239
Turnbull National Wildlife Refuge, 194, 232
Twin Lakes, 214, 220
Twin Sisters Rock, 149

U

U.S. Army Yakima Training Center, 69, 72, 131
Umatilla Rock, 89, 90
Umtanum Creek Canyon, 36
Umtanum Creek Falls, 34, 35, 36, 37
Umtanum Ridge, 16, 39, 44, 50, 56
Umtanum Road, 34, 39, 43, 48, 54, 56

W

Wahluke Branch-10 Wasteway, 127
Wahluke Lake, 126

Wahluke Slope Wildlife Area (Wahl-
  uke National Wildlife Refuge), 116,
  118, 126, 127, 128, 131
Wall Lake, 205
Walla Walla River, 148, 149
Wallula Gap, 150
Wallula Habitat Management Unit,
  147, 148
Wanapum Dam, 72
Washtucna Coulee, 168, 169
weather, 20
Weikel Road, 76
Wenaha–Tucannon Wilderness Area,
  239
Wenas Lake, 44
Wenas Road, 41, 44
Wenas Valley, 48, 56, 58
Wenas Wildlife Area, 57
Wenatchee Basin, 78

Wenatchee National Forest, 54
Westberg Trail, 52
Westberg, Ray, 52, 53
Whiskey Dick Mountain, 67, 68
Whiskey Dick Wildlife Area, 66
White Bluffs, 116, 123, 124, 127, 129
Wild Horse Monument, 64, 66
Willow Lake, 190
Wilson Creek, 222, 224
Winchester Wasteway, 184, 186
Winslow Pool, 232, 233
Wooten Wildlife Area, 236

Y

Yakima Canyon, 36, 39, 73, 75
Yakima Rim, 74
Yakima River, 152, 155
Yakima Skyline Ridge, 38, 41, 43

ABOUT THE AUTHORS

Dan Nelson's personal and professional life focus on the great outdoors of the Pacific Northwest. He met his partner, Donna Meshke, in a Mountaineering-Oriented First Aid (MOFA) course in 1991 and they've been enjoying living and playing together ever since. Donna appears in all of his books–both in the photos and as the photographer of some of them.

Dan received a bachelor degree in history and political science from Washington State University. After a short stint as a newspaper reporter, Dan joined the staff of the Washington Trails Association (WTA) as the editor of *Washington Trails* magazine. During his eleven years at WTA, he was "required" to spend considerable time each year out hiking and enjoying the backcountry trails of Washington. Currently, Dan serves as the public information officer for Olympic Region Clean Air Agency—an agency charged with ensuring the air remains clean, clear, and healthy on the beautiful Olympic Peninsula.

In addition to his love for walking in wild country, Dan is an avid fly fisher, canoeist, snowshoer, telemark skier, and paraglider pilot. If he's not out enjoying the backcountry, he's indoors writing about it. Dan is a regular contributor to *The Seattle Times*, *Backpacker* magazine and *Men's Journal*, specializing in Northwest destinations and outdoor equipment reviews. He launched a number of popular guidebook series with The Mountaineers Books, notably the new Day Hiking series (*Day Hiking Mount Rainier, Day Hiking Snoqualmie Region* and *Day Hiking South Cascades*), the Best Hikes with Dogs series (*Best Hikes with Dogs: Western Washington*) and the Snowshoe Routes series (*Snowshoe Routes: Washington*). Dan's other titles include *Best of the Pacific Crest Trail: Washington, Best Loop Hikes: Washington, Accessible Trails in Washington*, and *Predators at Risk in the Pacific Northwest*.

Alan L. Bauer is a professional freelance photographer specializing in the natural and local histories of the Pacific Northwest, where he has been a resident and active in the outdoors his entire life.

Alan's work has been published in *Backpacker, Odyssey, Northwest Runner, Oregon Coast*, and *Northwest Travel* magazines as well as in numerous publications and books in fourteen countries. He was a featured "Master Photographer" in 2006 for his macro work in *Smart Photography*, the top-selling photography magazine in India. He regularly provides images for CD covers, textbooks, websites, and research and corporate materials. He has been the co-author or photographer for many books in the Day Hiking series, as well as *Best Hikes with Dogs: Inland Northwest*.

Alan resides happily in the Cascade foothills east of Seattle with his caring family and border collie. For further information and to see samples of his work, please visit *www.alanbauer.com*.

THE MOUNTAINEERS, founded in 1906, is a nonprofit outdoor activity and conservation club, whose mission is "to explore, study, preserve, and enjoy the natural beauty of the outdoors. . . . " Based in Seattle, Washington, the club is now one of the largest such organizations in the United States, with seven branches throughout Washington State.

The Mountaineers sponsors both classes and year-round outdoor activities in the Pacific Northwest, which include hiking, mountain climbing, ski-touring, snowshoeing, bicycling, camping, kayaking, nature study, sailing, and adventure travel. The club's conservation division supports environmental causes through educational activities, sponsoring legislation, and presenting informational programs. All club activities are led by skilled, experienced instructors, who are dedicated to promoting safe and responsible enjoyment and preservation of the outdoors.

If you would like to participate in these organized outdoor activities or the club's programs, consider a membership in The Mountaineers. For information and an application, write or call The Mountaineers, Club Headquarters, 7700 Sand Point Way NE, Seattle, WA 98115; 206-521-6001. You can also visit the club's website at www.mountaineers.org or contact The Mountaineers via email at clubmail@mountaineers.org.

The Mountaineers Books, an active, nonprofit publishing program of the club, produces guidebooks, instructional texts, historical works, natural history guides, and works on environmental conservation. All books produced by The Mountaineers Books fulfill the club's mission.

Send or call for our catalog of more than 500 outdoor titles:

 The Mountaineers Books
1001 SW Klickitat Way, Suite 201
Seattle, WA 98134
800-553-4453
mbooks@mountaineersbooks.org
www.mountaineersbooks.org

The Mountaineers Books is proud to be a corporate sponsor of The Leave No Trace Center for Outdoor Ethics, whose mission is to promote and inspire responsible outdoor recreation through education, research, and partnerships. The Leave No Trace program is focused specifically on human-powered (nonmotorized) recreation.

Leave No Trace strives to educate visitors about the nature of their recreational impacts, as well as offer techniques to prevent and minimize such impacts. Leave No Trace is best understood as an educational and ethical program, not as a set of rules and regulations.

For more information, visit www.LNT.org, or call 800-332-4100.